COMMUNITY COLLEGE

W9-DGD-669

SEX AND CONSEQUENCES

SEX AND CONSEQUENCES

ABORTION, PUBLIC POLICY, AND THE ECONOMICS OF FERTILITY

Phillip B. Levine

PRINCETON UNIVERSITY PRESS

PRINCETON AND OXFORD

PUBLISHED BY PRINCETON UNIVERSITY PRESS, 41 WILLIAM STREET,
PRINCETON, NEW JERSEY 08540
IN THE UNITED KINGDOM: PRINCETON UNIVERSITY PRESS,
3 MARKET PLACE, WOODSTOCK, OXFORDSHIRE OX20 1SY

LIBRARY OF CONGRESS CATALOGING-IN-PUBLICATION DATA

LEVINE, PHILLIP B.
SEX AND CONSEQUENCES : ABORTION, PUBLIC POLICY, AND THE ECONOMICS
OF FERTILITY / PHILLIP B. LEVINE
P. CM.
INCLUDES BIBLIOGRAPHICAL REFERENCES AND INDEX.
ISBN 0-691-07098-9 (CL. ALK. PAPER)
1. ABORTION—GOVERNMENT POLICY. 2. ABORTION—LAW AND LEGISLATION.
3. FERTILITY, HUMAN—ECONOMETRIC MODELS. I. TITLE.
HQ767.L48 2004
363.46—DC22   2003060065

BRITISH LIBRARY CATALOGING-IN-PUBLICATION DATA IS AVAILABLE.

THIS BOOK HAS BEEN COMPOSED IN SABON TYPEFACE

PRINTED ON ACID-FREE PAPER. ∞

WWW.PUPRESS.PRINCETON.EDU

PRINTED IN THE UNITED STATES OF AMERICA

1 3 5 7 9 10 8 6 4 2

To Heidi

WITH LOVE

CONTENTS

FIGURES

TABLES

PREFACE

MY INTEREST in abortion policy and its behavioral impact began somewhat inadvertently. A coauthor (David Zimmerman) and I were working on an unrelated project regarding the impact of maternal welfare receipt on children's well-being. Over the course of that project we were worried about a potential statistical problem with our analysis. We were concerned that decisions regarding family size may be made in conjunction with the level at which parents are willing to "invest" in their children. Technically, we were concerned that family size is endogenous. A standard statistical solution to this problem is to predict family size based on some other factor (called an "instrumental variable") that is unrelated to the child's outcome. We had thought that we could use state abortion policies as these instrumental variables. Without any particular knowledge of abortion policy or the literature examining it until that point, we assumed that more restrictive abortion policies would increase the number of unwanted births.

In the next step of the research process, I had my research assistant at the time (Amy Trainor) collect data on abortion policies across states through the late 1970s and 1980s and estimate the relationship between these policies and the birth rate. The results of this preliminary analysis provided no indication that states which enacted moderate restrictions on abortion access experienced an increase in the birth rate relative to other states that had no such change. The contrast between this result and my expectations led us to the initial conclusion that if births were unaffected, then perhaps these restrictions are not strong enough to have any impact on the abortion rate either. If not, then it would make sense that births would be unaffected. But subsequent preliminary analyses indicated that abortions did become less frequent when a restriction was imposed. Further investigation continued to provide the same qualitative results.

At that point it became clear that this question was no longer one about a statistical technique to be incorporated into another analysis, but an interesting and important question on its own. It became one of the main components of my research agenda for the next decade. I focused my attention on the discrepancy between the results that I had been expecting and those that I was obtaining. Was I thinking about the question in the right way? In particular, my prior expectations regarding the impact of abortion policy on fertility had little grounding in economic analysis. Further reflection in this regard suggested that perhaps the results I had been obtaining were consistent with the implications an economic model would provide.

At the time, I was on leave from Wellesley College and in residence at the National Bureau of Economic Research (NBER) in Cambridge. Doug Staiger was also on leave from his university and in residence at the NBER during the same time. Coincidentally, he was in a similar position regarding his analysis of abortion access and teen births, which he was conducting with Tom Kane. That year was very fruitful in developing my thinking on this topic and subsequent collaboration with Doug has helped to solidify it.

Based on reviews of the literature and my own subsequent research (much of which was coauthored), it became clear that the preliminary findings that I had initially found confusing could be supported by quite a bit of evidence. Moreover, minor extensions of standard economic models provided predictions that were consistent with these findings. Based on the weight of the evidence, my thinking about the impact of changes in abortion policy on individual behavior has changed. The results of this process are reflected in the contents of this book.

One question that I have been asked regarding my research in this area is whether or not I have received any funding and, if so, from whom. At one point, Doug Staiger and I did receive an award from the Kaiser Family Foundation to provide a literature review on the impact of abortion policy on fertility outcomes. Some of the material from that research has been incorporated into this book. I have also received some limited internal funding from Wellesley College to conduct research on this topic. Other than that, this research has been unfunded.

It is also important to recognize that this book has been written for a broader audience than just professional economists. As much as possible, I have attempted to review economists' methods in as intuitive a manner as possible before they are used, to clarify all of the assumptions being made, to describe the strengths and weaknesses of those methods, and to define any jargon that is introduced. It should be accessible to social scientists in other disciplines, others interested in public policy, and students in economics classes.

ACKNOWLEDGMENTS

IT GOES without saying that the undertaking of writing a book cannot be conducted without a great deal of assistance; I certainly have benefited tremendously from the input of others. First, I would like to thank my previous coauthors (Jon Gruber, Tom Kane, Doug Staiger, Amy Trainor, and David Zimmerman) on papers to which I have contributed that address the issue of abortion policy. They have each contributed greatly to my thinking on the topic. Although each of these individuals has been influential, I owe a special debt of gratitude to Doug Staiger, with whom I have worked the most in this area. During the course of the writing of this book, Doug has also been a useful sounding board for different ideas.

Others have provided valuable input in the form of comments provided on earlier drafts of the manuscript as well as in discussions that followed. Kristin Butcher and Melissa Kearney read through the entire manuscript at early stages, helping to point out flaws in my reasoning and weaknesses in exposition. Kristin dedicated many commuter train rides to focusing on my work, and for that I am extremely grateful. As for Melissa, I am very fortunate to have a talented new colleague just down the hall with whom I can share ideas on issues of common interest, including this one. Ted Joyce and Jim McCarthy provided formal reviews through Princeton University Press and both went above and beyond their formal requirements. Both clearly dedicated a great deal of time to their reviews, thinking hard about the issues raised and providing extensive comments that were quite helpful. I also received useful suggestions from participants in academic seminars at the University of North Carolina (at the Carolina Population Center and at the Triangle Health Economics Seminar) and Princeton University (at the Office of Population Research) based on an early draft of this book. I have also presented numerous academic seminars over the years drawing upon earlier abortion-related research projects and those discussions were also quite helpful in shaping my thinking. Of course, any remaining errors or omissions remain my own responsibility.

Over the years a number of other friends have also provided important contributions that helped to improve this book. Diane Whitmore and I began a project on teen fertility that never came to fruition, but vestiges of that research were incorporated in subsequent work that I completed along with this manuscript. Over the years, Ted Joyce has always been the first person to whom I send new work in this area, asking for comments. Although Ted and I do not always completely agree, the dialogue is always at a high level, and I look forward to being challenged by him. I have also benefited from casual conversations, usually taking place over lunch, with Jon Gruber about my research and this book.

I am also grateful to those who provided me with data necessary to write this book. Larry Finer and Stanley Henshaw of the Alan Guttmacher Institute provided me with the necessary data to estimate the distribution of women's distance to the nearest abortion provider. Marianne Bitler provided me with data on adoption rates in the early 1970s. Doug Staiger and Ted Joyce provided me with data necessary to replicate figures in their original papers (permission has been received from their respective publishers to reproduce them).

A number of others have made important contributions to this work as well. Jonathan Imber encouraged me to write this book and connected me with Peter Dougherty, the economics editor at Princeton University Press, which instigated the writing process. Peter, Kevin McInturff, and Ellen Foos at the Press have been very helpful in its production. Linda Truilo did an outstanding job of copyediting and Meredith Szwed's proofreading was very helpful. Nancy Dussault and Pat Sjostedt provided indispensable administrative assistance throughout the course of the project. My other Wellesley colleagues (particularly Kyle Kauffman) also provided valuable sounding boards, listening to me develop my arguments over the course of the past decade. Students in my "Economic Analysis of Social Policy" classes were also subject to preliminary expositions of the material in this book and class discussions were helpful in refining my thoughts. I am also extremely grateful to my family for providing me with the background support necessary to pursue my work and for occasionally diverting my attention to the matters that are more important than scholarship.

SEX AND CONSEQUENCES

Chapter One

INTRODUCTION

PUBLIC DISCUSSION regarding abortion policy in the United States tends to focus on the ideological extremes. Active participants in the debate typically align themselves with a pro-life or pro-choice position. To generalize, pro-life supporters view a fetus as a form of life with its own rights, so that abortion represents the taking of a life. Women who get pregnant with babies they do not want should carry the pregnancy to term and give up the child for adoption. Pro-choice activists believe in a woman's right to control her own body, and the ability to have an abortion represents an expression of that right. Whether or not a fetus is a person is a complicated question that each individual should be able to answer personally, and so each woman, not the government, should be allowed to weigh the trade-off regarding ending the pregnancy and what is best for her. Of course both positions can be argued far more elaborately and others hold positions intermediate to these, but these broad extremes frame the debate.

The clash in these ideologies has resulted in an impasse so great that only infrequently is the topic seriously addressed in public debate. Occasional flare-ups sometimes erupt, like that regarding "partial birth abortion" or the approval of RU-486, also known as the "abortion pill" or Mifepristone. But, for the most part, positions regarding abortion have become so deeply entrenched and the arguments so routine, that one can accurately forecast the course of an argument about abortion based on an individual's first few words. It is unnecessary to continue to fill in the rest since everyone knows what the details are going to be.

The 2000 presidential election provides a perfect example of this. Three debates between Vice President Gore and Governor Bush were held that year, each lasting an hour and a half. In the course of these debates, the candidates answered questions about abortion just once. During the one interchange that took place, Vice President Gore stated, "The main issue is whether or not the *Roe v. Wade* decision is going to be overturned. I support a woman's right to choose; my opponent does not" (Commission on Presidential Debates, 2002). Subsequently, Governor Bush affirmed that position, indicating "I am pro-life." With little additional detail regarding the broader issue of abortion availability, that exchange characterized the extent of the debate on a very complex issue.

Yet within this polarized environment, it is ironic that the majority of Americans do not hold views that are consistent with either of these ideological positions. The Gallup Organization routinely surveys the nation regarding individuals' views on abortion policy; some of its survey results are presented in more detail in chapter 2. Periodically they survey a random sample of the population regarding the circumstances under which abortion should be legal. The majority of Americans (57 percent in January 2003) routinely report that the specific circumstances matter. The rest are roughly evenly split between those supporting abortion in any circumstance or under none. If the circumstances matter so much for so many people, then the issue for them cannot be solely about ideology.

President Clinton provided one expression of this more pragmatic view of abortion policy, stating at the 1996 Democratic National Convention that "abortion should not only be safe and legal, it should be rare." This centrist view focuses more on behavior than ideology. Although women should have the right to have an abortion, one would prefer that they do not exercise that right too often; avoiding pregnancy in the first place would be preferable. From this perspective, the outcome of interest is the behaviors (pregnancy and abortion), not the support of a philosophical argument.

Such a behavioral perspective has taken on additional importance in light of a recent U.S. Supreme Court decision. In 1992, the court ruled in *Planned Parenthood of S.E. Pennsylvania v. Casey* that restrictions on abortion access would be deemed constitutional so long as they do not impose an "undue burden" on women. This decision is controversial in the sense that no specific definition was provided for what this standard specifically entails. The court only provided the additional comment that "an undue burden exists, and therefore a provision of law is invalid, if its purpose or effect is to place substantial obstacles in the path of a woman seeking an abortion before the fetus attains viability." Although it may be difficult to identify whether an undue burden is present, one approach would be to determine the ways in which women's behavior would be altered if the restriction were imposed. For instance, if the restriction led women to give birth to children that they did not want, then perhaps this would satisfy the condition for an undue burden.

The manner in which abortion policies alter women's behavior represents a series of questions that can be objectively answered. How does a change in the legal status of abortion alter fertility outcomes? Does it alter the frequency of abortion? Does that lead to a change in the number of births? More abortions would necessarily reduce births if a policy change altered abortion behavior, but not the likelihood of a pregnancy. However, the policy change may alter the likelihood of a pregnancy, so one could also ask whether pregnancies become more or less prevalent through changes in levels of sexual activity and / or contraceptive use.

Once one has answers to questions like these, one can take that information and use it to inform a debate about abortion policy from an alternative perspective. In other words, a discussion of abortion policy may be centered on the types of behavioral responses that are brought about by changes in policy rather than based upon philosophy.

The purpose of this book is to apply the tools of economic analysis to understand better these behavioral responses and their implications for policy. It is not intended to supplant in any sense the important philosophical issues on which the traditional debate has focused. In fact, for those who believe deeply in the philosophies supporting either pro-life or pro-choice positions, my approach would be unconvincing and inapplicable. But for others, it may help contribute to their thinking on the topic and inform the debate.

The main hypothesis that I present is that the availability of abortion may be viewed in some ways as a form of insurance. Economists have developed standard models of insurance in which the primary feature of its availability is that it provides those who purchase it with protection against downside risk. If an individual has car insurance and his or her car is stolen or is involved in an accident, the insurance will help pay for it to be replaced or repaired. However, if the insurance provides complete protection, it may bring about behavioral changes for those who purchase it in that it may lead to riskier behavior. If an individual's insurance provided full reimbursement for repair costs or full replacement value if the car were stolen, that person may drive more recklessly or park it in higher theft neighborhoods than he or she would have otherwise. Insurance companies try to minimize this form of behavior by charging deductibles and copayments so that the insured bears some of the cost of a loss, providing some incentive to prevent it from occurring.

The availability of abortion shares some of the features of a standard economic treatment of insurance. The primary feature of abortion is that it provides protection from downside risk in the form of giving birth to a child that is unintended, either because the timing for having a child is bad or because additional children are not desired. On the other hand, if this form of insurance is available at very low cost, it may lead to changes in behavior that increase the likelihood of its being needed. In other words, it may alter decisions regarding sexual activity and contraception that would affect the likelihood of becoming pregnant.

This framework provides specific behavioral predictions that would result in response to changes in abortion policy. If a very restrictive abortion policy is in place, relatively few women may choose to have an abortion. For those women who are pregnant with children that they do not want, they largely may be forced to give birth anyway in this environment. If abortion policies were made less restrictive, women may choose to abort a pregnancy rather than give birth to an unwanted child. This represents the protection from downside risk that abortion availability can offer. But at some point, abortion availability may become sufficiently unrestricted that most or all women who would otherwise give birth to an unwanted child will choose to abort. If additional restrictions were removed, few, if any, unwanted births would be averted.

On the other hand, as abortion becomes even more readily available, the scope for changes in the likelihood of a pregnancy grows. Since using contraception or abstaining from sexual activity may be viewed as costly, women / couples may choose to do so less frequently, in essence substituting abortion for contraception, as abortion becomes even more accessible. Moreover, the availability of relatively low-cost abortion provides another benefit to women / couples in that it enables some time to pass between conception and the point at which a decision needs to be made regarding an abortion. This allows the decision makers to obtain additional information regarding the value of giving birth, such as the response of family members, the strength of the couple's relationship, or just the woman's or couple's own feelings about having a child. In this way, getting pregnant with the option to abort is actually advantageous and does not necessarily result solely from the substitution of abortion for contraception.

The implications from viewing abortion in this insurance framework suggest that different types of public policies may have very different types of effects. For instance, outlawing abortion may lead to a significant increase in unwanted births. On the other hand, comparatively smaller restrictions may not increase unwanted births much at all despite reducing the number of abortions performed. The reduction in abortion would be brought about by greater use of contraception and/or less sexual activity, resulting in fewer pregnancies.

Empirical research that has tested these predictions using data from the United States and other countries generally supports these predictions. In the United States, the process of abortion legalization in the early 1970s represented the biggest change in policy; studies of the impact of this policy-change suggest that birth rates fell considerably in response. Since then some states have instituted different forms of restrictions on abortion access, like Medicaid-funding restrictions, parental involvement laws, and mandatory delay laws that make it somewhat more difficult for women to obtain abortions. The reduction in the number of abortion clinics over time in some areas represents another form of moderately restricted abortion access. Overall, there is little evidence to indicate that these forms of restrictions increase the birth rate despite the fact that abortions are found to decline, suggesting that pregnancies become less common in response.

Similar evidence is available from an analysis of changes in abortion policy in other countries. Many countries in Eastern Europe, in particular, have experienced changes in abortion policy over the past two decades largely, but not exclusively, linked to political changes in those countries. Almost all of these changes resulted in liberal abortion laws, but the degree to which abortion used to be restricted varied quite a bit. The evidence shows that in countries where abortion was severely restricted, a broad legalization led to a reduction in births. On the other hand, in countries where previous restrictions were relatively modest in scope, legalization did not result in fewer births despite the fact that abortions increased, suggesting that pregnancies rose. Taken as a whole, these findings are consistent with the view that abortion acts like a form of insurance.

In what way can these findings be used to address the question of the appropriate design of abortion policy? At this point, the analogy of abortion as a form of insurance breaks down. As I described earlier, copayments and deductibles are appropriate methods to deal with the incentive issues that result from complete insurance in standard cases. With car insurance, for example, society as a whole is better off if excessive car thefts and accident rates can be reduced since they impose additional costs on society beyond those paid by the owner of the car. A straightforward extension to abortion policy might lead one to think that some form of moderate restriction would be appropriate. By imposing a small cost on the insured as a means to prevent excess use of the insurance, it would reduce "excessive" abortions.

But this implication may not be appropriate here. For instance, women / couples will choose the method of fertility control that is least costly (in terms of money or other factors) for them. If abortion is chosen more often because of its lower cost relative to contraception or abstinence, then it is valuable to them. Therefore, if the abortion decision only had an impact on the couple themselves, abortion should be unrestricted.

The problem with this view is that abortion decisions may also lead to something that economists call an "externality," in which the behavior of one individual has implications for the well-being of others. Such externalities in the car insurance example include the police expenditures and harm to others brought about by greater rates of car theft and accidents. In the present context, however, that externality may be positive or negative for society. Other individuals may promote a couple's ability to make the most informed choice possible or they may decry the outcome of their decision. In fact, violating a woman's right to privacy or taking away a child's life represent extreme examples of externalities that one could incorporate into this decision should one want to reintroduce these philosophical arguments. Either way, incorporating this externality significantly complicates the determination of appropriate public policy. Arriving at a solution requires weighing the advantages received by some against the hardships imposed upon others; a definitive solution to this problem is beyond the scope of economic analysis.

In a sense, the analysis presented here mimics the strengths and weaknesses that economic analysis brings to any policy discussion. Economists make a distinction between "positive" and "normative" questions. A positive question asks "what is" and a normative question asks "what should be." For instance, one could ask whether the minimum wage increases unemployment. This is a positive question and economic analysis can provide a strong framework for evaluating this claim (although, in this case it still generates quite a bit of controversy!). The answer to this question, along with other positive questions like the extent to which minimum-wage jobs are held by poor people, could help inform the normative question of whether we should increase the minimum wage.

Typically, economists have far more success addressing positive questions. We can generally offer some insight into how to use the answers generated by positive questions to evaluate the normative question, but the answer to that normative question may remain unresolved. This is the position I find myself in with the analysis of abortion policy in this book. I can attempt to clarify the circumstances under which one would favor a certain set of policies over others, but in the end it is impossible to state definitively what the best set of policies is. Nevertheless, the findings can serve as a reasonably agreed on set of facts that can be used in a broader discussion about the normative question of what form abortion policy should take.

Some of the ideas expressed in this book have been described earlier by others, and particularly by Posner (1992). Posner also treats abortion restrictions as a cost and discusses the impact of changes in its legal status on the likelihood of pregnancy. Moreover, he describes a process of weighing the social costs and benefits of the unwanted births that may result if abortion were illegal, in determining how abortion policy should be set. But there are two main differences between the research presented here and that in Posner (1992). First, his economic analysis is provided at an intuitive level that is consistent with basic economic premises, but the lack of detail overlooks some of its nuances. For instance, no recognition is made of the distinction between minor abortion restrictions and an outright ban in discussing the impact of abortion policy. Second, no empirical evidence is presented to support his hypotheses. It is the combination of economic modeling and empirical evidence that is presented in this book that considerably strengthens the conclusions drawn.

The remainder of the book will provide the material necessary to support and interpret these conclusions based on the theoretical and empirical evidence. Chapter 2 will provide the institutional background in the United States necessary to place the contents of much of the rest of the book in context. I will briefly review the legislation and judicial decisions that have shaped the history of abortion policy in the twentieth century. This information will be crucial for the design of the quasi-experiments described in subsequent chapters. I also present an extensive array of statistics regarding abortion in the United States, including, for example, its incidence, trends over time, and the characteristics of those who abort as well as their reasons for doing so.

Chapters 3 through 7 present the main theoretical and empirical analyses. Chapter 3 presents the theoretical framework that provides predictions regarding the impact of changes in abortion policy on individual behavior. The concept of abortion as insurance is derived from this analysis. In chapter 4, I provide an overview of the empirical methods employed to assess whether changes in abortion policy have a causal impact on an individual's behavior. The empirical evidence to be presented will extensively use quasi-experimental methods, and this chapter will provide a primer in their use. Although these methods provide significant benefits for the study of abortion policy, they are not perfect and appropriate caveats are required in order to adequately interpret the findings that come from them. Therefore, I will describe the methods and review both their strengths and weaknesses. I present empirical results for the United States in chapters 5 and 6. The former examines the impact of abortion legalization itself and the latter considers relatively minor restrictions like Medicaid funding and parental consent laws. These results are largely based upon previous research, although some new analyses are reported as well.

Up until this point the analysis has narrowly investigated abortion policy in the United States, but chapter 7 broadens the discussion into the international arena. In particular, I focus on Europe separately, examining Eastern and Western European countries. Initially I present a brief overview of the institutional environment, reviewing legislative changes, judicial decisions, and the statistical background necessary to interpret subsequent analyses. I then conduct empirical exercises analogous to those regarding the United States to investigate the impact of changes in abortion policy on individual behavior.

Although this book will cover a great deal of territory in evaluating the impact of abortion policy, there are still a number of questions that remain unanswered. Chapter 8 will identify some of those questions, describing what we do know about them and what still remains to be understood. The topics covered in that chapter include the impact of abortion policy on other outcomes, like life-cycle fertility, marriage, and the well-being of children, and the impact of welfare reform on abortion. In addition, I will briefly address other abortion policy issues, like the impact of RU-486, partial birth abortion, and the impact of improvements in contraceptive technology compared to changes in abortion access.

The final chapter summarizes the findings and discusses their implications for policy. After reviewing the findings presented earlier in the book, I will take up the normative question regarding the implications of the positive analysis for abortion policy. As I indicated earlier, this discussion will leave us with a useful framework to help think about appropriate public policy in this area, but it will be limited in its ability to draw specific conclusions regarding what the "right" policy should be. Although I do not conclude with specific policy prescriptions, this book offers the significant contribution of shedding new light on an old question with the hope of stimulating fresh discussion.

Chapter Two

ABORTION LAW AND PRACTICE

IT IS IMPOSSIBLE to undertake an examination of any public policy issue, let alone one as intricate as abortion policy, without a thorough understanding of its background. This chapter begins with a relatively brief description of the judicial decisions and legislative history over the past half century of the particular policies that will be addressed subsequently in this book.[1] The topics covered here include the original legalization of abortion in the early 1970s, and then the main forms of restrictions imposed on abortion since then, including Medicaid funding of abortion, parental involvement laws, and mandatory delay laws.

Following this, I will present a statistical overview describing the practice of abortion in the United States today. This section will characterize the extent to which abortion is utilized, how abortion services are provided, and the characteristics of women who choose to abort. I conclude this chapter with a brief overview of public opinion regarding support for legal abortion under various circumstances and for restrictions imposed upon it. The remainder of the book will draw on many of the facts presented here.

Judicial Decisions and Legislation

Abortion was not outlawed in the United States until the late 1800s, when public health concerns led states to institute bans on the procedure. These laws allowed for a legal abortion only under very specific instances, notably if carrying the pregnancy to term would endanger the life of the mother. They remained in effect, mainly unaltered, for decades (c.f. Calderone 1958; and Garrow 1994). In the 1960s, however, the process that eventually led to the 1973 *Roe v. Wade* decision, legalizing abortion across the nation, began in earnest. Ever since the *Roe* decision, legislatures and courts have extensively grappled with restrictions on abortion access, with much of the attention focused on three types of restrictions: Medicaid funding, parental involvement, and mandatory delay. This section of the chapter will characterize the legislative and judicial developments over the past half century that have resulted in our current legal environment regarding abortion.

Abortion Legalization

It is well known that the Supreme Court's 1973 decision in *Roe v. Wade* established the right of women to obtain legal abortions under most circumstances. This decision marked the continuation of a radical departure from earlier court decisions regarding women's sexuality and fertility. As recently as the *Poe v. Ullman* decision in 1961, the court upheld a lower court ruling in favor of a Connecticut law that outlawed contraception even for married individuals (see table 2.1 for highlights of relevant Supreme Court decisions regarding the legal status of abortion as well as the restrictions imposed upon its access discussed subsequently). The state did not enforce this law, which was the argument made by the court for its decision. Nevertheless, at this point the majority of the Court did not support a woman's right to privacy, which became the backbone of the *Roe* decision, although dissenting opinions did raise the idea.

That right was not recognized until the court's 1965 decision in *Griswold v. Connecticut*. That case also pertained to the Connecticut law that prevented married women from obtaining contraception. In response to the *Poe* ruling, family planning activists in Connecticut opened a birth control clinic and were immediately arrested. Such action by the state contradicted the Supreme Court's reasoning in *Poe*. The case progressed through the legal system until it finally reached the United States Supreme Court. In 1965, the court ruled in this case that the Connecticut law was unconstitutional because it violated individuals' right to privacy.

Although the *Roe* decision in 1973 would represent the next major Supreme Court action on the path to legalized abortion, considerable action was taking place at the state level directed at reducing or eliminating the restrictions on abortion in the interim. These actions significantly altered the landscape regarding a woman's ability to obtain an abortion. The first set of state changes were attributable to reform proposals originally made in 1962 by the American Law Institute (ALI). At that time, the ALI proposed lifting restrictions on abortion in the following cases: (1) if the pregnancy affected the physical or mental health of the mother; (2) if there was a fetal deformity; or (3) if the pregnancy resulted from rape or incest. These reforms were adopted by a dozen states between 1967 and 1970; these states, along with the year in which the reforms were adopted, are reported in table 2.2.

During this period courts at the state level were also handing down decisions that created some ambiguity in the status of abortion laws. The most dramatic of these decisions came in California, where the State Supreme Court ruled in 1969 that the state's pre-1967 law prohibiting abortion was unconstitutional. This decision led to a "de facto" legalization of abortion,

TABLE 2.1.
Summary of Judicial Decisions Regarding Abortion

Supreme Court Case	*Laws Challenged*	*Decision Regarding Law*	*Comments*
Legality of Abortion			
Poe v. Ullman (1961)	Connecticut law banning contraception	Upheld	Law had not been enforced previously, so ruling had little immediate consequences.
Griswold v. Connecticut (1965)	Connecticut law banning contraception	Reversed	First decision based upon a woman's right to privacy, which was important in the *Roe v. Wade* decision.
Roe v. Wade (1973)	Texas statute prohibiting abortion	Reversed	No state intervention in the first trimester; intervention in second trimester limited to matters regarding maternal health only; after viability, state may restrict abortion to cases of life endangerment.
Doe v. Bolton (1973)	Abortions performed in certain hospitals only; abortions approved by committee; residency requirement	Reversed	All three provisions defeated. State may not intervene in the decision to have an abortion and where a first-trimester abortion can be performed.
Restrictions on Medicaid Funding of Abortions			
Harris v. McRae (1980) *Williams v. Zbaraz* (1980)	Hyde Amendment	Upheld	State may exclude abortion from Medicaid coverage, even if the abortion is medically necessary.
Webster v. Reproductive Health Services (1989)	No state funding for counseling on abortion; public employees and facilities prohibited from performing abortions	Upheld	Reaffirms earlier rulings allowing states to choose not to use their own funds to pay for abortion services and /or counseling.
Parental Consent			
Planned Parenthood of Central Missouri v. Danforth (1976)	Parental consent	Overturned	Blanket parental consent requirement may not be imposed for all minors.
Bellotti v. Baird (1979)	Parental consent	Upheld	Decision itself was about procedural issues, but the court offered reasoning that applied to subsequent cases. Every minor must have judicial option to abortion decision, which does not require parental intervention; a minor found mature enough by court to make her own decision must be allowed to do so, without being subject to veto of parents.

TABLE 2.1. (*cont'd*)

Supreme Court Case	*Laws Challenged*	*Decision Regarding Law*	*Comments*
Parental Consent (*cont'd*)			
H.L. v. Matheson (1981)	Parental notification	Upheld	Law is valid because it does not give power of veto over decision to parents.
Planned Parenthood of Kansas City v. Ashcroft (1983)	Parental consent	Upheld	First formal ruling that a parental consent law with judicial bypass option is constitutional.
Ohio v. Akron Center for Reproductive Health (1990)	Parental notification	Upheld	Statute requires notification of one parent 24 hours prior to procedure with judicial bypass option.
Hodgson v. Minnesota (1990)	Parental notification	Upheld	Statute requires notification of both parents 48 hours prior to the procedure with judicial bypass option; requirement will be waived if one parent cannot be located, minor is victim of physical or sexual abuse, or emergency situation exists.
Planned Parenthood of S.E. Pennsylvania v. Casey (1992)	Parental consent	Upheld	Statute upheld because requirements do not pose an "undue burden."
Informed Consent and Mandatory Delay			
City of Akron v. Akron Center for Reproductive Health (1983)	Informed consent and waiting period	Overturned	Information presented to women seeking abortions should be nonpersuasive; waiting period is not necessary in ensuring the safety and health of the pregnant woman.
Thornburgh v. American College of Obstetricians and Gynecologists (1986)	Informed consent	Overturned	Statute struck down because the court felt its purpose was to convince women not to have an abortion.
Planned Parenthood of S.E. Pennsylvania v. Casey (1992)	Informed consent and waiting period	Upheld	Statute upheld because requirements do not pose an "undue burden."

which could be observed by the frequency in which abortions were conducted in the state by 1970 (c.f. Garrow 1994; Potts et al., 1977; and U.S. Department of HEW, Public Health Service, Center for Disease Control, 1971). The legality of abortion in eight other states became ambiguous as well between 1969 and 1972 following lower court rulings invalidating earlier anti-abortion laws. However, there was no obvious, dramatic impact of these lower court rulings on the availability of abortion in these

TABLE 2.2.
Summary of Abortion Liberalization in the United States

Category	*State and Year of Liberalization*
Repeal States (5): States in which abortion was legally available prior to *Roe v. Wade.*	Alaska (1970), California (1970),[1] Hawaii (1970), New York (1970), Washington (1970)
Reform States (12): States that implemented modest reforms prior to *Roe v. Wade* making it legal for women to obtain abortions under special circumstances.	Arkansas (1969), Colorado (1967), Delaware (1970), Florida (1968), Georgia (1968), Kansas (1969), Maryland (1968), New Mexico (1969), North Carolina (1967), Oregon (1969), South Carolina (1970), Virginia (1970)
"Court" States (8): States in which lower level court decisions left status of abortion policy somewhat ambiguous.	Connecticut (1972), District of Columbia (1969), Illinois (1971), Michigan (1970), Missouri (1971), New Jersey (1972), South Dakota (1970), Vermont (1972)
Control States (26): States in which abortion laws were unchanged until *Roe v. Wade.*	Alabama, Arizona, Idaho, Indiana, Iowa, Kentucky, Louisiana, Maine, Massachusetts, Minnesota, Mississippi, Montana, Nebraska, Nevada, New Hampshire, North Dakota, Ohio, Oklahoma, Pennsylvania, Rhode Island, Tennessee, Texas, Utah, West Virginia, Wisconsin, Wyoming

Source: Alan Guttmacher Institute (1989), Garrow (1994), and Merz et al. (1995).

[1] California is categorized as a repeal state starting in 1970 even though no formal repeal legislation was passed. This coding is based upon the 1969 State Supreme Court's decision that the pre-1967 state abortion law was unconstitutional and evidence that legal abortions were commonly practiced in the state by 1970 (c.f. Garrow 1994; Potts et al. 1977).

states like there was in California (c.f. U.S. Department of HEW, Public Health Service, Center for Disease Control 1971, 1972, 1974).

The clearest and most dramatic changes in abortion policy preceding the *Roe* decision took place in four states (New York, Washington, Hawaii, and Alaska) that in 1970 enacted legislation repealing their abortion bans. Because of its size, New York was perhaps the most important site of these policy changes. The formal legalization of abortion in New York effectively enabled many women in the densely populated East Coast to abort an unwanted pregnancy as well, since they could fairly easily travel to New York to do so.

But the legislative process that led to abortion legalization in New York was not a smooth one, and legalization could not have been considered in any way to be an anticipated outcome. The law repealing the existing legislation outlawing abortion passed by one vote because one member of the state assembly changed his vote at the last minute. That assemblyman stated, "I realize, Mr. Speaker, that I am terminating my political career, but I cannot in good conscience sit here and allow my vote to be the one that defeats this bill (Garrow 1994, 420)." The bill was signed into law on April 11, 1970 and went into effect on July 1st of that year. Although abortion had been legalized and began to be practiced openly, its future legal status was far from clear. Two years later, both houses of the New York State legislature passed a bill revoking the 1970 repeal law, but the governor vetoed it.

For the remainder of the country, no more states legalized abortion prior to the U.S. Supreme Court decision in *Roe v. Wade* in January of 1973. The *Roe* case challenged a Texas law that prohibited abortions except where the life of the pregnant woman was endangered by carrying the pregnancy to term. In its decision, the Supreme Court ruled that states were not allowed to intervene in the abortion decision during the first trimester of pregnancy, and that during the second trimester intervention would be limited to matters regarding maternal health, such as the quality of the abortion facility or physician. Finally, after viability of the fetus had occurred, the state would be allowed to restrict abortion to life threatening cases. The basis of this decision was the right to privacy, which the court's majority recognized is not explicitly mentioned in the Constitution, but has evolved as a matter of case law.[2]

On the same day as the *Roe* decision the court also ruled on a case, *Doe v. Bolton*, that challenged a Georgia abortion statute which imposed restrictions on where an abortion could be performed and which required that abortions be approved by a three-doctor hospital committee. The statute also included a residency requirement, which established that abortions would not be performed on women who had not been residents of the state for a minimum period of time. The court struck down all three of these provisions as well.

Although these two cases attempted to define the legal ability of a state to restrict abortion access, the boundary within which restrictions could be imposed was somewhat ambiguous. Many states went ahead and enacted their own restrictions. These laws were typically challenged in the courts and many eventually found their way up to the Supreme Court. Subsequent court decisions helped further define the bounds regarding the types of restrictions that would be allowed. The legal development of the most common form of these restrictions—including restrictions on Medicaid funding of abortion, parental involvement before a minor can abort, and mandatory delay before an abortion could be performed—is discussed next.

Medicaid Funding Restrictions

Medicaid is the government program that provides health insurance to poor people. It is largely administered at the state level, although its financing is split between the federal and state governments. In each annual budget, the federal government needs to approve the expenditures to be made to the states to pay its share of the Medicaid bill. In the immediate aftermath of abortion legalization, the Medicaid system would cover the costs of abortion for Medicaid recipients. In 1976, however, Senator Henry Hyde of Illinois sponsored an amendment (known as the "Hyde Amendment") that would prohibit federal funds from being used to pay for abortions; this amendment was passed in that year (to commence for the first time in 1977) and in every subsequent year. Therefore, the Medicaid system could only pay for abortions if the state government where a woman lived chose to pay the full monetary price. At present, seventeen states do so (some voluntarily and some in response to state court orders), meaning that poor women in thirty-three states and the District of Columbia do not have access to public funds to pay for abortions.

When the Hyde Amendment was initially enacted in 1976, it was immediately contested in the courts, and an injunction was imposed blocking its implementation. About a year later, that injunction was lifted while the courts continued to hear cases contesting it. Finally, in June of 1980 the U.S. Supreme Court ruled in *Harris v. McRae* and *Williams v. Zbaraz* that the Hyde Amendment was constitutional. This history can be roughly characterized by three separate periods. In 1974–76 Medicaid funding for abortions was generally available. Between 1977 and 1980 the status of the law was unclear, triggered on and off by a series of judicial decisions at both the federal and state levels. A woman making fertility decisions would have had difficulty perfectly forecasting the court's behavior and would have to incorporate this uncertainty into her decisions. By late 1980, the Supreme Court's rulings eliminated all ambiguity, and states that wanted to restrict Medicaid funding clearly could do so. After these rulings, twenty-seven states almost immediately instituted definitive, enforceable Medicaid funding restrictions. Ever since then a handful of states have added restrictions and a few states have removed theirs (largely attributable to court decisions at the state level), but most of the movement in public funding of abortion took place right after these 1980 U.S. Supreme Court rulings. Table 2.3 details the states that have imposed these restrictions over time.

TABLE 2.3.
Enforced Abortion Restrictions and Years in Which Restrictions Were in Effect

State	*Medicaid Funding*	*Parental Involvement*	*Mandatory Delay*
Alabama	1981–present	1987–present	
Alaska			
Arizona	1977–present		
Arkansas	1981–present	1989–present	2001–present
California			
Colorado	1985–present		
Connecticut		1990–present	
Delaware	1981–present	1995–present	
District of Columbia	1988–1993, 1998–present		
Florida	1981–present		
Georgia	1981–present	1991–present	
Hawaii			
Idaho	1981–1993	2001–present	1995–present
Illinois	1981–1993		
Indiana	1981–2000	1984–present	1997–present
Iowa	1981–present	1996–present	
Kansas	1981–present	1992–present	1992–present
Kentucky	1978–present	1994–present	2000–present
Louisiana	1981–present	1981–present	1995–present
Maine	1981–present	1989–present	
Maryland		1992–present	
Massachusetts		1979–present	
Michigan	1989–present	1991–present	1999–present
Minnesota	1981–1993	1981–1986, 1990–present	
Mississippi	1981–present	1993–present	1992–present
Missouri	1981–present	1979–present	
Montana	1981–1994		
Nebraska	1981–present	1991–present	1993–present
Nevada	1981–present		
New Hampshire	1981–present		
New Jersey			

TABLE 2.3. (*cont'd*)

State	*Medicaid Funding*	*Parental Involvement*	*Mandatory Delay*
New Mexico	1981–1994		
New York			
North Carolina	1996–present	1995–present	
North Dakota	1978–present	1981–present	1994–present
Ohio	1981–present	1985–present	1994–present
Oklahoma	1981–present		
Oregon			
Pennsylvania	1985–present	1994–present	1994–present
Rhode Island	1978–present	1982–present	
South Carolina	1981–present	1990–present	1995–present
South Dakota	1981–present	1997–present	1994–present
Tennessee	1981–present	1999–present	
Texas	1981–present	1999–present	
Utah	1981–present	1974–present	1994–present
Vermont	1981–1983		
Virginia	1981–present	1997–present	2001–present
Washington			
West Virginia		1984–present	
Wisconsin	1981–present	1984–present	1996–present
Wyoming	1978–present	1989–present	

Note: Parental Involvement laws include parental consent and parental notification laws as well as laws that require mandatory counseling for teens. The "present" is defined to be September 2002. Medicaid funding restrictions that are listed as being instituted in 1981 really began late in 1980.

Parental Involvement

The history of parental involvement laws is less discrete in nature, partly because court rulings on this issue have evolved over time. Parental involvement laws can either require minors, typically under the age of 18 to obtain consent from their parent or guardian before an abortion can be performed or they can require minors simply to notify them of their intention to have an abortion.[3] The first major case involving such a law was decided in 1976 in *Planned Parenthood of Central Missouri v. Danforth*. That case involved a Missouri law whose main provisions required written consent by the patient, as well as spousal consent for married individuals and parental consent for minors, before an abortion could be performed. The court ruled that the parental consent provision was unconstitutional because of the universal nature of its enforcement.

The ability of a minor to circumvent parental intervention, if so desired, became a major theme in subsequent court decisions regarding parental consent. This view was first expressed in *Belloti v. Baird* (1979), which addressed a Massachusetts law that required parental consent but also allowed a minor to obtain an abortion without parental consent if court approval was provided instead. But these arguments were made within the context of a case regarding a procedural issue; it was not a ruling on the constitutionality of the law itself. But similar reasoning was provided in *H.L. v. Matheson* (1981). In this case, the court ruled on a Utah law requiring notification of a minor's parents before an abortion could be performed. Because the parents held no veto power in the abortion decision, the court ruled, such a policy was ruled to be constitutional. *Planned Parenthood of Kansas City v. Ashcroft* (1983) represented the first case in which this reasoning was applied to a parental consent law. Since the law allowed the minor to seek the approval of a judge rather than her parents, the court ruled that it was constitutional. Subsequent Supreme Court rulings in *Ohio v. Akron Center for Reproductive Health* (1990) and *Hodgson v. Minnesota* (1990) reaffirmed the reasoning in these earlier cases, ruling that parental notification of one or both parents with judicial bypass is constitutional. The court's ruling in *Planned Parenthood of S.E. Pennsylvania v. Casey* (1992) placed the issue of parental involvement within the context of broader guidelines on abortion restrictions, indicating that restrictions would be deemed constitutional so long as they do not impose an "undue burden" on women. Parental consent with judicial bypass does not impose such an obstacle, the court ruled.

The increasing clarity with which the court supported the constitutionality of these laws over time led to a gradual progression of the number of states implementing them. As shown in Table 2.3, at present thirty-three states have parental involvement laws in place, with these laws becoming more common over time.

Mandatory Delay

Another form of restriction that some states attempted to implement would require those seeking an abortion to wait a specified period between the time when they requested an abortion and the time when the procedure could be performed. These laws typically also require that information be provided to the women regarding fetal development, the abortion procedure, alternatives to abortion, etc., so that the women could provide "informed consent" before the procedure could be performed.

The development of the law in this regard is perhaps the most dramatic in that the court actually reversed its thinking on the topic. In its 1983 ruling in *City of Akron v. Akron Center for Reproductive Health*, the court ruled that a waiting period does not satisfy "any legitimate state interest," and that the information required to be provided cannot be specifically designed to persuade a pregnant woman away from having an abortion. Similar reasoning regarding informed consent was offered in *Thornburgh v. American College of Obstetricians and Gynecologists* in 1986.

But this reasoning was explicitly contradicted in the court's decision in *Planned Parenthood of S.E. Pennsylvania v. Casey* (1992). In establishing a broader framework for introducing restrictions on abortion, the court stated that such restrictions are constitutional so long as they do not pose an "undue burden" on a woman's ability to have an abortion. The majority opinion goes on to define an undue burden as one whose "purpose or effect is to place substantial obstacles in the path of a woman seeking an abortion before the fetus attains viability." The court held that mandatory delay would make abortion "more expensive and less convenient," but that this did not impose an undue burden. It specifically stated that "the premise behind (*City of Akron v. Akron Center for Reproductive Health*'s) invalidation of a waiting period between the provision of the information deemed necessary to informed consent and the performance of an abortion . . . is also wrong."

The development of constitutional law in this regard strongly shaped the pattern of implementation of mandatory delay laws. Prior to 1992, no states enforced such laws since they were explicitly prohibited by earlier court rulings. Subsequent to the *Casey* decision in 1992, however, a number of states have enacted and enforced them, the majority of which came about within a few years of *Casey* (shown in table 2.3). Currently seventeen states enforce such laws.

Abortion in Practice

This section of the chapter will switch gears away from the legislative and judicial environment and present a descriptive analysis of the practice of abortion in the United States. I will present a series of statistics designed to characterize the frequency with which abortion is practiced along with its monetary price, the characteristics of abortion providers, and the characteristics of those who obtain abortions. From the perspective of economics, each of these topics can be thought of as a different component of a market outcome. In any market, there are those who demand a product or service and those who supply it. They come together in a marketplace and their interaction leads to an outcome where a certain amount of the product or service is bought and sold at a certain price. With abortion, women demand abortion services, providers supply those services, and the utilization of abortion along with its price represents the market outcome. The statistics presented here will describe each element of this marketplace separately.

Sources of Abortion Data

Before I present this descriptive analysis, it is important to understand where data on abortions come from, along with strengths and weaknesses of this information. This discussion will help us interpret those data presented subsequently.

The main difficulty in obtaining data on abortions is that it is a sensitive topic for which it is difficult to obtain accurate reports, ruling out large-scale surveys of individuals. The two main sources of national data on the incidence of abortion are the Alan Guttmacher Institute (AGI) and the Centers for Disease Control and Prevention (CDC). Both rely on sources other than individual women to obtain their statistics, improving their reliability. The AGI conducts surveys of abortion providers, inquiring about the number of procedures performed in the past year (or in the year before that). Because AGI has an extensive list of abortion providers, including those who perform a very small number of abortions per year, these data are generally recognized as the most accurate available. The CDC obtains information from state health departments along with limited surveys and other estimation procedures to obtain its count of the number of abortions. Their approach does miss some abortions, however, and the abortion count obtained by AGI averages 15 percent higher than that obtained by CDC (Alan Guttmacher Institute, 1997).

Along with the counts of abortions provided, both AGI and CDC collect additional information regarding abortion patients that is consistent with the sources used. The "*Vital Statistics*" nature of the CDC data means that it is also possible to obtain information on demographic status of women who abort, the length of gestation at the time of the abortion, the method used, and the number of previous abortions and pregnancies. The provider-based nature of the AGI survey makes it feasible also to collect data on the type of provider (hospital, clinic, etc.), the cost of the abortion, distance traveled from the patient's residence to the abortion provider, etc. In the statistics that follow, I will utilize data from AGI if it is available because it more accurately represents the population of abortion patients. If those data are unavailable, however, I will rely on CDC data instead.

Despite the availability of CDC and AGI abortion data, these data alone are not sufficient to provide a complete picture of the practice of abortion in the United States. Yet other "standard" data sources that also collect survey-based information on abortion are generally so weak for this purpose that their use must be significantly limited. For instance, the National Survey of Family Growth (NSFG), which is conducted periodically, most recently in 1995, surveys women of childbearing age and asks them about their entire pregnancy history, including abortion as an outcome. However, data from this survey under-reports abortion at the rate of about 50 percent, making it difficult to use these data to describe the characteristics of women who abort. I will use these data in some analyses later in the book, but their use requires appropriate assumptions and recognition of their potentially serious limitations. Beyond that I will also rely here on data collected by AGI in additional surveys that are not regularly conducted. For instance, AGI surveys have located national samples of abortion patients and obtained information on their characteristics. Another AGI survey similarly obtained information on the reasons why women obtained abortions. Data from these additional sources will be utilized subsequently in describing the characteristics of women who abort (the demand side of the market).

The Incidence and Price of an Abortion (the "Market Outcome")

The trend over time in the frequency of abortion, along with that of births and pregnancies, is presented in figure 2.1. In each case, rates are presented that indicate the number of events per 1,000 women of childbearing age. The use of rates is useful for this purpose because it creates a base representing those who are at-risk of the event before making comparisons over time. In 2000, the last year for which AGI abortion data are available, the abortion rate was 21.3, meaning that there were 21.3 abortions performed for every 1,000 women between the ages of 15 and 44. In other words, 2.1 percent of women of childbearing age aborted a pregnancy in that year. Historically, as one might have expected, the abortion rate rose significantly in the 1970s in the aftermath of the *Roe v. Wade* decision. It virtually doubled between 1973 and 1980, rising from 16.3 to 29.3 (although some of this increase may have been attributable to more complete counts of abortions performed). Since that point, the abortion rate held relatively stable over the 1980s and has declined somewhat in the 1990s.

These trends can be compared to the rates of birth and pregnancy over this period as well. There are obvious implications for changes in the frequency of abortion for the trend in births if pregnancy behavior remains unchanged; every additional abortion would prevent an additional birth.[4] This pattern is somewhat supported in the 1970s as the increase

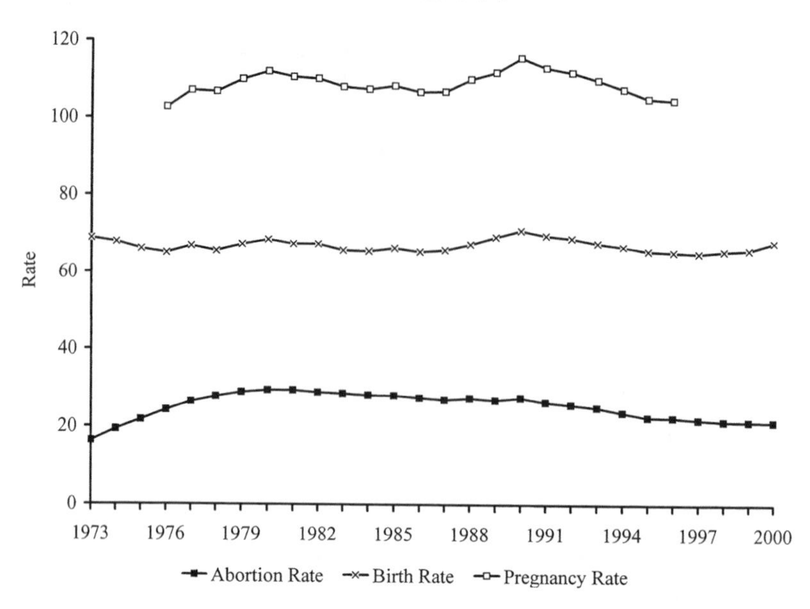

FIGURE 2.1. Abortion, Birth, and Pregnancy Rates (rates per 1,000 women age 15–44). *Source*: Ventura et al. (2000), Martin et al. (2002b), and Finer and Henshaw (2003).

in the abortion rate is matched with a slight decline in the birth rate. But the decline in the birth rate is relatively small compared to the increase in the abortion rate, suggesting that pregnancies increased over the period as well. This is precisely the pattern observed through 1980 in figure 2.1. Therefore, a significant component of the increase in abortions over this period was an increase in pregnancies, not a reduction in (presumably) unwanted births. Although these data themselves cannot tell us whether or not abortion legalization caused the increase in pregnancies, I will return to this issue in chapter 5. Similarly, through most of the 1990s, the abortion rate declined concurrently with the birth rate indicating that pregnancies must have declined as well, which is supported by the data. Although the reason for these patterns is not clear at this point, it is useful to recognize at this point in the analysis that abortions and births are not necessarily substitutes because the likelihood of pregnancies can change as well.

Another important observation from figure 2.1 is that the rate of abortions is reasonably high compared to the rate of pregnancies. To illustrate this more clearly, figure 2.2 displays the percentage of pregnancies that resulted in an abortion between 1976 and 1996. Through the end of the 1970s, that percentage climbed to 27 percent; more than one in four preg-

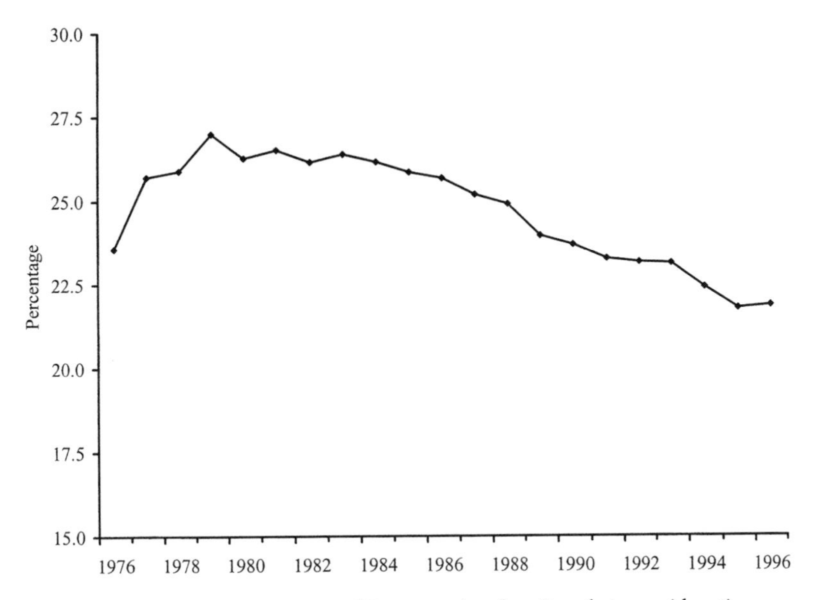

FIGURE 2.2. Percentages of Pregnancies that Result in an Abortion. *Source*: Ventura et al. (2000).

nancies resulted in an abortion at that time. Since then, this percentage has declined steadily, but in 1996 still more than one in five pregnancies (specifically 21.9 percent) resulted in abortion.

Figures 2.3 and 2.4 present the same information separately for teens. The patterns in the trends in abortion, birth, and pregnancy rates in figure 2.3 are similar to those for all women of childbearing age, but are more dramatic for the teens. Abortion rates climbed through the 1970s before stabilizing at a level of just over 40 abortions per 1,000 teens (or 4 percent of teens per year) and then falling off considerably in the 1990s to a rate of 27.5 in 1996 (almost 3 percent per year). In the 1970s, abortions and births moved in opposite directions, while pregnancies rose somewhat. In the 1990s both abortions and births fell, brought about by a dramatic decline in the pregnancy rate, which fell by over 20 percent (from 117.1 to 93) between 1989 and 1996.

The percentage of pregnancies that resulted in an abortion also declined sharply in the 1990s, falling from 39 percent in 1989 to 29.6 percent in 1996, representing a decline of 24 percent (see figure 2.4). If one looked at this figure alone and saw that fewer pregnancies resulted in an abortion, one may infer that this reduction in abortions among pregnant women must have resulted in more births to teens. This inference would be incorrect, however, since we know from figure 2.3 that births to teens actually

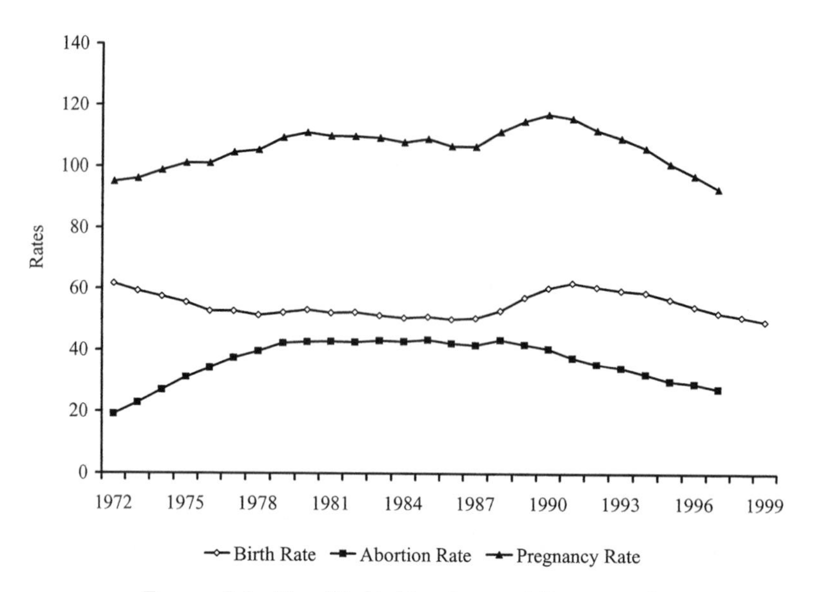

FIGURE 2.3. Teen Birth, Abortion, and Pregnancy Rates (rates per 1,000 women age 15–19). *Source*: Henshaw (2001).

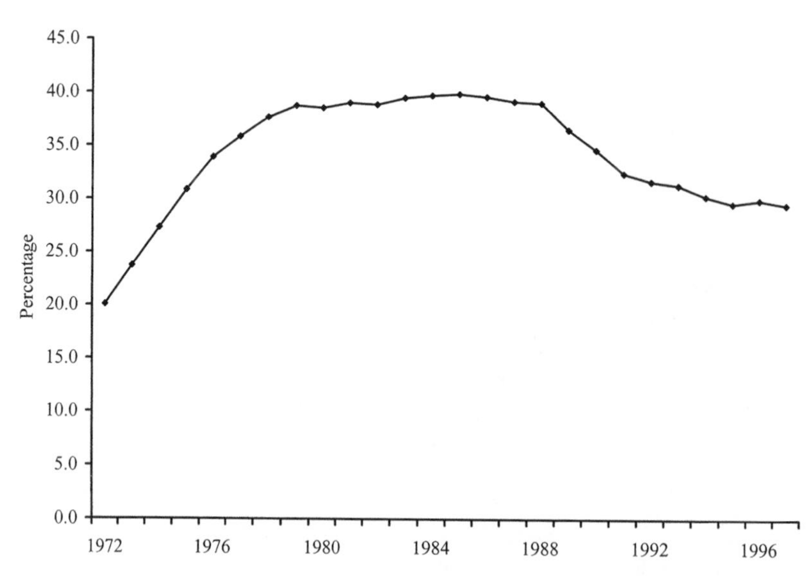

FIGURE 2.4. Percentage of Teen Pregnancies that Result in Abortion. *Source*: Henshaw (2001).

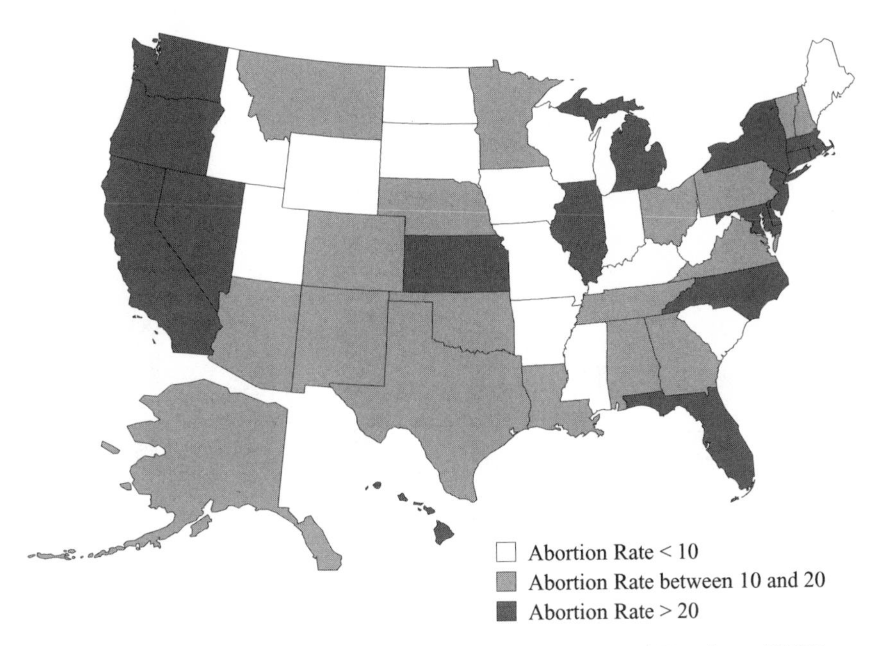

FIGURE 2.5. State Abortion Rates, 2000. *Source*: Finer and Henshaw (2003).

fell as well over the period. To explain this, what must have happened is that there was a greater reduction in pregnancies among those teens that would have been more likely to abort had they gotten pregnant. In this way, the population of teens that got pregnant was composed of those less likely to abort, which would explain the declining percentage of teen pregnancies resulting in abortions in the 1990s.

Beyond the patterns over time in the incidence of abortion, there is also a great deal of geographic variation in its incidence even at a particular point in time. Figure 2.5 presents a map of the United States, categorizing each state by the frequency of abortion in 2000. With the principle exception of Texas, most of the larger states—like New York (39.1), California (31.2), Florida (31.9), Illinois (23.2)—have abortion rates above the national average of 21.3. These rates are considerably higher than those in other states, like Wyoming (1.0), Kentucky (5.3), South Dakota (5.5), Mississippi (6.0), and Utah and Missouri (6.6 in each state). The pattern in teen abortion rates across states is not shown here, but can be found in Henshaw and Feivelson (2000). It is similar to that for all women, although the levels tend to be uniformly higher. The variation in abortion rates across states and over time will be used extensively in the empirical work reported in subsequent chapters.

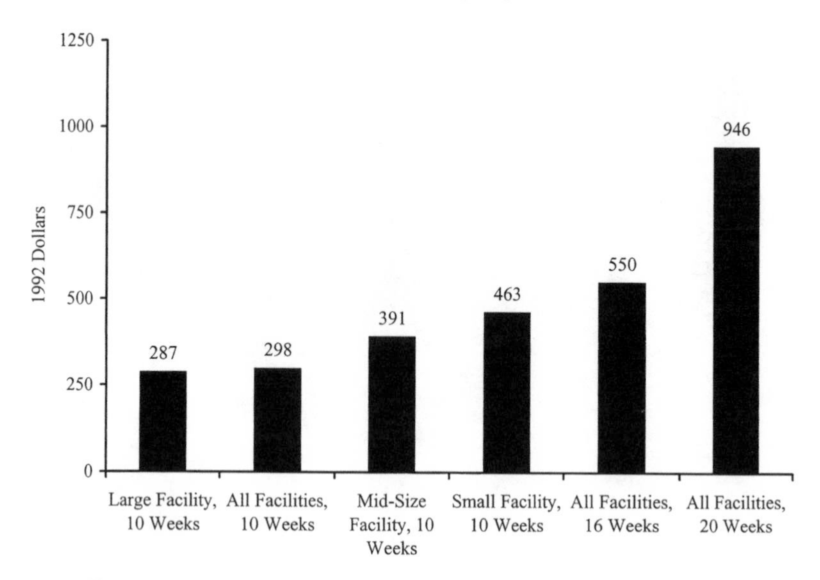

FIGURE 2.6. Monetary Price of Non-hospital Abortions, by Facility Size and Gestation. *Source*: Henshaw (1995a).

The information presented so far represents different indicators of the number of abortions performed, and this is one way to characterize the outcome in a market for abortion services. The other outcome of this market is the price that women pay to obtain an abortion. Data on the amount charged to obtain an abortion is available from the 1992 AGI survey of abortion providers (Henshaw 1995a). Because the abortion procedure becomes more complicated at later weeks of gestation, the price of the procedure depends upon the duration of the pregnancy. Also because larger facilities may be able to take advantage of their size and lower the average cost of their operations ("economies of scale"), the size of the facility also matters in terms of the price charged.

Figure 2.6 displays the median monetary price of abortions performed in a non-hospital setting by the size of the facility, measured as the number of abortions performed in that year, and by the length of gestation, measured in weeks. Among all abortions performed at 10 weeks of gestation, the median charge was $298.[5] This compares to a figure of $550 at 16 weeks of gestation and $946 at 20 weeks. For those abortions performed at 10 weeks of gestation, very large clinics (those that performed 5,000 or more abortions in 1992) charged $287, mid-size clinics (30 to 390 abortions) charged $391, and small clinics (30 or fewer abortions) charged $463. Although these levels may not be that high for the average individual, for lower-income women they may be significant. In addition,

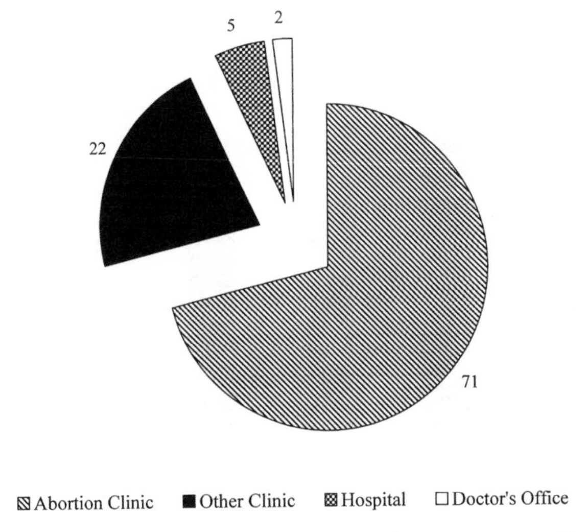

FIGURE 2.7. Where Abortions Are Performed, 2000. *Source*: Finer and Henshaw (2003).

the monetary price of an abortion is just one component of the total cost of an abortion to an individual, who has to face many other challenges in going through with the procedure. This issue will be discussed in more detail in later chapters.

Abortion Providers (the "Supply Side of the Market")

The market outcomes just described reflect the interaction of the willingness of providers to offer abortion services and the desire of individuals to obtain them (i.e. supply and demand). This section and the following one regarding the characteristics of abortion patients reflect the two components of the market.

One feature of the supply side of this market that matters is the type of facility in which abortion services are provided. As the previous section showed, charges for abortions performed in a non-hospital setting are not that high. Presumably, hospitals would charge considerably more since their costs of operation are likely to be much greater than those of a clinic specializing in the procedure. Therefore, the preceding discussion may have been misleading if a substantial fraction of abortions were performed in hospitals.[6] The data do not support this notion, however, as figure 2.7 shows; here we see that only 5 percent of abortions are performed in hospitals. Those abortions are likely to take place after longer

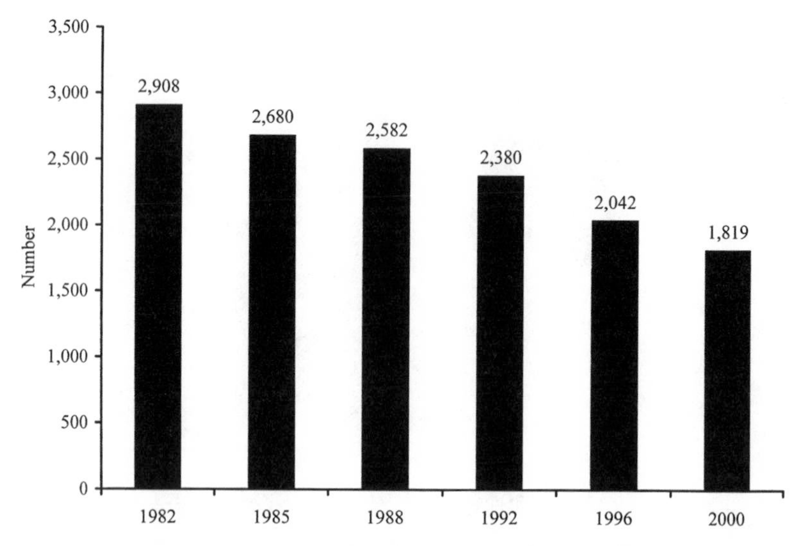

FIGURE 2.8. Number of Abortion Providers in the United States.
Source: Henshaw and Van Vort (1990) and Finer and Henshaw (2003).

gestations as well. The vast majority of abortions (93 percent) are performed at abortion clinics and other forms of clinics that presumably have considerably lower costs.

But access to abortion services is not just a function of the price. The difficulty in locating an abortion provider and potentially traveling to obtain the service also matters. The easier it is to find a provider and the shorter the distance that has to be traveled to get to one certainly lowers the overall cost (monetary and otherwise) of obtaining an abortion. In fact, the data show that the number of abortion providers has been falling steadily over the past two decades (see figure 2.8). According to data from AGI, there were 37 percent fewer abortion providers in 2000 compared to those performing the procedure in 1982.

One may be tempted to argue that the declining number of providers has contributed to the declining rate of abortion, documented earlier in the chapter. Such a conclusion would be premature, however, since the number of providers practicing the procedure is a function of both their willingness to supply abortion services and patients' demand for those services. Factors like clinic protests may have led practitioners to leave the field (or restricted the entry of others), and this may have contributed to the decline in abortions. On the other hand, for a variety of potential reasons individuals may have altered their behavior in a way that reduces their need for abortion services; the reduction in the number of providers may simply reflect this reduction in demand. The descriptive statistics presented so far do not enable us to distinguish between these two competing explanations.

Beyond the number of providers performing abortion services, access to abortion is also determined by their geographical distribution. Travel distance to a provider may be an important constraint, both in terms of finding out that those services are available and of the ability to afford the time and monetary cost of travel. Again, one needs to be careful in evaluating the statistics available in this regard. For instance, statistics indicate that 87 percent of counties have no abortion provider at all (Finer and Henshaw 2003), which would lead one to believe that access to abortion in the United States is very limited. Abortion providers, however, tend to be located in those areas where a lot of people live so that, in fact, only 34 percent of women live in counties without an abortion provider.

Since one way to delineate access to services would be to determine how far a woman has to travel to obtain an abortion, the latter number is more informative but still incomplete. Figure 2.9 presents the distribution of women by the distance from her county of residence to the closest county with an abortion provider who had performed at least twenty abortions per year.[7] This condition was not imposed by Finer and Henshaw (2003); I do so here to recognize that some providers may perform only limited, emergency procedures. The availability of these facilities may be unlikely to alter the abortion decisions of women in nearby locations. The statistics indicate that most women do not have to travel far to get to a provider. In these data, 62 percent of the population have an abortion provider in their county, an additional 26 percent have to travel less than 50 miles to a provider, and another 10 percent have to travel between 50 and 100 miles. Therefore, almost 90 percent of women live within, say, about an hour drive of an abortion provider and virtually all women live within perhaps a two-hour drive. Although these data indicate that most women reside within reasonably close proximity to an abortion provider, it may also be the case that knowledge of providers' availability may be incomplete if the women are not local, and this could limit access.

Characteristics of Abortion Patients (the "Demand Side of the Market")

Abortion patients represent the demand side of this market, and this section presents a description of their characteristics. Table 2.4 displays some of the findings from a recent survey of abortion patients conducted by

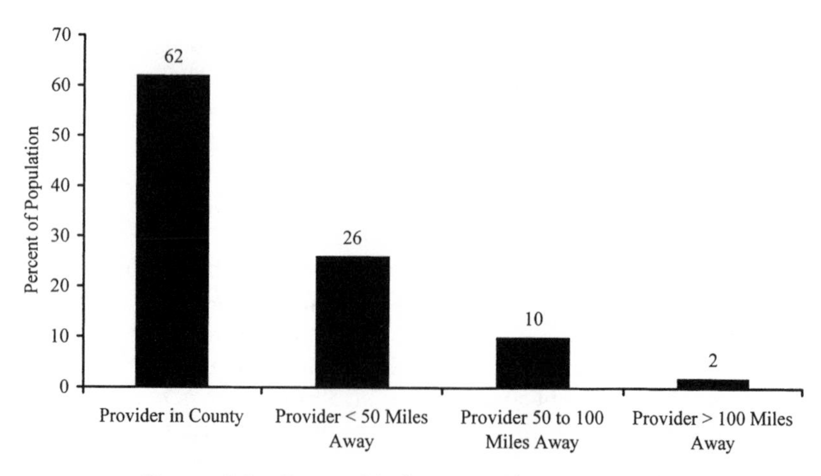

FIGURE 2.9. Geographic Access to Abortion Providers.
Source: Author's calculations using AGI date on counties with abortion providers and data from the 2000 Census. *Note*: The distance is defined as the miles between the population center of one county and the population center of the nearest county with an abortion provider.

AGI and reported in Jones et al. (2002a). It reports averages on a number of characteristics for abortion patients along with similar statistics for all women between the ages of 15 and 44. Analogous information is also available in Martin et al. (2002a) regarding the characteristics of women who gave birth; I report these statistics as well to provide an additional comparison. Based on these statistics, we see that 12 percent and 33 percent of abortion patients are 18–19 years old or 20–24 years old, respectively, even though only 6.5 percent and 15.1 percent of all women of childbearing age are in these age groups, respectively. This tells us that women in these age groups abort at about twice the rate that one would expect if their behavior was merely representative of the size of their group. They also are overrepresented relative to women giving birth.

Other comparisons are interesting as well and will further help identify who has abortions. White, non-Hispanic women receive the greatest share of abortions, but their share is considerably less than what one would expect based upon the population share of this group. On the other hand, black, non-Hispanic and Hispanic women have more abortions than one would expect simply based upon their population size. The ethnic / racial composition of births is roughly comparable to each group's population share. About two-thirds of abortion patients are never-married despite the fact that they represent about 40 percent of the population of women of childbearing age. Two-thirds of births occur to married women. Catholics do not abort any more or less than one would expect

TABLE 2.4.
Selected Characteristics of Abortion Patients and Women Giving Birth, 2000

	Percentage of Abortion Patients	*Percentage of All Women, 15–44*	*Percentage of Women Giving Birth*
Age Group			
15 to 17	6.5	9.5	3.9
18 to 19	12.0	6.5	7.7
20 to 24	33.0	15.1	25.1
25 to 29	23.1	15.6	26.8
30 to 34	13.5	16.5	22.9
35 to 39	8.1	18.5	11.1
At least 40	3.1	18.4	2.3
Race/Ethnicity			
White, Non-Hispanic	40.9	68.2	58.8
Black, Non-Hispanic	31.7	13.7	15.0
Other, Non-Hispanic	7.5	5.3	5.8
Hispanic	20.1	12.8	20.3
Marital Status			
Married	17.0	47.7	66.8
Separated/Divorced	15.6	11.5	NA
Never-Married	67.3	40.8	NA
Religion			
Protestant	42.8	51.0	NA
Catholic	27.4	27.5	NA
Other	7.6	5.4	NA
None	22.2	16.2	NA
Education			
Less than HS	12.7	11.2	21.7
HS Graduate	30.3	30.9	31.8
Some College	40.6	32.5	21.8
College Grad	16.4	25.5	24.7
Poverty Status			
< 100%	26.6	12.8	NA
100–199%	30.8	17.5	NA
200–299%	18.0	17.9	NA
300%	24.6	51.8	NA

Source: Jones et al. (2002a) and Martin et al. (2002a)

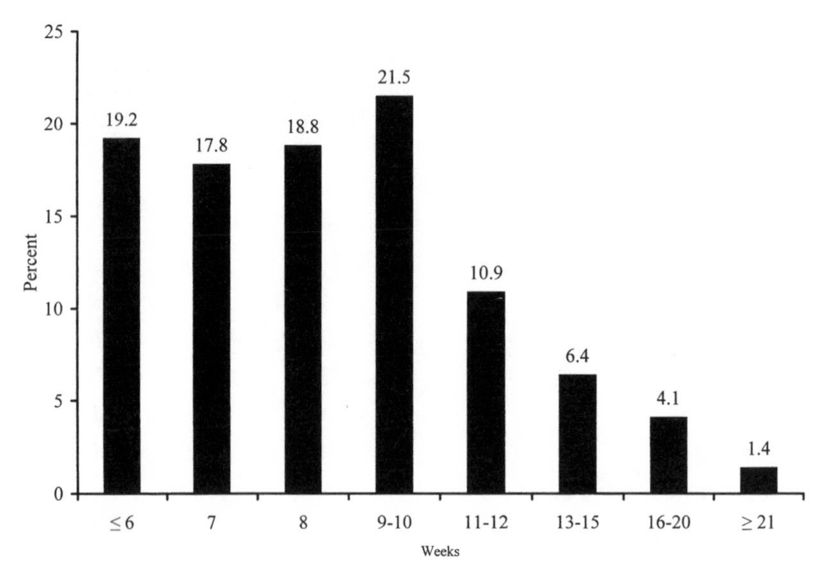

FIGURE 2.10. Weeks of Gestation at Time of Abortion.
Source: U.S. Centers for Disease Control and Prevention (2002).

based upon their share of the population. Finally, women whose families have low levels of income (measured relative to the poverty level) are over-represented among those who abort and women with high levels of income are under-represented among abortion patients.

Figure 2.10 presents the distribution of abortion patients by the gestation of their pregnancies. The statistics reported here indicate that most abortions occur relatively early in a pregnancy. Just over three-quarters take place within ten weeks and almost 90 percent within the first trimester of pregnancy. This is important because the medical complications of the procedure are considerably less significant at such an early stage and because the procedure is relatively inexpensive at this stage as well, as shown earlier in figure 2.6.

It also seems that those who abort are reasonably likely to do so more than once. Among the women in a 1994–95 survey of abortion patients conducted by the Alan Guttmacher Institute, just over half had never had an abortion before (see figure 2.11). This means that almost half of all abortion patients have had multiple abortions. Although this statistic seems high, it is important to recognize exactly what this statistic really tells us.[8] In particular, it does not mean that most women who abort have multiple abortions. If a cohort was followed over time, the distribution of abortions for each woman would likely indicate that more women have only one abortion. But those women who have only one abortion over

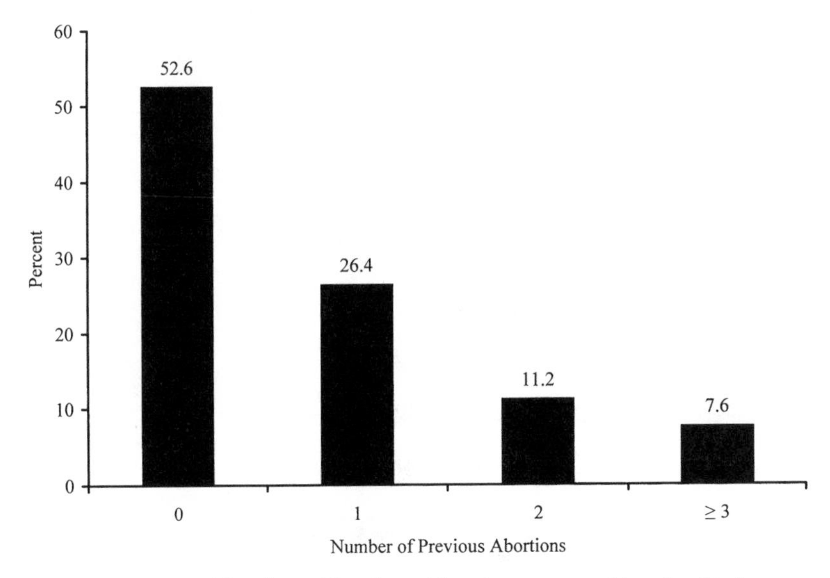

FIGURE 2.11. Number of Previous Abortions among Abortion Patients. *Source*: U.S. Centers for Disease Control and Prevention (2002).

their lives are less likely to be present at the abortion clinic at the time a survey is being conducted. This sample will tend to comprise more of the women who have had multiple abortions since they are more likely to appear at an abortion clinic over a particular period of time.

The reasons women report for having an abortion are presented in figure 2.12. The most common answer that women give is that they want to postpone childbearing. Unfortunately, this answer may not be sufficient for some purposes since it is unclear why these women wanted to wait to have a child. It may have been for any of the other reasons that women offer. Among the remaining reasons women provide, 21 percent indicate that they cannot afford to have a child, 14 percent indicate that they are having problems with their partner, and 12 percent report that they are too young and / or their parents object. Only about 6 percent report a reason related to the health of the mother or fetus.

Figures 2.13 and 2.14 present information regarding the contraceptive use of those women seeking abortions. Figure 2.13 indicates that just over half (53.7 percent) of these women were using some form of contraception, but this means that a sizeable minority (46.3 percent) were not. Figure 2.14 reports the specific methods used, both by abortion patients and, for the purpose of comparison, by all women of childbearing age. Abortion patients are more likely to use no form of contraception, or to use the condom and withdrawal, and less likely to use the pill, which make sense since the former choices are more likely to lead to a pregnancy.

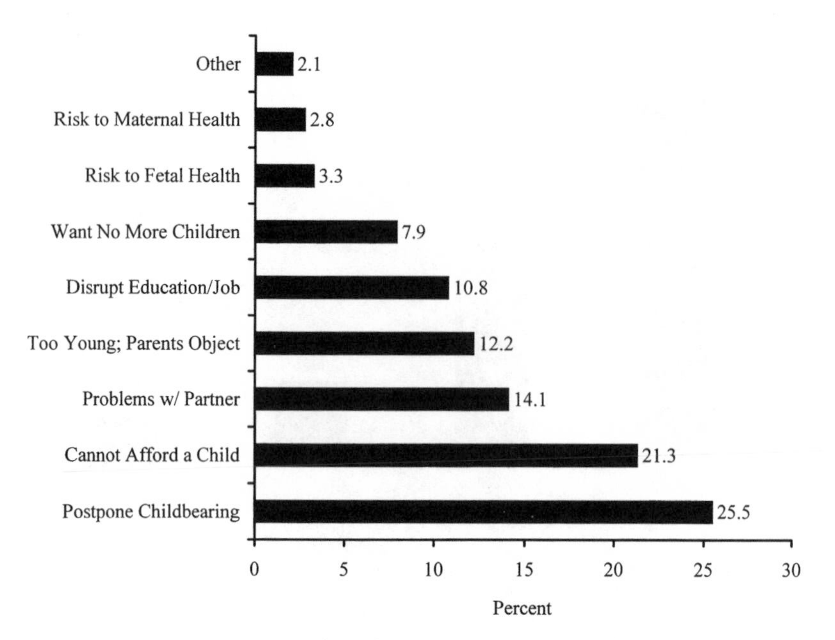

FIGURE 2.12. Reasons for Abortions. *Source*: Bankole et al. (1998).

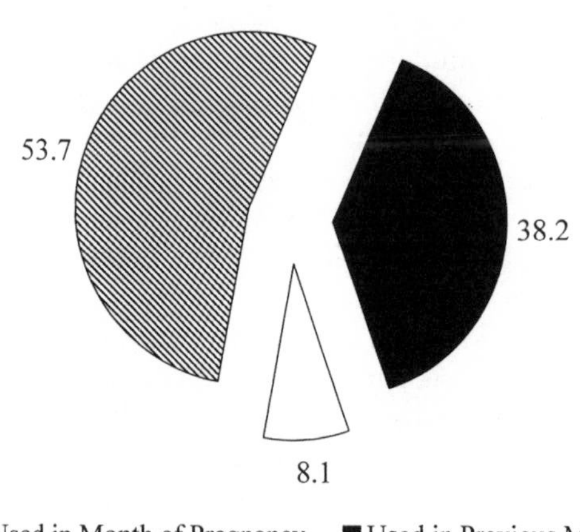

FIGURE 2.13. Contraceptive Use among Abortion Patients in 2000. *Source*: Jones et al. (2002b).

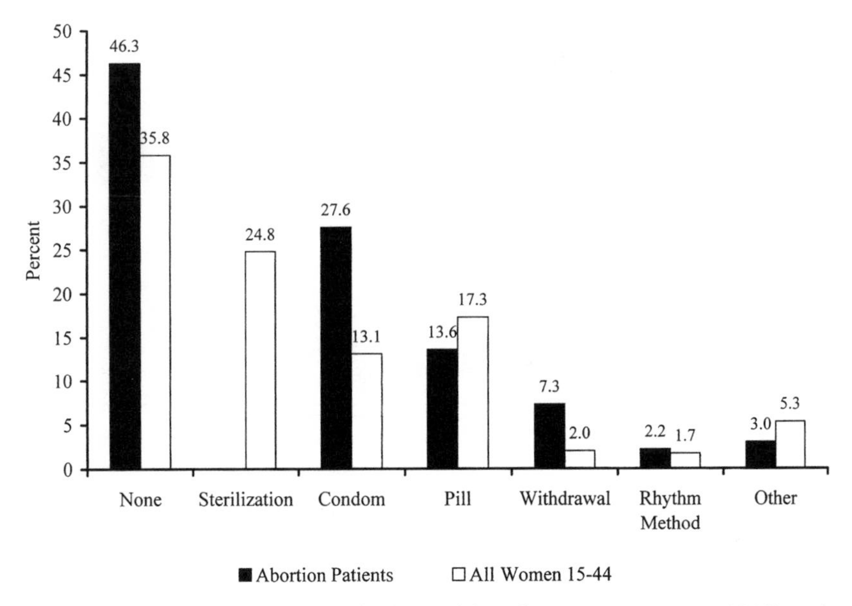

FIGURE 2.14. Contraceptive Methods Used by Abortion Patients (in 2000) and All Women (in 1995). *Source*: Jones et al. (2002b) and Abma et al. (1997).

Public Opinion Regarding Abortion

The material presented in this chapter has reviewed the legal history of abortion policy and provided a statistical description of the abortion marketplace. The last institutional feature of abortion in the United States that may help inform subsequent discussions is the public's opinion regarding various aspects of abortion policy. Public opinion polls are routinely conducted to examine the attitudes of the country regarding abortion. Pollsters ask respondents a plethora of questions regarding how people label themselves, what their own views really are, what their opinion is of others' views, the appropriate role of public policy in this dimension, and more.[9] In this discussion, I will focus on the overall support for abortion, the circumstances under which people believe it is acceptable, and the government policies that are sometimes proposed to restrict its access.

Figure 2.15 presents a broad representation of the circumstances under which individuals support abortion. As described in chapter 1, it shows that a relatively small minority, 18 percent, believe that abortion should be illegal in all circumstances, which is less than the 24 percent who believe that it should be available in all circumstances. However, the major-

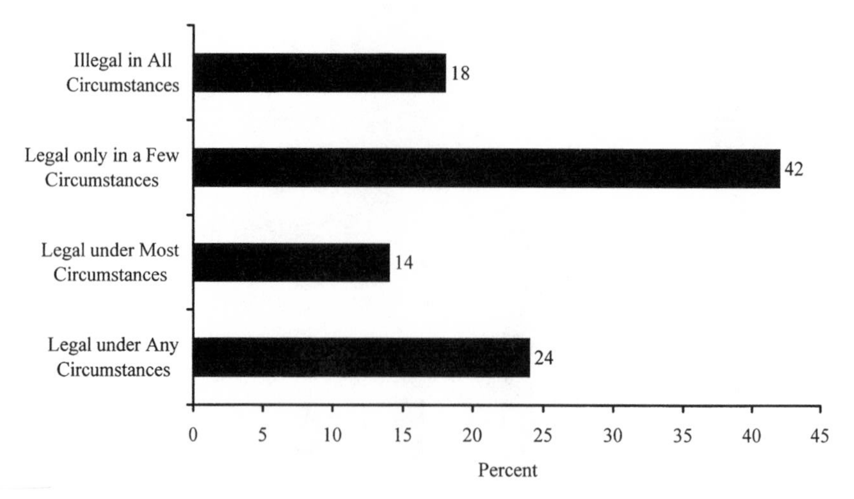

FIGURE 2.15. Percent Supporting Abortion, January 10–12, 2003. *Source*: Gallup Organization (2003).

ity of the population believes that it should only be legal in limited circumstances. Among that group, three times as many believe that it should be legal in a few circumstances (42 percent of the population) compared to those who believe it should be legal in most circumstances (14 percent of the population).

Figure 2.16 presents more detail regarding what those circumstances might be in which abortion would be supported. The majority of Americans support legal abortion when there is a serious health risk to the mother or baby or if the pregnancy resulted from rape or incest. For the most part, though, the American public is less inclined to support legal abortion for social or economic reasons. Fewer than 40 percent of the population would support legal abortion if the baby would interfere with a woman's career, if the family wants no more children, or if the family could not afford the baby.

Individuals' views regarding restrictions on abortion access are consistent with the limited circumstances under which individuals support legal abortion. At least 70 percent of the population support laws that require spousal notification, parental involvement, waiting periods, and informed consent (see figure 2.17). As described earlier in this chapter, court rulings have ruled out the introduction of spousal notification laws, but many states have instituted the other types of restrictions (where the mandatory delay laws described earlier typically include informed consent provisions).

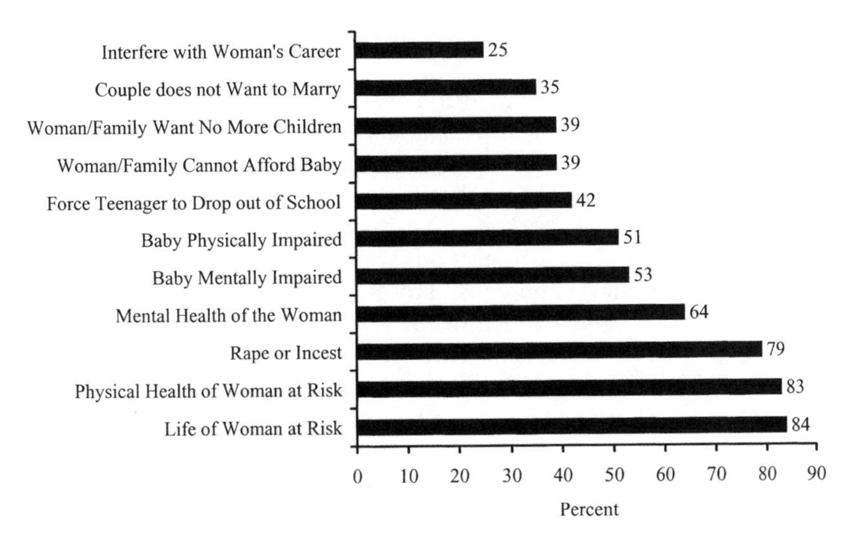

FIGURE 2.16. Percent Supporting Legal Abortion, Selected Circumstances. *Source*: Saad (2002). *Note*: Reported percentages reflect the average rate of support across mulitple surveys and survey organizations between 1996 and 2001.

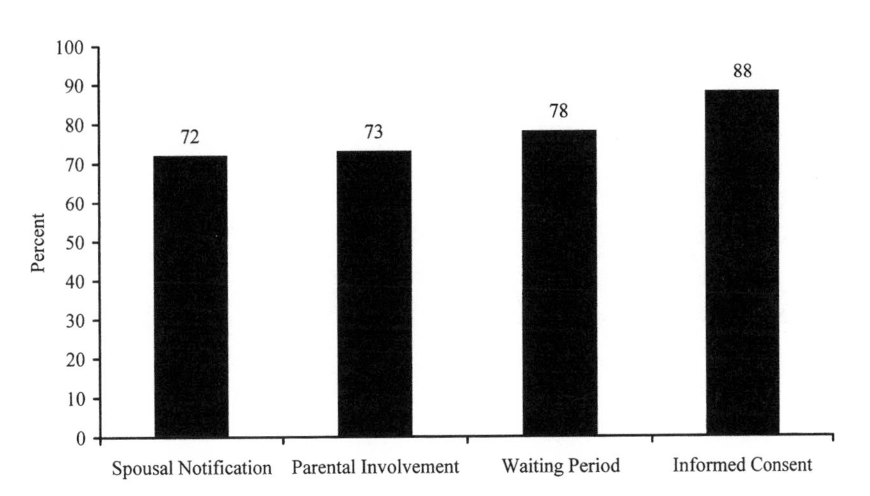

FIGURE 2.17. Percent Favoring Abortion Restrictions in United States. *Source*: Gallup Organization (2003).

Overview

The current environment of abortion availability in the United States has resulted from a great deal of judicial and legislative wrangling, both at the federal and state levels. This chapter began by describing the process that has led us to the set of laws that are in place today and the differences that exist across states in their provisions. This legal environment certainly must have had some impact on the market for abortion services; to characterize that market outcome, I also presented an extensive array of statistics in this chapter. Much of the remainder of the book examines the extent to which policy changes have had a causal impact on fertility outcomes. The variation in policies over time and across states will be used extensively in the subsequent analysis; the methods for doing so will be described in detail in chapter 4. The institutional detail provided here will also help place the results of the subsequent analysis into context.

Chapter Three

ECONOMIC MODELS OF FERTILITY AND ABORTION

OVER the past several decades, American policymakers have been active in changing the rules regarding the availability of abortion. As the last chapter documented, steps were first taken to modify its general prohibition in the late 1960s, and it was outright legalized under most circumstances in the early 1970s. Ever since then, states have frequently experimented with restrictions on the procedure, which are met at every turn with legal challenges and an eventual Supreme Court ruling that defines the limits within which the restrictions may be imposed, if at all. The three main restrictions that have survived court rulings and have been adopted by a sizeable number of states are Medicaid funding restrictions, parental involvement, and mandatory delay.

The introduction of each of these policies certainly has the potential to influence the decisions of women and their partners regarding whether or not they have an abortion. One of the central messages of this book is that it may also influence their behavior that would lead to a pregnancy. Changes in the availability and accessibility of abortion have the potential to change sexual activity and / or contraceptive behavior as well, and a thorough understanding of the impact of changes in abortion policy requires an understanding of all these potential effects.

This chapter will discuss the ways that economic modeling can help provide a framework for evaluating these implications. The approach taken here is to start from well-established models regarding women's fertility behavior and the factors that affect it. These models ignore the availability of an abortion and simply assume that all pregnancies are intentional. I then discuss subsequent developments in economic modeling that have incorporated the possibility that some pregnancies are unintended and that abortion is available as an option. At this point I am able to make a first set of predictions regarding the impact of changes in abortion policy on women's behavior. Following this, I describe more recent models that incorporate another layer of uncertainty in the fertility process brought about by additional information obtained following a pregnancy. These models provide further predictions that should be taken into consideration.

Background

The Role of Assumptions in an Economic Model

Before presenting these models, I want to raise several preliminary issues that will aid in their interpretation. The first issue addresses why economists make so many assumptions in our models. Critics can point to these assumptions and the extent to which they may deviate from a more complete description of reality, dismissing the value of the exercise. Why advance models that may not fully reflect all of the complexities of the real world? What can we learn from them?

The answers rest in the purpose of formulating a model in the first place. A main goal of formulating an economic model is to make predictions. If one thing changes, how will it affect something else? Economists make assumptions because it is impossible to incorporate all of the complexities of the world and put together a model that can yield any predictions. Otherwise, we would be unable to understand what to expect if something in the world changes; the answer would depend upon so many factors that we would never be able to learn anything. The key to economic modeling is to make the assumptions that you need to make the model "tractable" (i.e., able to yield predictions), without assuming away important elements that can alter those predictions.

One of the key assumptions made by economists is that of rationality. Economists assume that agents act to maximize their own self-interest. It is important to recognize that this does not mean economists believe that everyone is selfish; it may improve the well-being of one person if another person's well-being is improved. For instance, individuals give to charity because it makes them feel good to help others, not because they benefit directly themselves. If we do not assume that individuals act rationally, we cannot hope to predict anyone's behavior any better than basing our predictions on the flip of a coin.

The "Cost" of Abortion

One component of these models that will be crucial in understanding the implications of abortion policy is something that I will refer to as the "cost" of abortion. Because of its central focus in the models that will be presented, it is important to understand exactly how that term is being used here. Obtaining an abortion entails costs that are incurred in several forms. The easiest thing to measure is the monetary cost; we saw in the preceding chapter that this cost averages about $300 for the procedure itself.

But an abortion may be costly in many additional dimensions. The procedure may be physically unpleasant for the patient. She may need to take time off from work and spend time traveling to an abortion provider that may not be local. When she gets to the provider's location, there may be protesters outside the clinic, making her feel intimidated or even scared. If her family and / or friends find out about it, she may feel some stigma. Finally, it should not be overlooked that the procedure may be very difficult psychologically for a woman in a multitude of ways that cannot be easily expressed. The woman's partner or perhaps a close friend or whoever is going through the experience supporting her may experience some of these issues as well. All of these factors make getting an abortion difficult for a pregnant woman; these factors are what the model would refer to as the "cost" of the procedure.

Importantly, changes in the legislative environment surrounding the availability of abortion affect its cost. If abortion is illegal, this does not mean that one cannot obtain an abortion, it just means that the cost of the procedure is very high. We know that women did have abortions before it was legal, but the risks of that procedure in many dimensions (not the least of which was the risk of death) were extensive, which is reflected in the high cost. The legalization of abortion, then, amounted to a significant reduction in its cost.

Relative to this change in the legal environment, the restrictions that are debated and sometimes enacted now are modest in scope, yet they also represent a change in the cost of obtaining an abortion. If a minor becomes pregnant and needs the permission of her parents before obtaining an abortion, this could be costly for her. In fact, one could view the court's requirement of judicial bypass as a means to limit this cost in case telling her parents would be excessively costly. Mandatory delay laws impose a time cost and Medicaid funding restrictions increase the monetary cost of the procedure. In the models described below, all of the factors just described, legal or otherwise, will be included in the cost of an abortion.

Decision-Making Framework

In a model of fertility outcomes, one must include all the steps leading there, including sexual activity, contraceptive intensity, and the decision whether or not to abort a pregnancy should one result. These decisions certainly may be made by a woman and her partner jointly, but this need not be the case and it is the woman's behavior that is easier to observe. Therefore, in the discussion that follows, the decision maker will be referred to as a woman.

The decisions that women have to make with regard to sexual activity and contraception along with the decision to abort or give birth if pregnant are even more difficult to think about within the context of an economic model than some other decisions. The reason for this is that the outcomes of these decisions are, by nature, uncertain. If a woman engages in sexual activity without using a perfect form of contraception, she will get pregnant with only some probability. If she gets pregnant, she needs to evaluate the outcomes if she gives birth or has an abortion, which is also difficult to do. In addition to the difficulties in evaluating what it would be like if she gives birth or aborts, things in her life may change that would alter her perceptions over the course of the pregnancy. For instance, a fetal defect may be detected, a parent may unexpectedly support the birth, or a boyfriend may choose to marry a woman who becomes pregnant. Besides the complexity of the decision-making process if everything were known in advance, in this case decisions need to be made in the presence of uncertainty.

Economic analysis has standard methods that deal with decision making when outcomes are uncertain that can be applied to the present problem. If there were no uncertainty, rational economic actors would be assumed to maximize their own well-being, or utility. In the presence of uncertainty, economists assume that decision makers take into consideration their well-being given each of the possible outcomes in the world and maximize the average of those, weighted by the likelihood of them occurring. This is known as the "expected utility hypothesis."

A classic example of this approach is deciding whether or not to place a bet. If the individual wins a bet, then she will get some money and this will entail a certain improvement in her well-being. If she loses, money will be lost and this will result in a reduction in well-being. According to the expected utility hypothesis, individuals determine the value of making the bet by computing their level of well-being averaged across the outcomes of winning and losing, weighted by the respective probabilities. If this weighted average level of well-being is greater than that from not making the bet, then, according to this hypothesis, the bet will be made.

Is This Realistic?

This framework just described imposes a substantial burden upon the decision maker. Individuals are assumed to assess how they think they will feel under different scenarios of the world, assign probabilities to the likelihood of each of these outcomes, and then weigh them against each other. Yet we know that this is not how we actually choose the course of our actions. It is unrealistic to expect that people actually undertake the sort of complicated computations that this decision-making framework imposes upon them.

Then why do we use it to characterize such personal and complicated problems like fertility decisions? The answer brings us back to what we are trying to accomplish by setting up an economic model. We are trying to simplify the world in such a way that we are able to make predictions regarding the impact of changes in it. We are not stating that we think people actually make decisions in this way, but we are just using a mathematical approach to characterize those actions as if that were the way people make choices.

The following example may help clarify this issue. Suppose you are driving down a single lane highway at 60 miles per hour and you come upon a car in front of you that is only traveling at 40 miles per hour. You would like to pass this car, but off in the distance on the other side of the highway there is a car coming at you. You need to decide at the speed you are traveling (or the speed you are able / willing to go) whether or not you can pass the slow-going car on your side of the road before the oncoming car reaches you. If you were a physicist, you could write down a mathematical model of the problem facing the driver and solve it to determine whether or not it makes sense to attempt to pass the slower car. This is a very complicated problem that few among us would be able to solve. Yet we do solve such problems all the time when we drive and generally come up with the right answer. In this situation, drivers are acting like they are solving a very complicated mathematical problem, but in fact they are not doing so.

This is exactly how economists think that individuals "solve" the sorts of problems we are addressing here, in choosing the actions that maximize their own well-being. The mathematical approach to the problem is merely a representation of what people are actually doing that can be used to make predictions. We do not actually believe that people specifically make their decisions this way.

Yet this view that individuals act rationally when it comes to decisions regarding fertility and its antecedents is frequently criticized by others. For instance, in reference to teen childbearing Luker (1997) sarcastically characterizes an economic approach to these problems along with her opinion of that approach in the following way: "Michelle (a teenager) is the calculating, knowing, 'rational actor' of neoclassical economics: she coolly assesses the costs of having a baby, analyzes the benefits of welfare, and 'invests' in a course of action that will get her what she wants . . . the thought of women being self-centered rational actors in the intimate realms of sex, childbearing, family, and home is a rather chilling one" (4, 5). Much of this criticism is attributable to a fundamental misunderstanding of economic modeling and its contributions. As the earlier discussion suggests, nobody believes that individuals actually make the calculations that these models suggest, but that these models yield predictions regarding individual behavior, and that is the goal. Because of the assumptions and simplifications incorporated into such models, the predictions also require empirical support before strongly emphasizing them.

In fact, many of the reasons that economic models are criticized are often easily incorporated into them. For instance, in providing examples to disprove rationality, Luker (1997) states "teenage mothers, like other mothers, have also been known to get pregnant hoping that the pregnancy will solidify a partnership, making a couple out of two individuals. Many of them choose to forgo an abortion because they have moral objections, and because they feel a commitment to this new person in the making. Most poignantly, in the vast majority of cases, giving birth while still a teenager is a pledge of hope, an acted-out wish that the lives of the next generation will be better than those of the current generation, that this young mother can give her child something she never had" (5). As the remainder of this chapter will make clear, all of these features have been incorporated into the models presented. Just because moral objections are labeled as costs and a pledge of hope is labeled a benefit does not change the underlying premise of the behavior being described. Given this prelude, the remainder of the chapter presents a theoretical framework for determining the impact of changes in abortion policy on individual behavior.

Standard Economic Models of Fertility

This discussion begins with models that make the most extreme set of assumptions. We then see what we can learn from them, and proceed by relaxing those assumptions in stages. The simplest models of fertility make very strong assumptions about the information available to women and their ability to control their fertility. Despite the significant degree to which these assumptions deviate from reality, these models are able to make important predictions regarding fertility behavior that are born out in the real world based upon empirical evidence. This work is largely attributed to Gary Becker, whose 1992 Nobel prize in economics was partially attributable to this work.[1]

Within these models, women are assumed to have complete information regarding all possible outcomes from giving birth. A birth has some value, be it positive or negative, to the mother. In terms of benefits, perhaps in more traditional societies they may take the form of work performed around the house in childhood or from monetary transfers from adult children to their parents. But regardless of culture, children may bring about non-pecuniary benefits, and they are counted as well.

Having children, however, also involves many costs that may extend throughout childhood (or even later). Again, these costs need not be restricted to those that are monetary, although the cost of diapers, clothes, and food certainly would be included. For example, caring for a child requires a significant time commitment by the primary caregiver (typically assumed to be the child's mother), which represents what economists call an "opportunity cost." This is costly because the primary caregiver had to give up some valuable activity to raise the child. The value of having a child and the costs of childrearing are all assumed to be known to the woman at the time she is contemplating whether or not to have a child.

Models within this class also assume that women have perfect control over their fertility. Should they decide they do not want to give birth, they can obtain perfect methods of contraception at zero cost. Therefore, the decision to give birth or not is independent of factors that could influence contraceptive choice. Either contraception is used or it is not, and one option is no more costly to the mother than the other. They make a decision whether or not to have a child and that outcome emerges from their actions. There is no such thing as an unintended pregnancy, medical complications, or the like.

These very strong assumptions lead to a straightforward decision-making process. Women decide to have a baby or not by comparing the costs of having a child to the benefits. If the value brought to the parents by having a child is greater than the costs of child-rearing, the woman chooses to get pregnant and have a baby. Otherwise she does not. This decision-making process is an example of utility maximization, but since there is no uncertainty it does not rely upon the expected utility hypothesis. In these models, there is no role for abortion since every pregnancy is planned and because the decision to become pregnant is made with complete information. In addition, these models generally do not consider the marriage decision explicitly, but rather focus on optimal fertility choices given that a woman is married (or unmarried).

Despite their strong assumptions, these models have a number of fundamental implications that are generally supported empirically. The focus of much of the literature has been on the important role played by a woman's wage, since it captures the opportunity cost of a woman's time required in raising children. Thus, increases in female education or in labor market opportunities for women are predicted to lead to smaller family sizes and delayed childbearing, both of which have been supported in empirical studies.[2] Similarly, factors that reduce other costs of raising children (e.g., tax deductions, education subsidies) have been found to increase fertility and affect birth timing.[3]

The impact of family income on fertility is less clear. As with any normal good, spending on children is expected to increase with income. However, this may take the form of more spending on each child rather than more children. Thus, as pointed out in Becker and Lewis (1973), increases in family income (through male wages) may lead to smaller family sizes, as higher income leads to a shift from spending on more children to spending more on those children already born. Similarly, a higher wage for the woman can lead to a similar shift in resources. This theory originated as an explanation for the demographic transition observed in many developing countries (when income rises while fertility falls). But, these implications are more broadly consistent with empirical work finding that family income and female earnings are negatively associated with family size and positively associated with measures of child well-being.[4]

Overall, the economic model of fertility has provided a powerful tool for understanding fertility behavior over time, across countries and across families. Moreover, careful econometric models based on these simple economic models have been found to outperform standard demographic models in terms of explaining and forecasting aggregate changes in fertility and birth timing (Heckman and Walker 1990). This evidence suggests that economic models, in which women make rational choices to maximize utility, may also provide a good guide to understanding other fertility-related behavior, including abortion.

This is not to say, however, that this model perfectly forecasts fertility behavior. For instance, the implications of this model are very clear regarding the impact of greater welfare generosity on fertility behavior. Since welfare receipt is largely associated with having children, more generous benefits provide women with an incentive to give birth. This theoretical prediction may be the one that has been empirically tested the most within the fertility literature, but the research conducted to date often provides conflicting results. In a recent survey of this literature, Moffitt (1998) concludes, "A neutral weighing of the evidence still leads to the conclusion that welfare has incentive effects on . . . fertility, but the uncertainty introduced by the disparities in the research findings weakens the strength of that conclusion" (p. 75). This illustrates the importance of incorporating the results of empirical evidence along with the predictions of economic theories before drawing conclusions regarding the impact of public policy on individual behavior.

Standard Economic Models of Abortion

Features of the Model

The economic models of fertility just discussed do not require individuals to make decisions regarding abortion because of two key simplifying assumptions: (1) women can perfectly control fertility at no cost, and (2) women have complete information regarding the costs and benefits of having a child before pregnancy. Within this framework every pregnancy results from the fact that a woman is better off having a child and nothing can change that decision once she arrives at it. Therefore, in these models there is no reason ever to abort a pregnancy.

Standard economic models of abortion deviate from this framework by relaxing the first of these assumptions. In particular, these models assume that contraception is costly and imperfect.[5] In these models, pregnancies may occur that would result in a birth that would impose costs rather than benefits if a birth resulted. Here I define these births as "unwanted" in the sense that costs are imposed; births that provide benefits would be "wanted." This use of the terms "wanted" and "unwanted" births differs somewhat from standard usage in the demography literature.[6] In that lexicon, pregnancies may be unintended either because a birth was unwanted or mistimed. An unwanted birth is one where the parents never wanted to have an additional child, and a mistimed birth is one that the parents did not want to have now. I use the term "unwanted" to refer to any birth that would impose a cost, and not a benefit, on the parents. Obviously, having a child may bring about both some costs and benefits, but here and elsewhere whether the birth would result in a cost or a benefit reflects the overall value, combining all these effects.

In these models, women can take steps to reduce the likelihood of a pregnancy, but each additional step becomes increasingly difficult. The choice of contraception is likely to follow a course in which the method that an individual feels most comfortable with is chosen first. If additional methods are desired to further reduce the risk of pregnancy, those methods would entail greater sacrifice. For the purposes of this discussion, I do not distinguish between the decision to engage in sexual activity or use birth control. This simplification just treats abstinence as a method of birth control that eliminates the probability of a pregnancy if practiced completely.

The Abortion Decision Tree

Using these assumptions, economists, as well as other social scientists, are naturally inclined to represent the process leading to an abortion or birth in the form of a tree. Figure 3.1 provides such a representation. At the top of the tree there is a box indicating that the contraceptive intensity decision needs to be made first. Again, for simplicity, sexual activity is incorporated into this analysis through abstinence, which represents a complete form of protection from pregnancy if practiced all the time. The actions chosen at this stage of the tree affect the likelihood of the outcome of these actions, pregnancy or not. If the woman is not pregnant, there

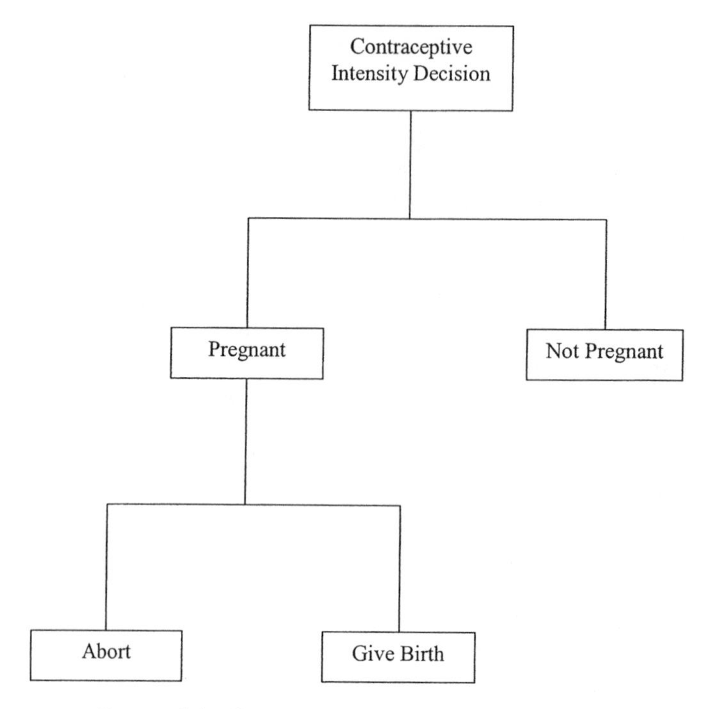

FIGURE 3.1. Contraceptive Intensity and Abortion Decision Tree.

are no subsequent elements of the tree, and she would go back to the top of it in the following month. If she does get pregnant, the woman needs to decide whether to give birth or have an abortion. This figure is called a decision tree because it represents all the decisions that an individual needs to make sequentially over time.

One element that is missing from this decision tree, but does represent a decision that women must make that is relevant in this context, is the decision to get married. The reason it is not included in this analysis is that it is difficult to determine exactly where in this tree that decision belongs. For those who promote abstinence until marriage, it should come at the top of the tree. At the other extreme, marriage may not occur until after a baby is born, if at all. It may also go anywhere in between. Because the marriage decision considerably complicates this analysis without necessarily being related to the process leading to a birth or an abortion, marriage is omitted from this tree.

At this point, the decision tree is merely a descriptive device that characterizes the decision-making process. But the application of game theoretic concepts to this decision tree, which economists have been doing for some time, provides additional insight into how these decisions should be made. These concepts indicate that we should make these decisions "backward" (i.e., moving up the tree). We should first address the decision to give birth or abort once pregnant and then tackle the issue of the choice of contraceptive intensity.

The Abortion Decision

The abortion decision is relatively straightforward to incorporate into an economic model. For women who become pregnant unintentionally, the birth would be viewed as costly if it took place. Abortions are costly too, though, so women will choose the least costly alternative. Although precisely evaluating the relevant costs may not be so easy in reality, for the purposes of this model I have imposed the simplifying assumption that they are known and decisions are therefore made accordingly.

Some interesting implications are obtained just from this simple model of the decision to have an abortion. In this model, all abortions are the result of unintended pregnancies that women would have been willing to pay some positive amount in order to avoid. The greater the cost of having a child, the greater is the likelihood that an unintended pregnancy will be aborted. Hence, one might expect abortion to be more common among teens, older women, unmarried women, women in poverty, or women at risk for having an unhealthy child (e.g., premature or with birth defects). Many of these predictions are consistent with the evidence, some of which was reported earlier in table 2.4.

The Contraception Decision

Deciding how intensively to use contraception is a more difficult problem because it incorporates an element of uncertainty, namely whether or not a pregnancy will actually occur. A chosen level of contraceptive intensity dictates the probability with which a woman becomes pregnant but does not determine whether or not a pregnancy will result. Greater contraceptive intensity simply reduces the likelihood of a pregnancy. Therefore, the specific outcome of the decision is not known; with some probability that a pregnancy will result and with some probability that it will not. Choosing the level of contraceptive intensity then becomes an exercise in choosing the likelihood a pregnancy will result.

The uncertainty involved in the outcomes in this decision process naturally leads to the application of the expected utility hypothesis. Here we assume that individuals choose a level of contraceptive intensity to maximize their average level of well-being, weighted by the relevant probabilities. With some probability, the woman will become pregnant and there is some payoff associated with that outcome. With some probability, she will not become pregnant and there is some payoff associated with that as well. The weighted average of these levels of well-being represents the expected "benefit" (which may be negative) that will result from her contraceptive intensity decision. In addition, using contraception is costly and these costs reduce her well-being. The choice of an appropriate level of contraceptive intensity requires one to balance these expected benefits and costs to maximize one's well-being.

The relevant measure of the cost of contraception that will be incorporated into the solution to this problem reflects the extent to which these costs rise as greater contraceptive intensity is used. This is called the "marginal cost" of contraception. As I described earlier, women who start using contraception will use the method they feel most comfortable with first, and additional efforts to reduce the likelihood of a pregnancy will require her to use less-preferred methods. This means that the additional cost associated with greater efforts to reduce the likelihood of a pregnancy should rise as contraceptive intensity increases. Mathematically, the marginal cost of contraception may be represented as:

$$MC = \frac{\Delta C}{\Delta P}$$

where MC is the marginal cost, Δ indicates a change, C is the overall cost of using a certain level of contraceptive intensity, and P represents the probability with which one *avoids* a pregnancy. In this expression, $\Delta C \ / \ \Delta P$ tells us the increase in the cost of contraception associated with a one percentage point increase in the likelihood of *avoiding* a pregnancy. This is how the marginal cost is defined.

The solution to this problem is best characterized by figure 3.2. This figure distinguishes between two separate cases, one in which the woman views the cost of abortion to be greater than the cost of birth, and the other assumes the opposite. From an earlier discussion, we know that if the cost of abortion is greater than the cost of giving birth (Case I), then the woman will give birth if pregnant, and she will choose the opposite course of action in Case II. Besides these costs, both figures also present the marginal cost of contraception, which is drawn to incorporate the assumption that it increases as contraceptive intensity increases. For simplicity, I have assumed that this increase is linear in these figures, but it need not be.

Figure 3.2 indicates that a woman will choose a level of contraceptive intensity that maximizes her expected utility at the point where the marginal cost of contraception just equals either the cost of birth or the cost of abortion, whichever is lower. It is the lower cost that is relevant because once it is clear that an unintentional pregnancy will result in, say, a birth, the cost of abortion becomes irrelevant in the decision-making process.

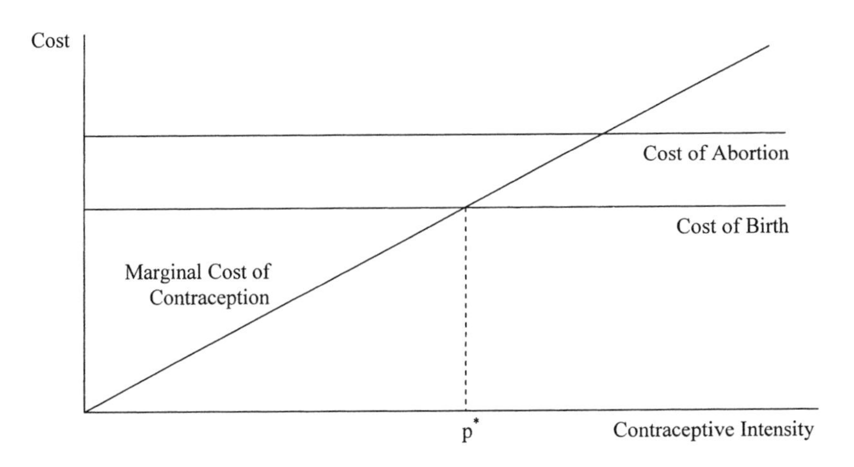

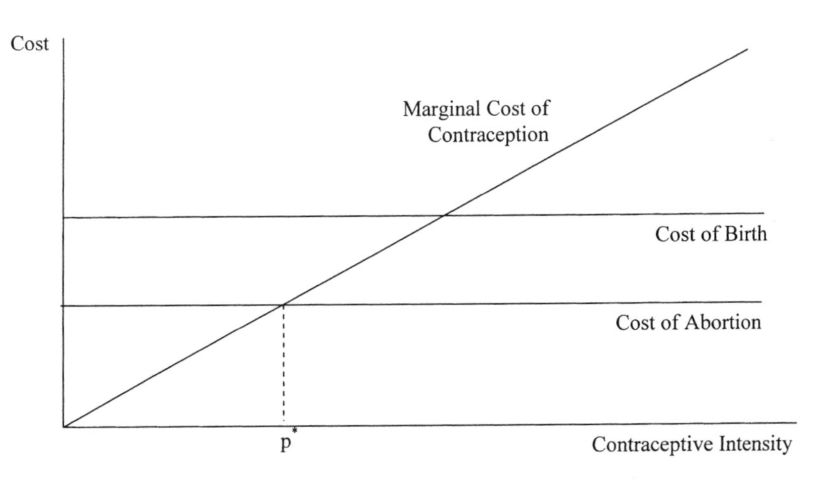

FIGURE 3.2. The Contraception / Abortion Decision.

The following example will clarify why this solution makes sense. Here, I will considerably simplify the process by arbitrarily assigning numbers to relevant costs just for illustrative purposes. Consider a woman for whom the cost of giving birth would be $1,000 if she experiences an unintended pregnancy. Assume that this cost is lower than the cost of an abortion, and so a pregnancy would result in a birth, not an abortion. Now suppose that she is trying to decide whether to increase her contraceptive intensity enough so that the probability of getting pregnant would decline by 10 percent (i.e., $\Delta P = 0.1$). Furthermore, suppose that the additional cost imposed upon her by increasing her contraceptive intensity was \$20 (i.e., $\Delta C = 20$). Should she adopt this technique? Based on these numbers, she can reduce the probability of incurring a \$1,000 cost by 10 percent, and so the expected savings from using this additional form of contraception would be \$100. But it only costs her \$20 to obtain this savings, and so she should certainly do so.

The next step that she would take to reduce the likelihood of pregnancy by an additional 10 percent costs \$30. By the same reasoning she would do this as well. Every increase in contraceptive intensity will lead to a greater increment to its cost. At some point the cost of reducing the likelihood of pregnancy by an additional 10 percent will cost an additional \$100 and this is the last step that should be taken. Beyond that the additional cost would be greater than the benefit and should be avoided.[7]

Therefore, the individual chooses a level of contraception where $\Delta C = \Delta P^* B$, with B representing the cost of giving birth (\$1,000 in this example). Rearranging this expression, the optimal level of contraceptive intensity is shown to be:

$$MC = \frac{\Delta C}{\Delta P} = B.$$

This is the decision rule represented in the top panel of figure 3.2, where the level of contraceptive intensity is determined by the intersection of the cost of giving birth and the marginal cost of contraception. If the cost of abortion is less than the cost of giving birth, then we have exactly the same decision process, but the cost of abortion would replace the cost of birth as the relevant comparison to the marginal cost of contraception. In other words, the individual would choose a level of contraceptive intensity where

$$MC = \frac{\Delta C}{\Delta P} = A$$

and A represents the cost of abortion. This is the decision process represented in the bottom panel of figure 3.2.

The Impact of Changes in Abortion Cost

As represented in figure 3.3, the impact of a fall in the cost of abortion depends upon the relationship among the initial cost of abortion, the magnitude of its decline, and the cost of giving birth to an unwanted child. First consider Case I, where the cost of abortion before its decline is above the cost of birth. Here, a woman who unintentionally gets pregnant

Case I: Fewer Unwanted Births

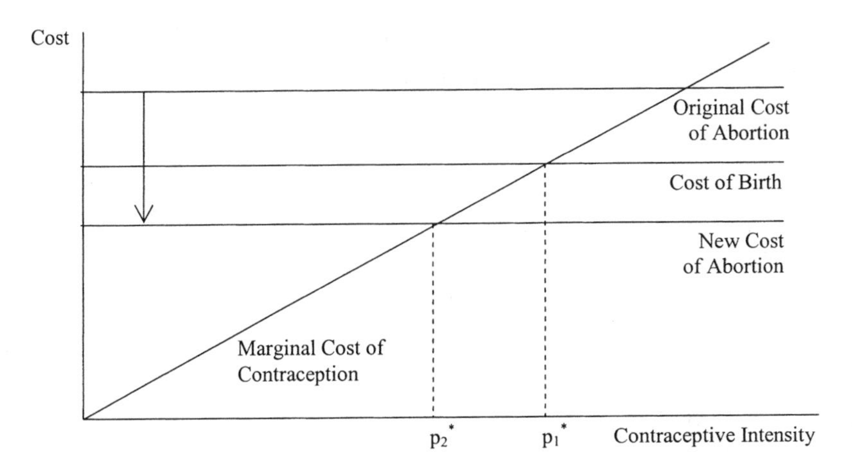

Case II: Lower Contraceptive Intensity

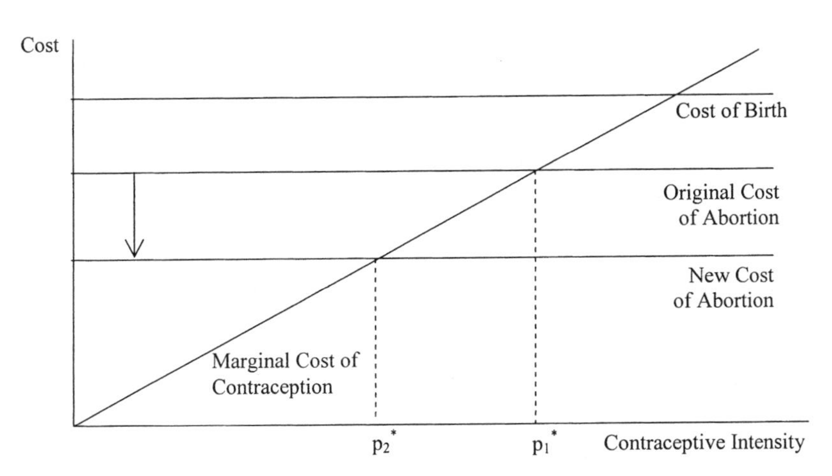

FIGURE 3.3. Effect of a Decrease in the Cost of Abortion.

would choose to give birth at the original cost of abortion. If its cost falls, however, and that decline pushes the cost of abortion below that of giving birth, then the woman would now choose to have an abortion. The main impact of the decline in the cost of abortion would be a substitution of abortion for unwanted births. There may also be an additional effect as well, though. As the cost of abortion continues to fall further below the cost of birth, contraceptive intensity will decline (from p_1^* to p_2^*). This will result in even more abortions, but these abortions will be the result of additional pregnancies brought about by less use of contraception. Although it is difficult to weigh the magnitude of these two effects, I simply presume that the substitution of abortion for unwanted births predominates.

On the other hand, if abortion is already less costly than having an unwanted child (Case II), an unintentional pregnancy would result in an abortion even at its original cost. Therefore, if that cost fell further it would have no impact on the number of unwanted births. But contraceptive intensity would fall and more unintended pregnancies would result. These additional pregnancies would all result in additional abortions, not more births.

Of course, an increase in the cost of abortion has the opposite outcomes of those just described, as shown in figure 3.4. If the cost of abortion starts out below the cost of an unwanted birth, but then rises above that level, additional unwanted births will result. On the other hand, if that increase results in a new cost of abortion that is still below that of an unwanted birth, then no additional births will result. Contraceptive intensity will increase, though, reducing pregnancies and the abortions that would have resulted from them.

Implications for Changes in Abortion Policy

In the context of an economic model, a change in abortion policy is reflected as a change in the cost of abortion. I will assume that the cost of giving birth to an unwanted child is independent of this policy change. Therefore, the impact of these changes in the cost of abortion depends upon two factors, its original level relative to the cost of an unwanted birth and the magnitude of the decline.

The difficulty in making predictions regarding the impact of such changes in the real world is that much of the cost of abortion and the cost of an unwanted birth are determined by the individual herself and by no means needs to be uniform across women. For instance, some women may find the idea of aborting a pregnancy quite distasteful and would assign a very large cost to the procedure regardless of its legal standing. Others may hold personal views that do not attribute a large cost to the procedure at all. Obviously there may be others with a more moderate position. Any prediction regarding the impact of abortion policy on women's behavior has to take into account this heterogeneity across women. Similarly, there exists a distribution in individuals' views regarding the cost of an unwanted birth, causing a slight inconvenience to some or a huge impediment to others.

Case I: More Unwanted Births

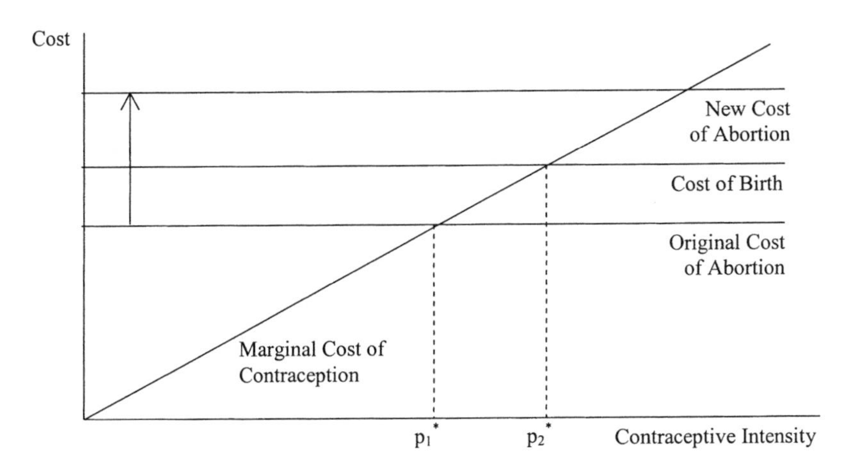

Case II: Greater Contraceptive Intensity

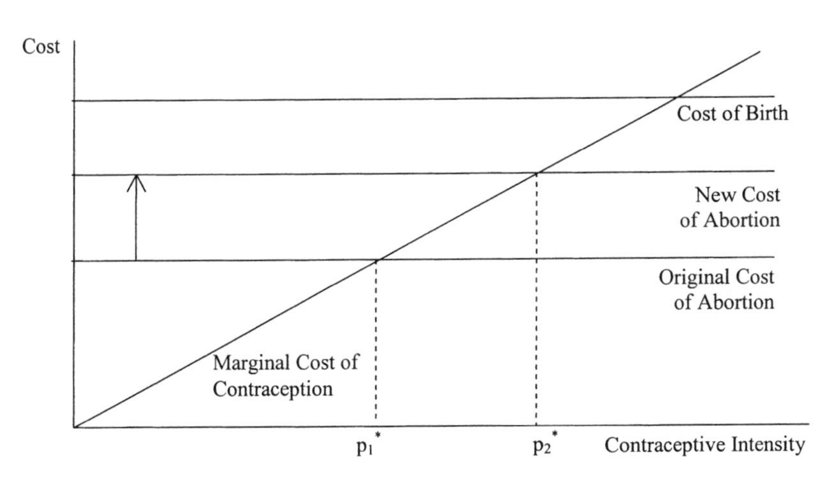

FIGURE 3.4. Effect of an Increase in the Cost of Abortion.

Changes in the cost of abortion brought about by changes in abortion policy differ in magnitude as well and these differences need to be taken into account. The legalization of abortion in the early 1970s can be thought of as a dramatic reduction in the cost of the procedure. The types of restrictions that are debated today may certainly represent substantial changes in the cost of abortion, but those changes are relatively small in relation to that brought about by abortion legalization. Even within types of policy changes, women may place different values on them. For instance, teens' parents may react (or be expected to react) differently upon being notified of their daughter's pregnancy. This means that even within the class of relatively moderate restrictions, the cost for some may be greater than the cost for others.

Based on this discussion, some additional assumptions are required to predict the impact of these changes in policy. First, I assume that when abortion was largely illegal, the cost of abortion, at least for most women, was greater than the cost of an unwanted birth. Its widespread legalization in the early 1970s led to a very large reduction in its cost, and for many women the cost of abortion fell below the cost of an unwanted birth. This would support the prediction that abortion legalization reduced unwanted births. In a legal abortion environment, however, I also assume that the types of restrictions that have typically been placed on abortion since then are unlikely to raise that cost over that of an unwanted birth for a large number of women. If this is the case, then these restrictions will not lead to many additional unwanted births, but will largely result in greater contraceptive intensity, resulting in fewer pregnancies and abortions.

Extended Model of Abortion

Features of the Model

I began this chapter with a model of fertility that assumed a woman can perfectly control her fertility at no cost and that women have complete information regarding the costs and benefits of having a child before pregnancy. In the preceding section I relaxed the first assumption regarding contraceptive technology, but maintained the assumption of perfect information. That model yielded important insights regarding the potential impact of changes in abortion costs on pregnancies, abortions, and births. In this section, I also relax the assumption of perfect information and examine additional implications for individual behavior that can be derived from such a model.[8]

The problem with assuming that a woman is perfectly informed regarding birth outcomes at the time of pregnancy is that additional information really is gathered beyond that point. In fact, a woman learns much during the early stages of pregnancy, ranging from health information about the pregnancy (e.g., through amniocentesis) to the amount of support she can expect from the father and her family and friends. Evidence presented in chapter 2 provides some support for this proposition; figure 2.12 presented the reasons why abortion patients chose their course of action. About a third of women reported that they chose to abort for reasons that appear to be related to additional information received after the pregnancy (they had problems with their partner, their parents objected, or there were fetal or maternal health issues).

Thus, the feature that truly makes abortion unique, as opposed to other forms of birth control, is that it allows a woman to delay the decision to give birth until she is better informed. By relaxing the assumption of perfect information, we are now able to incorporate into our model the fact that decisions regarding sexual activity and contraceptive intensity are made at one point in time and then the decision to continue a pregnancy or have an abortion comes subsequently. The fact that a time lag exists over which this information arrives enables a pregnant woman to "change her mind" from what she might have been expecting before getting pregnant.

In this extension to the standard abortion model, people are assumed to be able to assess the probabilities of these uncertain outcomes brought about by acquiring additional information. Some of the information received may make her more likely to give birth ("positive information") and some of it may make her less likely to give birth ("negative information"). There are clearly gradations of each type of information as well, but for simplicity I assume that the information received is either favorable or unfavorable, and I ignore any variation within categories.

Each of these possibilities occurs with some probability and it is clearly difficult to know precisely what the risks are. Yet one may also suspect whether an outcome is likely or unlikely and could incorporate those suspicions into their decision-making process. Consider a married woman who wants to start a family with her husband. She may be fairly certain that once pregnant she would not receive any negative information. A fetal defect is certainly a possibility, however, so she could not be completely assured of this. Similarly, other individuals may be fairly certain that a pregnancy will not result in a "wanted" birth, but circumstances could arise that may change their mind. For instance, a college student planning on a career and on starting a family later in life may unexpectedly find her partner and / or family very supportive of continuing a pregnancy and may choose to give birth if she becomes pregnant.

The simplifying assumption that is made here is that these suspicions can be assigned specific probabilities so that we can act as if they are known for certain in modeling individual behavior. In fact, we can distinguish between different groups of women according to their likelihood of receiving positive or negative information. "Low-risk" (of negative information) women would be those who want to have a baby and are unlikely to receive any information that might change their mind. "High-risk" women are those who are fairly certain they do not want a child right now and are also unlikely to receive any information that might change their mind. Of course, there may be a group of women between these two

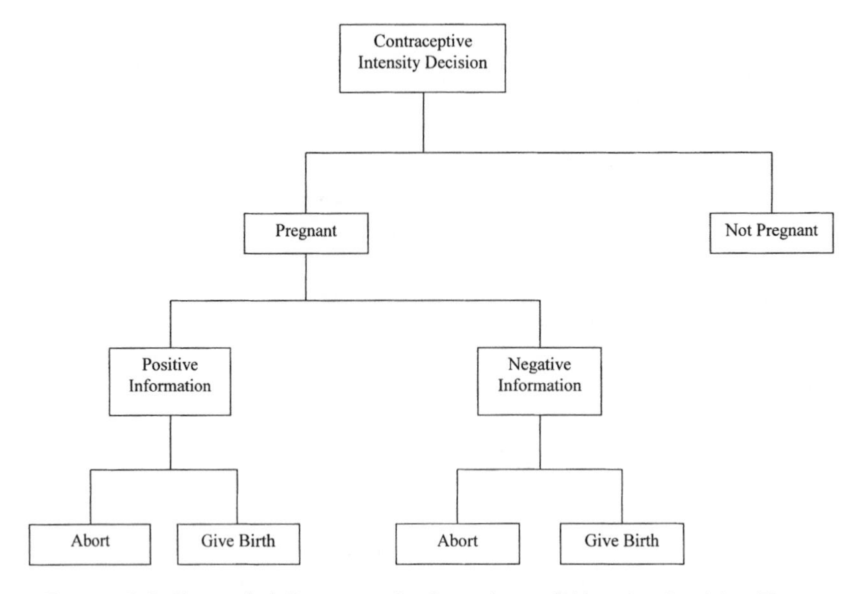

FIGURE 3.5. Expanded Contraceptive Intensity and Abortion Decision Tree.

extremes for whom the value of having a child at this moment is less clear, and they may be labeled "medium-risk" women. The implications for behavior in response to changes in abortion policy differ for each of these three groups of women.

The Decision Tree and the Abortion and Contraception Decisions

Although the decisions that a woman needs to make in this model are the same as those in the standard model, an additional level of complexity needs to be incorporated into the decision tree, as depicted in figure 3.5. In this model if she becomes pregnant, time will pass between the point at which she learns of her pregnancy and the point at which she needs to choose whether to give birth or abort. Over this period, information will be learned regarding the outcome of her pregnancy that will help assist in her decision. As I assumed for simplicity earlier, this information is either positive or negative. Once this information is obtained, regardless of its content, the woman needs to decide whether to give birth or have an abortion.

The decision to abort or give birth conditional upon a pregnancy is similar to that in the standard model. If the cost of giving birth is greater than the cost of having an abortion, one should have an abortion and vice versa. When positive information is received, this decision is obvious since giving birth does not impose a cost at all, but represents a benefit, so a birth always results. Only when negative information is received do the relevant costs need to be weighed.

The decision process gets more complicated when we move up the tree to focus on choosing a level of contraceptive intensity. At this stage, the decision maker is facing important elements of uncertainty, both in the probability that a pregnancy results and in the likelihood of receiving positive information, making it difficult simply to weigh the costs and benefits of a particular activity. This is where the expected utility hypothesis comes into play. As in its application in the standard model of abortion, we assume that individuals choose a level of contraceptive intensity to maximize their average level of well-being, weighted by the relevant probabilities. There, we were concerned only with the probability of a pregnancy, but now the probability of receiving positive or negative information needs to be incorporated as well.

The details of this solution are beyond the scope of this book, but I characterize it and attempt to provide some intuition here. In the standard model, we saw that the level of contraceptive intensity is set where the marginal cost of contraception just equals either the cost of birth or the cost of abortion, whichever is lower. Here, the solution indicates that women set the level of contraceptive intensity where the marginal cost of contraception just equals the expected value brought about by a pregnancy. Previously, we knew whether or not a birth or abortion would result if a pregnancy occurred, but here that outcome depends upon the probability that positive or negative information is received. The expected value of the outcome of a pregnancy before it takes place is just the average of the values of those outcomes weighted by the probabilities that each occurs.

The intuition for this solution is similar except that one is always comparing the marginal cost of contraception to the "expected cost" resulting from a pregnancy and not the actual cost. If one can increase the level of contraception at a cost that is less than the reduction in the expected cost of a pregnancy, then more contraception should be used. As more contraception is used, the increase in costs associated with greater levels of contraception are greater, so that at some point these additional costs will just equal the reduction in the expected cost of a pregnancy and at this point, no additional contraception should be used.

The Impact of Changes in Abortion Cost and Abortion Policy

Many of the predictions regarding changes in abortion cost described in the standard model follow here as well. For instance, if abortion costs are very high and then decline, they will eventually cross a threshold beyond which unwanted pregnancies will begin to be aborted rather than result in a birth. In addition, as abortion costs continue to fall, no subsequent reduction in births will take place, but contraceptive intensity will decline resulting in more pregnancies and more abortions. These are the main implications of the standard model and they follow here as well.

But there are other implications from this model that may help us gain additional insight into the behavioral impact of changes in abortion costs, potentially brought about by changes in abortion policy. Primary among them is that it may be possible for a reduction in abortion costs actually to increase the birth rate. In the standard model, once abortion costs fall below the cost of an unwanted birth, then those births no longer take place and there is no additional impact of further reductions in its cost on births. In the present model, however, a further reduction in the cost of abortion leads to more pregnancies and for some of those pregnancies positive information may unexpectedly be revealed, which would lead to a birth. If abortion were more costly, such pregnancies would not result so there could be no birth. In this way, lower abortion costs could actually *increase* births; all of these additional births would be "wanted." I refer to this result as counterintuitive because the conventional wisdom relates lower abortion costs to fewer births, and this reduction reflects those that would have been unwanted. Although this model does provide this prediction as abortion costs initially fall below the threshold of the cost of an unwanted birth, it also provides a counterintuitive prediction if abortion costs continue to fall significantly below that level.

This model also provides additional insight by distinguishing between different types of women and the different reactions they may have to changes in abortion policy. In the standard model we had assumed perfect information regarding the value of a birth from the time contraceptive intensity decisions are made. There, we could distinguish between those for whom births were wanted (i.e., provided benefits, not costs) and those for whom a birth was unwanted (i.e., costly). In that model, abortion was an irrelevant option for the wanted births. Predictions regarding the impact of changes in abortion costs only related to women whose births would be unwanted.

By relaxing the assumption of perfect information in the extended model, however, we can obtain a fuller picture of whose behavior may be affected. In this model, women differ in their probability that positive or negative information will result; no one can perfectly predict that their birth will be wanted or unwanted a priori. Although this probability would vary continuously across the entire population of childbearing-age women, for simplicity I have assumed three distinct types depending on the likelihood that they receive negative information: high-risk, low-risk, and medium-risk.

Changes in abortion policy have different implications for each group. One can show that low-risk women will not use contraception, which makes sense since they are virtually certain that they will want to have the baby if pregnant. Changes in abortion policy cannot have an impact on their contraceptive practices. Although negative information is unlikely, it is still possible (like a fetal defect) and then the cost of abortion may make the difference between giving birth or having an abortion.

Similarly, changes in abortion policy are unlikely to have much of an impact on the contraceptive choices of high-risk women. These women are fairly certain they do not want a child right now and are also unlikely to receive any information that might change their mind. Therefore, these women are likely to use contraception rather intensively and get pregnant relatively infrequently. If they do happen to get pregnant, however, a birth would be very likely to be unwanted, and so the cost of abortion could play an important role in determining whether they abort or have an unwanted birth.

The behavioral implications for changes in abortion policy are most interesting for those women at moderate risk of negative information. These women would benefit the most from a pregnancy in that it would reveal the information regarding its actual value. It is women in this group whose contraceptive behavior may be the most influenced by changes in abortion cost. As the cost of abortion falls for them, they may be more likely to reduce their level of contraceptive intensity in order to obtain this information. It is also for this group that births may actually rise if abortion costs fall low enough. Their additional pregnancies will result, with a moderate probability, in positive information, and these pregnancies will result in additional births. But these women are also subject to the possibility of having unwanted births if abortion costs are too high.

These predictions can be used to evaluate the potential impact of changes in abortion policy, again assuming that these policy changes can be represented by a change in abortion cost. As in the preceding section, however, we must recognize that further assumptions are required before doing so. This is because individual women vary in their own assessments of the cost of abortion even in the absence of government policy. Their valuation of the cost of an unwanted birth may also differ. As before, I will maintain the assumption that the legalization of abortion reduces the cost of abortion below the threshold of the cost of an unwanted birth, at least for most women. In addition, I assume that moderate restrictions on abortion access do not raise its cost above that threshold for many women.

With that said, the main predictions that resulted from the standard model earlier still stand here. Legalized abortion is predicted to reduce unwanted births, but imposing restrictions on abortion within a legal abortion environment is predicted to reduce pregnancies without increasing unwanted births. Moreover, we also have the additional prediction that births may actually rise if abortion costs get low enough and that any effects of abortion policy on contraceptive behavior should be most prevalent among women for whom the value of giving birth is the least certain a priori. Although this counterintuitive birth effect has received some empirical support, that support is not that strong. Therefore, in subsequent discussions I will not emphasize this prediction, leaving it mainly as an intriguing theoretical possibility.

Abortion as Insurance

The theoretical predictions brought about by changes in the cost of abortion (perhaps resulting from changes in abortion policy) reflect the application of traditional methods to the issue of pregnancy, abortion, and birth. These models stand on their own and do not require further interpretation within the broader context of other economic principles. Nevertheless, it may be useful to draw an analogy between the implications of these models and those that previous research has elucidated with regard to insurance markets. In some dimensions this analogy is better than in others, and I will highlight where it works well and where it does not. But the fundamental areas of similarity may help us interpret the behavioral responses that these models suggest.

To help draw this analogy, it is useful first to review some of the primary features of the economics of insurance markets. As with any market, it has a supply and demand side. The demand side of the market reflects consumers' behavior and their willingness to purchase insurance. Here, consumers have preferences for risk, and those who are risk averse would choose to purchase insurance because it protects them from incurring a loss. The value they place on certainty compensates for the insurance premium they need to pay, and so they decide to purchase insurance. Firms, on the other hand, are willing to offer insurance as long as they can sell enough policies that the risk they bear is minimal. By the law of large numbers, if a loss occurs with a certain probability and enough people are exposed to this risk, then the number of people who suffer the loss will be reasonably certain (the probability of the loss multiplied by the number at risk). Since the outcome for the insurance company is reasonably certain, they are willing to offer insurance as long as they can collect a premium sufficient to cover their expected payouts. Since some consumers are willing to buy the insurance and some firms are willing to offer it, a market for insurance exists.

An important feature of the market for insurance, however, is the possibility that complete insurance coverage may alter individuals' behavior. In particular, those with complete coverage may act in such a way that they increase the likelihood that the event being insured against actually occurs. Individuals with car insurance may drive more recklessly or park their cars in higher theft areas. Those with homeowners' insurance may be less likely to install smoke detectors that can limit the loss of a fire through early detection.

The fundamental problem created by this feature is that it creates a differential between the cost facing the individual with insurance and the cost to society brought about from suffering a loss. The individual still may face costs if his / her car is stolen, like the hassle associated with going to the police station, buying a new car, etc. But this cost does not reflect the true cost of the loss that society faces, like the cost of the police who try to solve the crime. Since the costs faced by the individual are less extensive than the costs faced by society, an individual making decisions based solely on his / her own costs will incur "too many" losses. Society would prefer it if the individual would be more careful, but this concern is not incorporated by the individual in his / her decision-making process. This outcome is considered to be "inefficient" from the point of view of economics.

In some dimensions, but not others, the availability of abortion is like the provision of insurance. In its most fundamental form, abortion provides protection from downside risk, just like insurance does. If a woman gets pregnant and that pregnancy would result in an unwanted birth, the availability of abortion provides an alternative resolution which prevents that cost from being incurred. Women will evaluate the cost of "purchasing" this form of insurance relative to the cost of the loss, and this will reflect the demand side of the market. The analogy breaks down on the supply side of the market, however, because abortion providers do not in any way act like insurance companies offering standard forms of insurance.

Another area where the analogy between traditional insurance and abortion may break down is the appropriate response to the presence of these behavioral changes associated with complete insurance. Recall that with standard forms of insurance, these behavioral changes introduce costs to society that are greater than the cost imposed upon the insured, so "too many" losses result. One way that insurance companies reduce this problem is by providing economic incentives so that insured individuals do not "overuse" the insurance. For instance, car insurance companies charge deductibles and firms that sell homeowners' insurance provide discounts for alarm systems. A direct extension of this approach to abortion policy would be to impose costs that lessen its use. Unfortunately, applying that principle directly to abortion may be inappropriate; I will discuss this issue further in the concluding chapter.

Conclusion

This chapter has provided alternative theoretical models that provide predictions regarding the way in which fertility outcomes would respond to changes in abortion policy. These predictions indicate that legalizing abortion would result in a significant reduction in unwanted births, but that imposing modest restrictions within a legal abortion environment will not bring about more unwanted births. Instead, they will lead to fewer abortions through a reduction in pregnancies.

These predictions fundamentally depend upon the assumptions underlying these models. Since some of those assumptions are rather strong and since I have no direct evidence regarding their validity, one could plausibly question the value of this theoretical exercise. Much of the remainder of the book will focus on empirical examinations of these predictions. If individuals respond to changes in abortion policy in the manner predicted, then these models can help provide a framework for understanding why. It is the combination of the empirical evidence in conjunction with the predictions of the model that enables us to understand better the impact of changes in abortion policy.

Chapter Four

METHODS FOR EVALUATING THE IMPACT OF POLICY CHANGES

IN THE PREVIOUS CHAPTER I introduced theoretical models suggesting that changes in abortion policy may be expected to alter individuals' behavior regarding pregnancy, abortions, and births. Based on the assumptions made there, I predicted that the primary impact of abortion legalization would be a reduction in the number of unwanted births. In that case, abortions would largely "replace" unwanted births. In contrast, relatively minor restrictions on abortion access, like parental involvement, mandatory delay, or Medicaid funding restrictions, would largely affect contraceptive intensity and the likelihood of a pregnancy. Abortions would decline because of the reduction in pregnancies, but births would not increase as a result and may even fall.

But these predictions depend on a number of fairly strong assumptions, suggesting that these conclusions are somewhat tenuous at this point. Their reliability could be considerably strengthened if they were subject to empirical evaluation indicating that individuals have indeed reacted in the predicted manner in response to previous changes in abortion policy. If so, the theoretical framework presented in the previous chapter may help us interpret the reasons for those behavioral changes. Moreover, it may give us greater confidence regarding the predicted impact of future policy changes.

The purpose of this chapter is to provide the background necessary to evaluate these predictions. Most of the empirical research that has been conducted recently regarding the impact of abortion policy relies on "quasi-experimental" techniques. These techniques use variation in abortion policies that typically result from changes in state laws. States experiencing a change in the law can be thought of as a pseudo-treatment group, and states in which there is no law change represent a pseudo-control group. Within this framework, a "treatment effect" can be established by comparing changes in outcomes in treatment group states compared to control group states. Of course, the application of these methods brings with it strengths and weaknesses as well. In this chapter I will elaborate on this technique along with a discussion of its beneficial attributes and its limitations. Although a background in statistics or econometrics helps one to understand these methods, the discussion will be presented in a manner that should be largely accessible even to those with limited exposure to these areas. The methods presented here will form the basis for much of the remainder of the book.

Controlled Experiments

Before moving on to a discussion of the use of quasi-experiments to examine the impact of changes in abortion policy on individual behavior, it is useful to describe the application of actual controlled experimental methods to similar, hypothetical exercises. The lessons learned here can be applied to quasi-experiments and can help identify some of the strengths and weaknesses of that approach.

A classic example of a scientific experiment is a drug trial. Pharmaceutical companies regularly develop new drugs in the laboratory and need proof that they are effective in treating the condition for which they were designed, before they are given approval by the Food and Drug Administration to be sold. Preliminary methods are employed to insure that no significant harm will be done to those who take the drug. Then an experimental design is typically implemented to test its effectiveness. The main element of this design is random assignment to a treatment group, whose members will receive the drug, and a control group, whose members will not receive the drug. In some instances the control group takes sugar pills instead to see whether it is the act of being treated rather than the treatment itself that matters. To test the effectiveness of the drug, one compares outcomes between treatment and control group members. If the drug is designed to treat an illness, then the drug is effective if more members of the treatment group get better compared to members of the control group.

One complication in all of this is that there is also some degree of chance regarding who gets better and who does not. We want to make sure we can distinguish between a differential in outcomes that is attributable to chance compared to one that is due to the drug itself. In other words, it may be the case that random variation in those who happen to get lucky and get better resulted in more members of the treatment group recovering from the illness compared to members of the control group. We need to distinguish this outcome from one in which the drug itself was the factor behind the improvement. To do this, we apply standard statistical tools of hypothesis testing. We reject the null hypothesis that the drug had no impact if the differential in outcomes between the two groups is "big enough." We do this when the likelihood that the differential that we observed is so large as to be very unlikely to be driven just by chance. When this is found to be true, we say that the difference is "statistically significant."

The key to the success of this experimental design is random assignment. When we randomly assign members to treatment and control groups, then it must be the case that the two groups are statistically identical in every dimension other than the presence of the treatment. The similarity between the two groups not only relates to those characteristics of individuals that we can observe, but extends to all characteristics including those that typically cannot be observed by the researcher. For instance, some individuals may have genes that would make them more resilient to the illness on their own and researchers may be unaware of this fact. If more of these individuals were in the treatment group, then more of them would recover naturally. In this case, the drug would appear to be effective, but in reality we should attribute the differential to the fact that the treatment group comprised more members who had this gene. But random assignment eliminates this possibility since individuals with this gene are equally likely to be in the control and treatment groups. In the absence of the treatment, we would expect the outcomes of the two groups to be statistically identical. Therefore, a simple comparison of outcomes (along with appropriate hypothesis testing and tests of statistical significance) is sufficient to determine whether the drug is effective.

Consider, for example, an experiment designed to test whether or not taking an aspirin a day can help reduce the occurrence of heart disease. Without random assignment the results of the experiment may be biased. If those who take the aspirin are less likely to smoke, for instance, then it would appear that the drug was effective even though the differential in heart disease would really have resulted from the difference in smoking behavior. But if individuals are assigned to treatment and control groups randomly, then the two groups will be statistically identical; any risk factor associated with heart disease (genetics, diet, smoking, and the like) will be the result only of random variation. The impact of the aspirin can then be identified by comparing rates of heart disease among the two groups of individuals. Then statistical tests can be conducted to determine the likelihood that any difference in outcomes just occurred by chance. If that likelihood is small, then we would conclude that the aspirin regimen was effective.

A very desirable feature of this approach is its simplicity. The statistical techniques required to estimate the effect of the drug are relatively straightforward. Means of outcomes for the two groups need to be calculated and appropriate hypothesis tests conducted. But no methods more complicated than that are required to determine the true, causal impact of the drug on the relevant health outcome.

Although ethical considerations completely rule out the possibility of implementing a true experimental design to examine the impact of abortion policy, it still would be useful to consider what such an experiment would look like. Recall that random assignment to control and treatment groups is the cornerstone of a true experimental design. Here we would select a sample of women and then randomly assign them to control and treatment groups where women in the treatment group would be subject to some change in abortion policy and women in the control group would not. Suppose, for instance, that abortion is largely illegal nationwide (as it was prior to 1970) and that we want to test the impact of legalization. Then women in the control group would be unable to receive a legal abortion, but women in the treatment group would be able to abort legally. Within this experimental framework, evaluating the impact of legalizing abortion would simply require a comparison of, say, the pregnancy, abortion, and birth rates of the treatment and control groups followed by appropriate hypothesis testing.

Controlled experiments do have a number of desirable properties (cf. Burtless 1995), but they are not without their limitations (cf. Heckman and Smith 1995). For instance, consider an alternative experiment where we tested the impact of criminalizing abortion in an environment where abortion was generally legal (i.e., the treatment group would be unable to obtain a legal abortion). Here, the treatment effect estimated from this experiment may be greater than that which would result if the policy were actually implemented. This is because a national ban on legal abortion may result in a network of illegal abortion providers, which would reduce the impact. If only a sample of women were subject to illegal abortion in the context of an experiment, no such network would emerge imposing greater constraints on women's fertility.

The Quasi-Experimental Approach

The Basics

Although we know how we would conduct a controlled experiment to test the impact of changes in abortion policy and how to evaluate the outcome of the experiment, one cannot be conducted for obvious ethical reasons. But suppose that we had data from the real world that had the same "look and feel" as data that would have been generated from a controlled experiment. If we could find such data, we could apply similar methods to them. Suppose, for instance, that some women in the country were, just coincidentally, suddenly subject to a different set of abortion policies to which other women were not subject. This would be called a "natural" or "quasi-experiment." Those women newly subjected to the policy changes would represent a pseudo-treatment group and those women who were not would represent a pseudo-control group. Changes in state laws provide an example where such conditions may hold.

In practice, we would have to make some modifications to this approach in recognition of the fact that these data were not truly generated from a controlled experiment. The main problem is that there was no random assignment. It was that feature that enabled us to assume that the control and treatment groups were statistically identical before the law changed and that they could be expected to have the same outcomes, on average, had no treatment occurred. We do not have actual randomization in a quasi-experiment, so additional methods need to be incorporated and assumptions made before we are able to use this approach.

Without formal randomization we have no way to be sure that the control and treatment groups (from now on I drop the "pseudo" for simplicity) are statistically identical before the policy change takes place. Suppose, for instance, that we are examining the impact of abortion legalization, which occurs in one set of states but not others, on the birth rate. It may be the case that the demographic composition of the states is different or cultural attitudes toward family size differ, and that would lead to different birth rates regardless of any differences in abortion policy. If we happened to see that the birth rate was lower in the states in which abortion was legal, it would be inappropriate to assign that difference to the legal status of abortion.

One way to circumvent this problem is to examine the change in the birth rate after the change in law, relative to its level beforehand in the states that legalized abortion. The fact that we are looking within this set of states would cause us to hold constant those long-standing differences between states that may make comparisons across states difficult. If the birth rate fell in states that legalized abortion in the years following the law change, we may be more confident that this reduction was actually attributable to that.

We may still be concerned about adopting this approach, however, because other things may have been changing in those states at the same time as the law change that may confound its impact. For instance, if cultural attitudes toward women's work were changing around the time of the law change and if this led families toward preferring fewer children, then it would appear that abortion legalization lowered the birth rate, but in reality it was the change in preferences.

But this approach does not exploit the fact that a control group exists: namely the set of states in which there was no law change. Suppose that the changing preferences toward smaller families were taking place across the nation at roughly the same pace. We can use the trend toward lower fertility in the control group states as a model for what we might have expected to happen in the treatment group states as well. Then we can look to see if birth rates fell by *more* in the treatment group states follow-

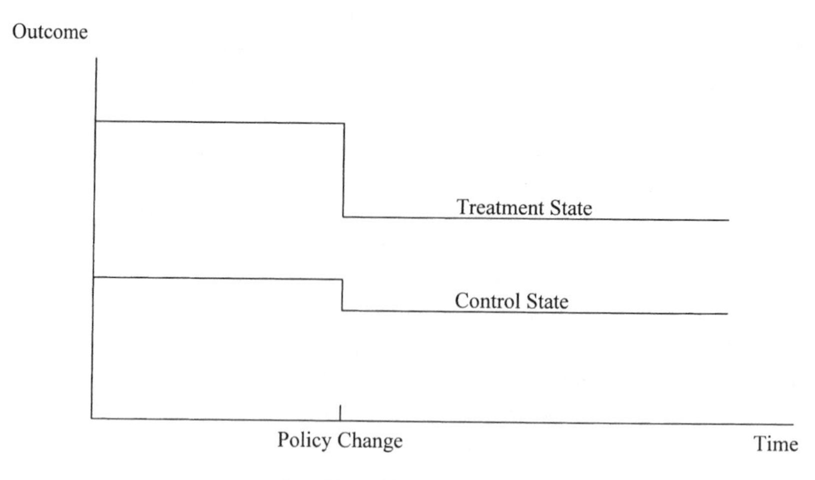

Panel II: Difference in Outcomes

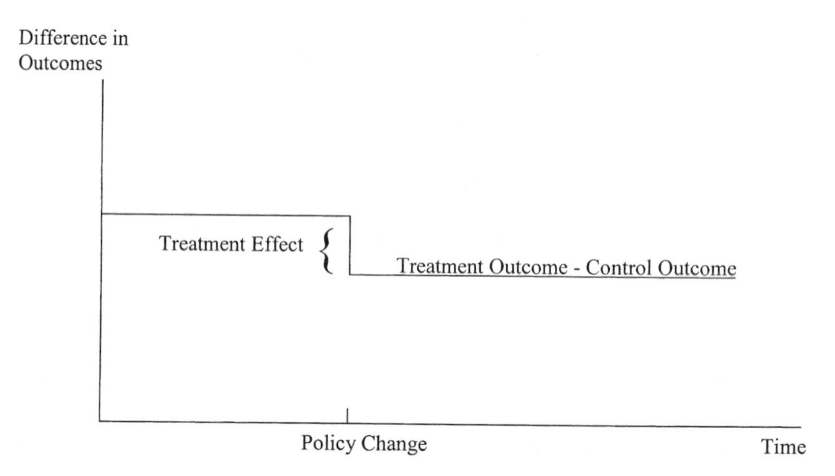

FIGURE 4.1 Illustration of the Use of Quasi-Experimental Methods.

ing abortion legalization than we would have predicted solely on the basis of the experiences of the control group states. This represents the treatment effect.

A Graphical Approach

This approach is illustrated in the two panels in figure 4.1. The top panel depicts two hypothetical patterns in some outcome, like birth rates, in treatment group states and control group states before and after some policy change. For simplicity, I assume that there is no trend or year-to-year variation in these data other than the year the policy change occurs. In the treatment group states, the level of the outcome is considerably higher than in the control group states well before any policy change takes place and this difference cannot be attributable to anything other than preexisting differences between the two sets of states. These differences are typically attributed to "state fixed effects," which reflect unspecified factors that lead to long-standing differences in behavior across states. At the time of the policy change, however, the level of the outcome in the treatment group takes a large, discrete drop and then stabilizes at a lower level for the remainder of the period. The difference between the post–policy change period from the pre–policy change period in those states controls for these state fixed effects.

But the difference in outcomes between pre- and post-policy change periods in treatment group states still may not accurately represent the true impact of the policy because other factors also may have changed at the same time. The pattern in outcomes in control group states, in which no policy change took place, can help us identify the impact of these other factors. In those states, we could similarly compare outcomes in the post-change period from the pre-change period. Since no policy change actually took place in control group states, any change in outcomes must be attributable to other influences, which are sometimes called "year fixed effects."

We can use this information to "adjust" the difference between post-change and pre-change outcomes observed in the treatment group states to isolate the impact of the policy change itself. To do this, we just need to subtract the change in outcomes in the control group states from the change in outcomes in the treatment group states. What remains is the impact of the policy abstracting from other changes taking place at that time. This approach is called a "difference-in-differences" estimator because what we are doing is taking the difference in outcomes in treatment group states and subtracting the difference in outcomes in control group states. As with controlled experiments, we would need to conduct a hypothesis test to determine whether this difference is statistically significant before we would be willing to conclude that the policy had some impact on behavior.

An alternative approach to considering this difference-in-difference estimator is presented in the lower panel of figure 4.1. In this panel, the line represents the difference in outcomes between treatment and control groups at each time period. In this format, the shock that occurred nationwide and affected the outcome at precisely the same time as the policy change but was unrelated to that change is differenced out directly. We

TABLE 4.1.
Illustration of Difference-in-Differences Approach

Group	*Period*	*Average Outcome in State/Period*	*Difference*	*Difference-in-Differences*
	after policy change	outcome = z + s + t + p		
Treatment Group			ΔO^T = t + p	
	before policy change	outcome = z + s		
				$\Delta O^T - \Delta O^C$ = p
	after policy change	outcome = z + t		
Control Group			ΔO^C = t	
	before policy change	outcome = z		

Note: p = policy effect; t = time- (year) specific effect (assumed to influence outcomes in all states after policy change); s = state-specific effect (assumed to influence outcomes in treatment group states relative to control group states at all times); z = baseline level of outcomes

also see that in the period before the policy change, the outcome level is consistently higher in the treatment group than the control group. After the policy change, there is still a positive difference in outcome levels between the two groups, but that difference is not as great as it used to be. The reduction in that difference represents the treatment effect.

A Mathematical Approach

The same information that is presented in the two panels of this figure can be represented mathematically as well and may help clarify how a difference-in-differences estimator works. This illustration is presented in table 4.1. There exists a control group of states that experiences some baseline level of an outcome that is denoted by z in this table. As in figure 4.1, assume some common shock comes along that shifts the level of that outcome in both control and treatment group states at precisely the time of the policy change, but is unrelated to the policy change. This is denoted by t in the table. Therefore, in control group states the average outcome level is equal to z before the policy change and $z + t$ after the policy change. Treatment group states are always different than control group states and would always exhibit a different level of outcomes regardless of the policy. This component is represented by s in the table. The policy itself has an effect, p, that alters the average outcome level in treatment group states after the policy goes into effect. Therefore, in treatment group states, the average outcome level is equal to $z + s$ before the policy change and $z + s + t + p$ after the policy change.

The goal of this exercise is to identify p, and a difference-in-differences approach accomplishes this. To see this, first suppose we take the difference in average outcomes over time within treatment group states. This is labeled ΔO^T in the table and would equal $t + p$. If we computed the comparable difference in control group states, we would get ΔO^C, which would be equal to t. If we took the difference of these differences, $\Delta O^T - \Delta O^C$, we would be left with p, which is the treatment effect. Therefore, this difference-in-differences approach enables us to hold constant long-standing differences that exist across states as well as factors that affect outcomes nationally at the same time, in an attempt to isolate the impact of the policy itself.

Extensions

This approach provides a useful framework for evaluating the impact of public policies and is sometimes utilized directly in policy evaluations. I will present several examples of its direct application in subsequent chapters. Nevertheless, it does impose strong assumptions that may be violated in reality. For instance, differences across states are assumed to be long-standing in nature and not changing at all over time. This assumption seems plausible in some instances but not in others. The weather is always warmer in Florida than in Massachusetts, but immigrants have been altering the demographic composition of Florida at a faster rate than in Massachusetts. Moreover, it assumes that any changes that take place over time other than the policy itself affect all states uniformly, and this assumption need not be true. For instance, a slowdown in the economy tends to have national repercussions, but some states may be affected more or less than others. California provides an example of this in the recession of the early 1990s; the slump there was greater and lasted quite a bit longer than that in the rest of the country.

The way that problems such as this are generally addressed is to use regression-based methods that can control for both state- and year-fixed effects along with a series of other variables that may differ both across states and over time.[1] Including variables like this in a regression model of this form still enables us to interpret the results within the context of a quasi-experiment and in difference-in-differences estimates. As always, hypothesis testing is also required in this framework before we are able to conclude that a policy had some impact. In the discussion to be presented in subsequent chapters, estimates obtained from both simple quasi-experimental methods along with a regression-based approach will be reported where appropriate.

Limitations of Quasi-Experimental Methods

Although quasi-experimental methods provide very powerful tools to evaluate the results of policy interventions in a relatively intuitive manner, they do possess some limitations that need to be addressed as well. Meyer (1995) presents a detailed discussion of these issues. The discussion here will summarize the main points that are most relevant to the issues that may arise in analyses of the effects of abortion policy. Where appropriate, the possible methods that can help overcome these limitations are discussed. All the problems would be resolved if random assignment were possible, but since it cannot be carried out in many of the circumstances in which quasi-experiments are employed, this solution usually is not applicable.

One significant problem that may arise in a quasi-experiment is that something else may have changed that alters outcomes around the same time as the policy. The quasi-experimental framework is able to identify the impact of a policy change based on the change in outcomes in treatment group states compared to the change in outcomes in control group states. Without randomization, we cannot rule out that some other change took place at about the same time as the policy change. If another change did occur in the world that affected only treatment group members after the policy intervention, we would be unable to distinguish between the causal impact of the policy and the impact brought about by this other factor. In fact, if we do not know that the other change took place, we would incorrectly attribute all of its impact to the policy itself. If the other factors that are changing are ones that we can observe and control for in a regression-based extension to the quasi-experimental design, then they would not bias the results. What would cause problems are those factors that are not controlled for, either because we do not have data that captures them or because they are inherently unobservable (like changes in preferences).

Another potential problem is something called "policy endogeneity" (cf. Besley and Case 2000). In a quasi-experiment, the policy change that takes place is assumed to be introduced as if it were a random event, uncorrelated with the outcomes in the state. However, one can imagine that policymakers monitor events that occur in their own jurisdiction and may respond accordingly. If, say, teen abortion rates are rising, policymakers may choose to implement a parental involvement law in an attempt to reverse that trend. In that event, quasi-experimental methods will yield biased estimates of the policy impact. Even if the parental involvement law had no impact on behavior, the ongoing trends may continue, and it would appear that the policy intervention led to rising abortion rates.

"Contamination" of the experimental framework is also a potential problem. In a controlled experiment, contamination would result if members of the control group managed to find a way to receive treatment. For instance, in randomized trials of an experimental cancer drug, if control group members realized that they were not receiving the drug they may go to another country to try to get it there. If they were successful in getting the drug and the drug were actually effective, the fact that they got better would reduce the estimated impact of the drug based on a comparison of the control and treatment groups. Similar problems exist in a quasi-experimental design. If one state legalizes abortion, for example, but neighboring states do not, then women in control group states may cross the state line and obtain an abortion, reducing the estimated impact of the law change.

Perhaps the primary solution to avoiding problems in quasi-experimental analyses is to find policy variation that occurs as if it were random, unrelated to changes in the outcome under consideration (called "exogenous variation"). If the policy change is truly exogenous, one should be more likely to accept that the results of such an analysis will provide estimates of the causal effect of the policy. It does not solve every problem (like contamination of the control and treatment group), but it certainly reduces many others.

In the context of abortion policy, the changes that take place do possess features that would lead one to believe they are exogenous. Abortion legalization in the early 1970s was certainly coming at a time of dramatic social change. But the precise timing of legalization in a handful of early legalizing states and of the Supreme Court's decision in *Roe v. Wade* were considered to be surprising developments at the time. Similarly, some of the subsequent variation in state policies imposing relatively minor restrictions on abortion access also came about as the result of Supreme Court decisions. Although those states that chose to implement them may not have been exogenous, these states usually have been in favor of such restrictions for some time and were only able to implement them after the court ruled that they were constitutional. Again, this makes the timing of their introduction plausibly exogenous and suitable for use in a quasi-experimental framework.

The use of multiple control groups can also be useful in addressing some of the limitations inherent in quasi-experiments. For instance, such an approach can help detect whether the control group has been contaminated. With multiple control groups, it is likely to be the case that contamination is more likely among some of them than others. If the pattern of results is consistent with this hypothesis, then we can gauge the extent to which contamination occurred. For instance, if one state legalized abortion earlier than others, then travel to the legal abortion state would be far greater among women closer to that state than among women further away. If separate control groups were arranged according to their distance to the legal state, this would help identify the impact of contamination.

A similar approach is to compare quasi-experimental estimates between subcategories of the population that one would expect to be differentially affected by the treatment. For instance, parental involvement laws should only affect the behavior of women below the age of 18. But the same quasi-experimental exercise can be conducted for older women, comparing changes in outcomes for those in control and treatment group states. If the estimated impact for older women is the same as that estimated for minors, then it is unlikely that the finding is causal. On the other hand, if we find no effect for the older women, but some change in behavior among minors, then this would indicate a causal treatment effect. Sometimes this is referred to as a "triple-difference" estimate since a third difference is taken between groups after standard difference-in-differences estimates are computed for each group.

Conclusion

Recent research that has been conducted regarding the impact of abortion policy has applied quasi-experimental methods extensively. Much of the rest of the book will take advantage of the insights gained from this research, so that the overview of the methods described in this chapter will be helpful in interpreting the discussion to come. Although these methods provide a valuable tool in estimating the impact of policy changes, like those regarding abortion access, they also possess some limitations as I have described here. These strengths and weaknesses should be kept in mind in interpreting the results to come.

Chapter Five

THE IMPACT OF ABORTION LEGALIZATION

IN THE PRECEDING two chapters I set forth predictions regarding the potential impact that changes in abortion policy would have on women's fertility behavior and described methods that can be used to assess those effects. Recall that moving from an environment that was very expensive, as it would be if abortion were illegal, to one in which the cost of an abortion fell considerably (i.e., through legalization) would primarily reduce the number of unwanted births. This would occur if the cost of an abortion fell below the cost of an unwanted birth. To the extent that the cost of an abortion continued to fall further, however, it is still possible that contraceptive practices would be altered, resulting in more pregnancies. Subsequent imposition of relatively minor restrictions on abortion access was predicted mostly to affect contraceptive behavior, since I assumed that these restrictions do not raise the cost of an abortion above the cost of an unwanted birth, at least for most women. These policy changes would then lead to fewer pregnancies and fewer abortions.

But these predictions relied upon a number of fairly strong assumptions and it would be imprudent to rely too heavily upon them without empirical evidence to support them. In the preceding chapter I described the quasi-experimental methods that have been used extensively in the past decade or so to examine these predictions. The next two chapters will focus on this empirical evidence, largely reviewing research that has already been completed, but also introducing some new evidence. This chapter will examine the impact of abortion legalization and the following chapter will focus on the three most common forms of restrictions: Medicaid funding, parental involvement, and mandatory delay. Both chapters will concentrate on the impact of abortion policy in the United States; the following chapter will broaden the examination to consider abortion policy in other countries.

In this chapter, the quasi-experimental techniques employed are greatly assisted by the history of abortion legalization in the United States, described in Chapter 2. In fact, this history sets up an even stronger test of the impact of abortion legalization on behavior since two experiments can be examined. Starting in 1970, abortion was legalized in a handful of states ahead of the 1973 United States Supreme Court decision in *Roe v. Wade*. This establishes naturally occurring treatment and control groups made up of women in states where abortion became legal and women in states where the status quo held. In 1973, however, the treatment and control groups were reversed. Women in states that had legalized abortion earlier experienced no law change and represent a control group that can be compared to women in states affected by the Roe decision. Since the timing of these law changes was quite unexpected during this period, both sets of changes reflect plausibly exogenous variation that can be used in a quasi-experimental framework. Although other limitations of that framework exist, and will be described later in this chapter, this set of experiments provides a useful starting point for evaluating the impact of abortion legalization on women's behavior.

I will use these quasi-experiments in this chapter to explore the impact of abortion legalization on three specific outcomes: the birth rate, the adoption rate, and the pregnancy rate. The models in chapter 3 make specific predictions regarding the birth rate and we will assess those here. The predictions in those models relate specifically to unwanted births, so I also consider the impact on adoption. If abortions take place when a pregnancy would have resulted in an unwanted birth, then abortion legalization should have reduced adoption.

I also examine the impact of abortion legalization on the likelihood of pregnancy itself, since it is possible that this policy change could reduce contraceptive intensity or increase sexual activity depending upon the extent to which the cost of abortion fell. Although data limitations somewhat weaken the analysis in this regard, under a certain set of assumptions we can use the available data to examine the impact on pregnancies. Along with the empirical results from this analysis, I will also present a test of the plausibility of the maintained assumptions.

Early Research

The use of quasi-experimental methods to study the impact of abortion legalization has become common within the past decade or so, but earlier research that generally used alternative methods addressed this question as well. Before describing more recent research, I begin with a review and critique of these earlier studies. This review, as with subsequent reviews of previous research, is designed to be illustrative of the techniques used and conclusions drawn by earlier researchers, but is not necessarily exhaustive in scope.

Not surprisingly, considerable research focused on the impact of abortion legalization just after it occurred in the early 1970s. The main, but not exclusive, focus of that work was its impact on birth rates. Some work adopted a "case study" strategy, comparing trends in birth rates in the

TABLE 5.1.
Earlier Research Examining the Impact of Abortion Legalization

Paper	*Outcome Measures*	*Data*	*Methodology*	*Findings*
Tietze (1973)	abortions and births	*Vital Statistics* data from New York	Compares outcomes in first two years following New York's 1970 legalization law.	Reports an increase in the number of abortions and a decline in the number of births.
Sklar and Berkov (1974)	births	*Vital Statistics*	Compares trends in birth rates between states that legalized/ liberalized abortion and other states.	Estimates that law changes reduced birth-rates by 4 percent.
Bauman, Anderson, Freeman, and Koch (1977)	births	*Vital Statistics*	Estimates rank order correlations between the difference in fertility rates between 1967 and 1971 and the abortion ratio in 1970.	Finds correlation was small before 1970, but then became big and negative.
Moore and Caldwell (1977)	1st intercourse, 1st pregnancy, and pregnancy outcomes	survey of almost 5,000 teens in 1971	Uses regression models relating outcomes to legal status of abortion in state in 1971.	Finds no relationship between availability and pregnancy, positive relationship between availability and abortion, and negative relationship between availability and nonmarital births.
Quick (1978)	births and infant health measures	*Vital Statistics* data from Oregon	Uses pre-post comparison of outcomes before and after Oregon's 1969 liberalization (not legalization) law.	Finds a lagged reduction in birth rates and low birth weight babies, but no impact on neonatal and infant mortality.
Tietze (1984)	maternal mortality	National Center for Health Statistics and Centers for Disease Control data	Uses deviation in maternal mortality after legalization from projected rates before legalization.	Concludes that abortion legalization prevented 1,500 pregnancy-related deaths.
Joyce and Mocan (1990)	births to white and black teens	*Vital Statistics* data from New York City	Uses advanced time-series econometric techniques to estimate the break in trend associated with the June 1970 legalization in New York City.	Estimates that abortion legalization led to a 14 percent and 19 percent decline in births to white and black teens, respectively.
Gohmann and Ohsfeldt (1994)	births	*Vital Statistics* and Alan Guttmacher Institute	Uses national time-series data from 1915 to 1988 and estimates impact of increase in abortion providers after 1970 on national fertility rates.	Finds strong positive relationship.

particular location before and after the law change (cf. Tietze 1973; and Quick 1978).[1] Results from these studies indicate that the birth rate dropped by roughly 25 percent in the period following legalization, and in applying a series of assumptions, suggested that perhaps one-quarter to one-half of this decline can be attributed to abortion legalization.

More recently, Joyce and Mocan (1990) have applied more sophisticated econometric techniques for the analysis of time-series data to examine the New York City experience regarding births to black and white teens. They found that legalization reduced the birth rate by 14 percent for white teens and 19 percent for black teens. Gohmann and Ohsfeldt (1994) use aggregate time-series data for the entire country between 1915 and 1988, relating fertility rates to the number of (legal) abortion providers, which obviously rose dramatically following abortion legalization. Comparing the entire pre- to post-legalization period, calculations based on their estimates suggest that births fell by about 10 percent.

A shortcoming of the case study approach is that it is unable adequately to capture the other changes taking place at the same time in that particular location. Particularly given the social upheaval taking place in the late 1960s and early 1970s, a pre-post comparison design largely ignores these changes. Although strategies can be developed that more accurately identify the underlying trends that may be occurring, as in Joyce and Mocan (1990), it is difficult fully to control for these changes, which may follow erratic time-series patterns, considering the ongoing social circumstances around that time.

A quasi-experimental approach helps address this problem and some early work had moved in this direction. Bauman et al. (1977) and Sklar and Berkov (1974) adopt such a strategy. Bauman et al. estimate rank order correlations between the 1967–71 change in fertility rates and the abortion ratio (the ratio of abortions to live births) in 1970 and find a significant negative relationship, although it is impossible to quantify the impact of legalization on fertility. Sklar and Berkov estimate the impact of legalization on fertility by taking the difference between the change in birth rates between 1965 and 1971 in states that had in any way liberalized their abortion law versus states with no legal changes. They conclude that births fell by about 4 percent as a result of legalization. Although this approach offers significant advantages, it still may confuse changes in the environment within specific states that led to liberalization with the law change itself. In addition, the fact that women traveled to states in which abortion was legal (Tietze 1973) will lead to an understated impact on fertility. More recent research provides methods to help reduce these problems as well.

Comparisons of outcomes before and after abortion legalization were similarly applied to address its impact on maternal mortality. For instance, Tietze (1984) compares the actual trend in maternal deaths attributed to abortion through the early and middle 1970s with the rate that would have been predicted had abortion not been legalized. He concludes that legalization prevented roughly 1,500 deaths to women who would have sought illegal abortions otherwise. This estimate is likely to be biased both by the absence of a comparison group that could provide an indicator of trends in the absence of legalization and by measurement error in the stated cause of death in the era before abortion became legal.

Some past work also considers the possibility that the legalization of abortion also had an impact on sexual activity, contraceptive use, and pregnancy behavior. Tietze (1973 and 1975) discusses the possibility of these effects in his work and rules them out, but provides no evidence and gives no references to specific data in this regard. Moore and Caldwell (1977) explicitly examine the impact of abortion policies on these outcomes using a special survey of teen women conducted in 1971. This work uses the cross-sectional variation in policies that existed at this time and estimated their impact along with other types of policies on the transition to first intercourse, abortion, pregnancy, and nonmarital births. They find that higher abortion availability increases the likelihood of an abortion, reduces the likelihood of a nonmarital birth, but has no effect on the likelihood of pregnancy or first intercourse. Although the availability of such an unusual dataset for its time is enviable, the strict reliance on cross-sectional data, which cannot distinguish true causal effects from cultural differences across states, weakens the impact of this study.

The Impact on Birth Rates

Quasi-Experimental Predictions and Description of the Data

Recent research using quasi-experimental methods overcomes many of the limitations of previous analyses and will be used extensively in the subsequent discussion. Before presenting the results of these exercises, it is useful to review what one might expect to find. Recall from the preceding chapter that we may infer that a policy had a causal impact if some outcome changed in treatment states following the policy change, but not in the control states, which were not subject to the policy change. Graphically, this was depicted in figure 4.1, which shows the trend over time in levels for the two sets of states and in differences between the two sets of states.

With abortion legalization, however, we have an even stronger method of determining whether or not the policy change had a causal impact. The reason for this is that we actually have two experiments taking place, not just one. In some states ("repeal states"), abortion became legal three years before it did in other states, setting up one quasi-experiment. But then in 1973, the experiment reversed and the rest of the country ("Roe states") legalized abortion. This means that the treatment group becomes those states that did not legalize abortion until the *Roe* decision and the early legalizers constitute the control group. If birth rates fell in response to legalization, then any gap in birth rates that was generated following early legalization in a handful of states should be eliminated when *Roe* came along.

This projected pattern can be represented graphically, as in figure 5.1, which is a modified version of figure 4.1. In the top panel, we see that birth rates are projected to decline in each set of states at the time abortion is legalized. In the bottom panel, we see that the difference in birth rates between the two sets of states shrinks when abortion is initially legalized in repeal states and then returns to its earlier level following the *Roe* decision.

The availability of two successive experiments helps us assess the extent to which the estimated impact is really attributable to changes in abortion policy rather than some other event that happened to take place at the same time. If the data exhibit the pattern reflected in the lower panel of figure 5.1, then any other factor besides abortion policy that could generate this result would have to occur at exactly the right point in time in both sets of states. The chances of this seem remote. Therefore, if we observe this hypothesized pattern, it is strong confirmation that the cause is the change in abortion policy.

There still remain a couple of important caveats in this analysis that should be taken into consideration before presenting the results of such an exercise. First, after the first set of states legalized abortion in 1970, women in other states had the option to travel to obtain an abortion. This activity would lessen the extent to which legal abortion will be observed to have reduced the birth rate. In the analysis below, besides comparing births in states that legalized early to births in states affected by the *Roe* decision, I will also separate states in the latter group into categories according to their distance to states that legalized early. Under the assumption that travel was more common among women closer to the states legalizing abortion early, comparisons against groups of states that differ according to their distance can provide an indication of the extent to which travel reduced the estimated impact of abortion legalization.

Second, the response to changes in abortion laws may not have been instantaneous, particularly in states affected by the *Roe* decision. In 1970, women in states that legalized abortion very quickly had access to those services, so their births may have declined starting in 1971 (biology limits any impact until several months after the law change). In 1973, however, women in Roe states may not have had instantaneous access to abortion. Because travel to a legal abortion state had been a possibility beforehand, excess demand for abortion services was not as great in these states at

Panel I: Levels of Birth Rate

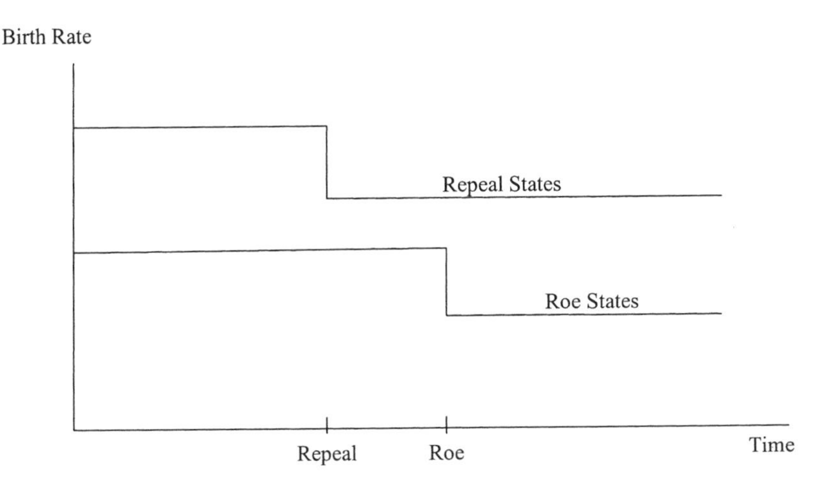

Panel II: Differences in Birth Rates

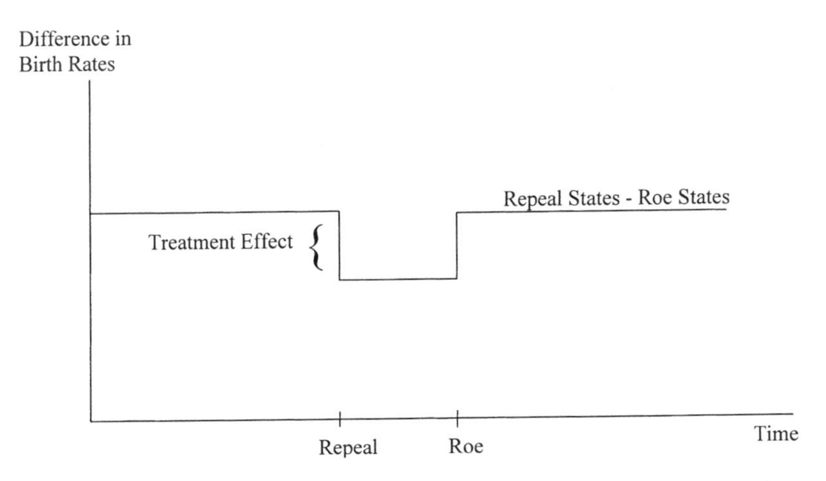

FIGURE 5.1. Illustration of the Impact of Abortion Legalization on Births.

the time of legalization. In addition, abortion advocates mobilized very quickly following the initial legalization to establish clinics in the handful of locations where abortion was allowed. Following *Roe*, it took considerably longer to set up a nationwide network of providers. Therefore, one may expect that the impact of *Roe* on birth rates may have developed more slowly than the initial impact of legalization.

Most of the data used to test these predictions come from *Vital Statistics of the United States*, published by the U.S. Census Bureau (various years). These data are obtained from birth certificates filed with state public health agencies and, therefore, reflect virtually complete data. Information obtained from the birth certificate enables an enumeration of births by state, age, and race; all of these data will be used below. Population estimates by age, race, and state of residence from the U.S. Census Bureau are also utilized for the denominator of the birth rate.

I also examine differences in the impact of abortion legalization by marital status, but *Vital Statistics* data are inappropriate for this exercise. Over the time period considered here, the marital status of the mother was not requested on birth certificates in all states, including California and New York. Since women in these states represent the vast majority of those affected by the early legalization of abortion prior to *Roe*, I cannot use these data here. Instead, I employ data from the 1980 Census of the Population. In those data, births over the 1965 to 1980 period can be observed as well; marital status at the time of birth is determined by comparing the mother's age at first marriage and the child's date of birth. This does not perfectly identify marital status at the time of birth, however. In addition, state of residence is defined as of 1980, not at the time the child was born. These problems with the data somewhat weaken this part of the analysis, but these are the best data available.

Aggregate Effect

Figure 5.2 presents the results of this quasi-experimental exercise, examining the impact of abortion legalization on birth rates for all women of childbearing age (15–44). This figure presents the percentage difference in birth rates between "repeal" states that legalized abortion in 1970 (New York, California, Washington, Alaska, and Hawaii—see table 2.2), and "Roe" states whose residents experienced no definitive law change until the *Roe* decision.[2] States that had liberalized their abortion laws are not included in this analysis. These states do not make for good comparisons because those law changes may have had an impact on birth rates there as well. To facilitate the estimation of the impact of abortion legalization, all percentage differences are normalized so that the 1970 value is equal to zero. In other words, all values in this graph have been shifted by the value of the percentage difference in 1970 so that the impact of abortion legalization can be measured directly on the y-axis.

The values reported in figure 5.2 strongly resemble the pattern predicted in the lower panel of figure 5.1. In actual data, it should not be surprising that year-to-year fluctuations exist in individual behavior and those movements are generally viewed as random. In the period leading

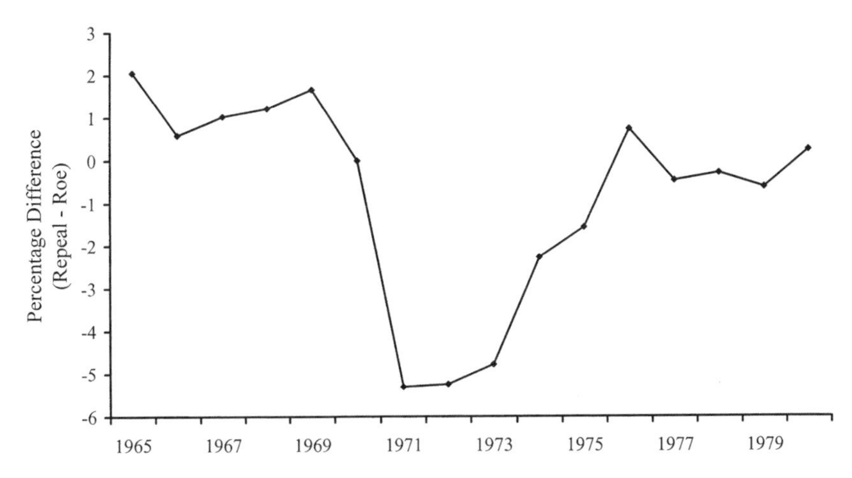

FIGURE 5.2. Impact of Abortion Legalization on Aggregate Birth Rates. *Source*: Reprinted from Levine, Phillip B., Douglas Staiger, Thomas J. Kane, and David J. Zimmerman. 1999. "*Roe v. Wade* and American Fertility." *American Journal of Public Health* 89 (2): 199–203, copyright 1999, with permission of the American Public Health Association. *Note*: The percentage differences have been normalized so that their values equal zero in 1970.

up to 1970, for instance, the difference in birth rates between repeal and Roe states was relatively constant, providing no evidence that fertility behavior in the two sets of states was diverging prior to that date. But in 1971 we observe a discrete decline in birth rates for women in repeal states of about 5 percent relative to birth rates for women in Roe states. That difference was largely stable between 1971 and 1973. In 1974 and 1975, the percentage difference began to narrow. By 1976 and in the following years, any difference that had emerged during the 1971–73 period had been eliminated. If we allow for slower growth in access to abortion services following the *Roe* decision compared to that following the earlier legalization efforts, the pattern reflected in figure 5.2 is exactly what we would have predicted if abortion legalization reduced the birth rate. These results would suggest that births declined by about 5 percent as a result.

Effects by Demographic Group

Figures 5.3 through 5.5 present analogous statistics separately according to women's age, race, and marital status at the time of birth, respectively. Differences in birth rates between categories of states by the age of the mother at the time of birth are reported in figure 5.3. Women are disaggre-

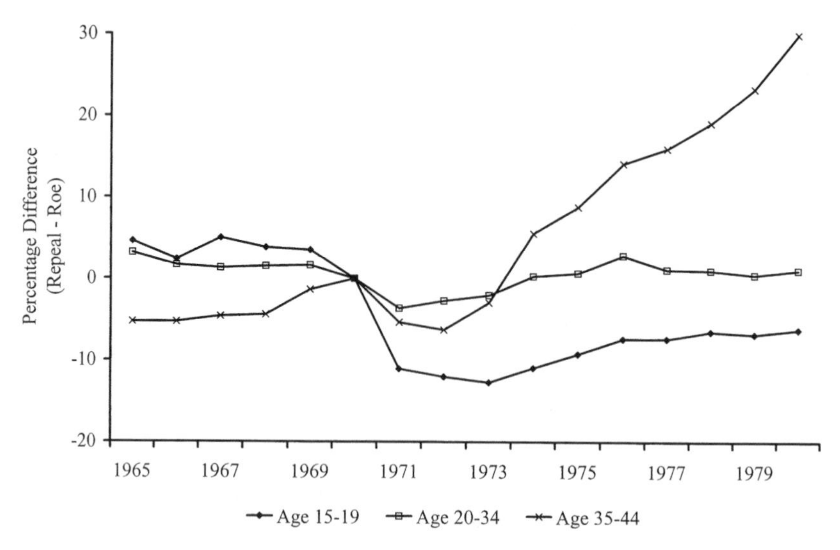

FIGURE 5.3. Impact of Abortion Legalization on Birth Rates, by Age Group. *Source*: Author's calculations. *Note*: The percentage differences are normalized so that their values equal zero in 1970.

gated into three age groups, 15 to 19, 20 to 34, and 35 to 44, and the percentage differences in birth rates over time are plotted separately for each group.

Overall, the results show the same dip in the difference in birth rates starting in 1971, with a rebound starting after that, supporting the general conclusion that abortion legalization had a causal impact on birth rates. The pattern for 20- to 34-year-old women looks the most like that for all women, which is not surprising since women in this group have a large fraction of all births. For them, one would conclude from this figure that births fell by perhaps 3 or 4 percent in response to abortion legalization.

The pattern for teens and the older women of childbearing age is not exactly what was predicted, however. For teens, the reduction in birth rates in repeal states relative to Roe states is striking in the years following early legalization.[3] For this group, births fell by, perhaps, 12 percent in response to the 1970 legal changes. Although a slow rebound is observed in 1974 and 1975 that stabilizes after 1976, the difference in rates in the latter period is not the same as it was in the late 1960s. One could infer from this that teens in Roe states did not utilize abortion services to the same extent as that observed among teens in repeal states. This may reflect differences in preferences for abortion services between teens in the two sets of states.

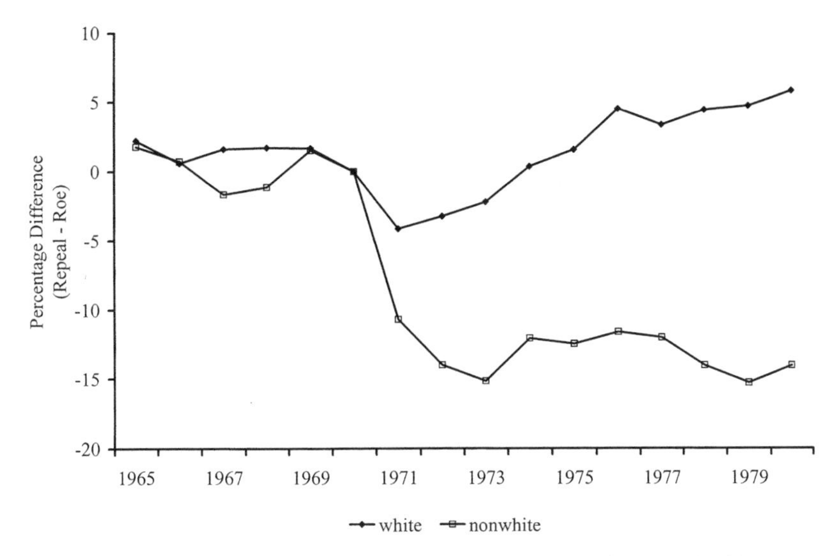

FIGURE 5.4. Impact of Abortion Legalization on Birth Rates, by Race. *Source*: Author's calculations. *Note*: The percentage differences are normalized so that their values equal zero in 1970.

A somewhat different pattern is observed for women between the ages of 35 and 44. For them, with the exception of the 1971 to 1973 period, there appears to be a general upward trend in this difference. Birth rates for all women in this age group were falling very rapidly over this period, perhaps in response to greater availability of effective methods of contraception or changes in preferences, possibly related to labor market activity. The upward trend in this difference suggests that the continuous decline in birth rates for this group was greater for women in Roe states relative to women in repeal states. For the present purposes, I maintain the assumption that this pattern is independent of the changes in abortion law. Nevertheless, we observe a discrete break from this upward trend in the 1971 to 1973 period. We see that the birth rate to women between 35 and 44 in repeal states fell by about 6 percentage points during this time. Although this evidence does suggest that abortion legalization had a causal impact on birth rates for women in this age group as well, a better estimate of the magnitude would probably incorporate the deviation from the upward trend. The regression-adjusted estimates reported below will do just that.

Similar figures by the race of the child are presented in figure 5.4. The pattern for white births is very similar to that for all births, shown in figure 5.2, which should not be surprising since whites represent such a large share of the population. For this group, we see that the birth rate

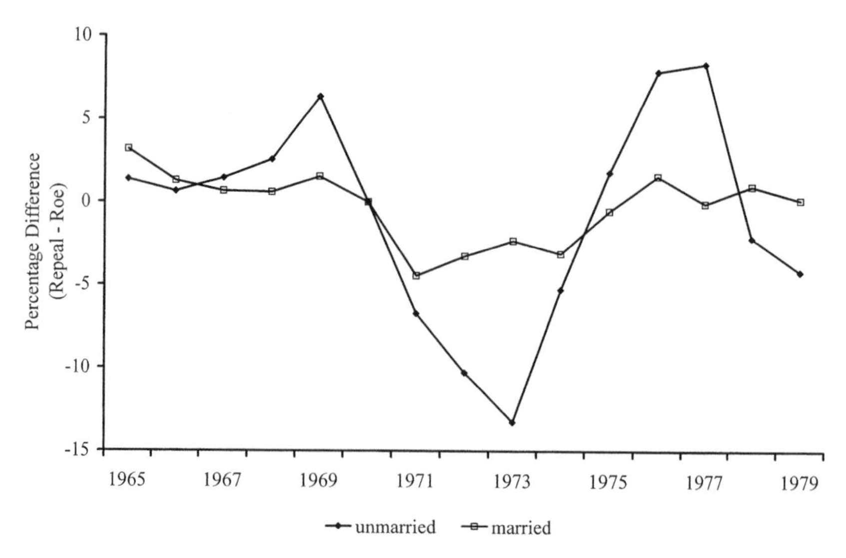

FIGURE 5.5. Impact of Abortion Legalization on Birth Rates, by Marital Status. *Source*: Author's calculations. *Note*: The percentage differences are normalized so that their values equal zero in 1970.

fell by perhaps 4 percent in response to abortion legalization in early repeal states and then more than completely rebounded in the mid to late 1970s, indicating that the *Roe* decision had a similar, or perhaps even greater, impact on women in states affected by it. The impact of repeal laws in early legalization states is shown to have been very large for nonwhite children (both black and other races, although this group is mostly black). Nonwhite birth rates to women in repeal states fell by 10 to 15 percent relative to women in Roe states over the 1971 to 1973 interval. As with teens, however, the rebound was not so great, suggesting that the *Roe* decision itself had less of an impact for nonwhite women in the states affected by it or something else was affecting birth rates for women in these states in that period. Again, differences in preferences for abortion services between nonwhites in the two sets of states may be able to explain this finding.

The impact of abortion legalization on birth rates for married and unmarried women is depicted in figure 5.5. Although nonmarital births were becoming a more significant fraction of total births over this period, the vast majority of all births were to married women. Therefore, it is not surprising that the impact of abortion legalization for married women is similar to that observed overall. Here we see that births fell by about 4 percent following the early legalization in repeal states and then completely rebounded in other states following the *Roe* decision. Because nonmarital births were less common and because the data used to estimate them came from a 5 percent sample from the Census and not the universe of births in *Vital Statistics* (described earlier), it is probably not surprising that the pattern in nonmarital births is somewhat erratic. Nevertheless, there is a noticeably large drop in the difference in birth rates between repeal states and Roe states in the 1971–73 period. On average, nonmarital births fell by about 10 percent in these years. This difference was eliminated in the late 1970s, suggesting that legalization had a causal impact on non-marital births on the order of about a 10 percent reduction.

Summary of Regression-Adjusted Effects

All of the results provided so far are based upon the direct application of quasi-experimental methods that do not allow for other factors to affect outcomes differentially in the treatment and control groups besides the treatment. But as I described in chapter 4, these methods may be biased to the extent that other factors exist that may have changed across states and over time. Therefore, one approach to control for this is to estimate regression models that replicate the basic design of the quasi-experimental approach, but also include other factors. These other factors may include observable characteristics, like economic, social, and demographic conditions in each state over time. But more generally, differential trends across states may be taking place that we cannot observe, like those that I hypothesized may explain the results in figure 5.3 for women aged 35 to 44. Regression models can also control for these state-specific linear trends in much the same way as they control for state fixed effects.

The results reported in table 5.2 examine the impact of abortion legalization on birth rates using such regression models. These models control for observable factors that vary over time and between states as well as differential state-specific trends.[4] The estimates reported here reflect the percentage reduction in birth rates in the 1971 to 1973 period relative to that between 1965 and 1970 after controlling for these other factors. They are obtained from Levine et al. (1999) and more details regarding this estimation as well as the results are available there.[5]

In this table, we see that the legalization of abortion in the early 1970s had vastly different effects on different groups of women. For instance, births fell by 12 percent for both teens and all nonwhite women, but only by 2 percent for women aged 20 to 34 and 3 percent for married and white women. Overall, these results indicate that the birth rate fell by about 4 percent in response to abortion legalization. Although not shown here, Levine et al. (1999) also provide evidence indicating that reform states, which liberalized their abortion laws but did not legalize abortion, experienced no statistically significant decline in birth rates in response.

TABLE 5.2.
Summary of Regression-Adjusted Estimates of the Impact of Abortion Legalization

Category	*Estimated Percentage Reduction in Birth Rate*
All Women of Childbearing Age	4.1
By Age Group:	
15–19	12.1
20–34	2.1
35–44	7.9
By Race:	
White	3.4
Nonwhite	11.6
By Marital Status:	
Married	3.1
Unmarried	5.5
By Distance to Early Repeal State:	
Less than 250 miles away	4.5
250 to 750 miles away	4.5
More than 750 miles away	10.8

Source: Levine et al. (1999).

Note: The estimates come from regression models of the natural logarithm of the birth rate for the relevant group on the legal status of abortion interacted with indicator variables for the 1971–73 period, for the 1974–75 period, and the 1976–80 period. Other explanatory variables include: the share of women 15 to 19, 20 to 24, and 25 to 34 among women of childbearing age; share of the state population that is nonwhite; per capita income; the crime rate; the insured unemployment rate; state and year fixed effects; and state-specific linear trends. The reported value of the estimated impact on the birth rate is the coefficient on the interaction between a repeal indicator and a 1971 to 1973 indicator variable.

Effects by Distance to Early Repeal States

Although these results indicate that abortion legalization had a substantial impact on American fertility in the early 1970s, the actual impact of the policy change was probably even greater than that just described. The reason for this is the travel between states that occurred for women to obtain an abortion during the period in which abortion was only legal in

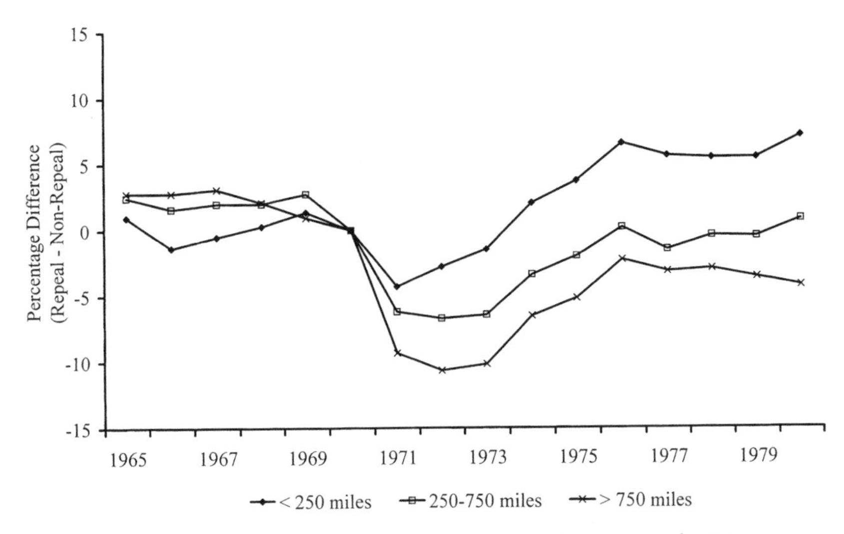

FIGURE 5.6. Impact of Abortion Legalization on Birth Rates, by Distance to Repeal States. *Source*: Author's calculations. *Note*: The percentage differences are normalized so that their values equal zero in 1970.

a few places. The methods used so far compare the decline in birth rates in the states that legalized abortion early to the birth rates in states that did not. If women in Roe states traveled to repeal states in the early 1970s, then legalized abortion in repeal states may have reduced the birth rate in Roe states as well. The decline in births in the comparison-group-states that is attributable to abortion legalization would make it look like the impact of the policy change was smaller than it really was.

To assess this problem, I categorize nonrepeal states according to their distance to repeal states. The distance categories chosen are states within 250 miles of repeal states, 250 to 750 miles of repeal states, and greater than 750 miles from repeal states.[6] For this analysis, since the impact of state abortion reforms that fell short of outright legalization were not found to have any impact, and to increase the sample of states within each of these distance categories, all nonrepeal states are considered together as comparison states. The underlying assumption of this analysis is that travel from the states far away from the repeal states was relatively uncommon. Therefore, using that group to compare trends in birth rates may provide an estimate of the impact of abortion legalization unaffected (or at least considerably less affected) by this problem.

The results of this analysis are reported in figure 5.6 and the bottom of table 5.2. Figure 5.6 presents the pure quasi-experimental exercise, similar to those reported earlier for differences by demographic group. In that

TABLE 5.3.
Abortion Utilization and Access after *Roe v. Wade* by Distance away from Repeal State

		Non-repeal States		
State Characteristics	*Repeal States*	*Less than 250 Miles to a Repeal State*	*Between 250 and 750 miles to a Repeal State*	*More than 750 Miles to a Repeal State*
Abortions per 1,000 women age 15 to 44, by state of residence, 1976	37.3	25.5	19.1	17.8
Percentage of women age 15 to 44 in 1976 living in counties with an abortion provider	96.8	77.0	52.1	55.9
Percentage of women age 15 to 44 in 1976 that were living in counties more than 50 miles from nearest county with an abortion provider	0.2	2.2	8.8	20.6

Source: Reprinted from Levine, Phillip B., Douglas Staiger, Thomas J. Kane, and David J. Zimmerman. 1999. "*Roe v. Wade* and American Fertility." *American Journal of Public Health* 89 (2): 199–203, copyright 1999, with permission of the American Public Health Association.

figure, we see that trends in birth rates are comparable between repeal and nonrepeal states in the period prior to legalization regardless of the distance separating them. At the time that abortion was legalized in the repeal states, however, birth rates begin to diverge between repeal and nonrepeal states and the extent of the differential grows with distance. Birth rates in repeal states fell by perhaps 3 to 4 percent relative to the closest comparison states, by about 6 percent relative to states 250 to 750 miles away, and about 10 percent compared to states farthest away. By the late 1970s, these differentials have all been largely eliminated, although the rebound was larger than the initial decline in close states and somewhat smaller than the initial decline in the far away states.

Evidence consistent with these findings is presented in table 5.3, which describes the level of abortion utilization and access in different parts of the country in 1976, three years after the *Roe* decision. By this date, any transitional issues involving the nationwide introduction of abortion services following *Roe* would have been largely (but perhaps not completely) overcome. In this table, states are distinguished by their repeal status and their distance to a repeal state, as I have done earlier. It is clear that abortion was much less available and much less utilized in areas of the country far away from repeal states. For instance, virtually all women in repeal states lived in a county with an abortion provider compared to just over half of women in the states most distant to them. The abortion rate was also about half the level in these most distant states compared to repeal states in 1976. These statistics support the finding in figure 5.6 of an incomplete rebound in further away states following the *Roe* decision.

Regression-adjusted estimates largely confirm these results in the bottom of table 5.2. There we see that birth rates fell in repeal states by 4.5 percent compared to the closest and the middle-distance group of states, but by 10.8 percent compared to the farthest group of states. The small differences between these results and those obtained from figure 5.6 would reflect the influence of the additional control variables, including state-specific linear trends, in these regressions.

Overall, these results indicate that travel between states dampened the estimated impacts of abortion legalization reported earlier. Perhaps a better estimate of the reduction in births brought about by abortion legalization had no travel occurred would be on the order of about 10 percent, obtained using the most distant states as a comparison. Although it is more difficult to estimate precisely these effects for specific demographic groups in a smaller set of comparison states, it is safe to say that the impact for these groups also would be greater than that reported earlier.

The Estimated Effect of Reversing "Roe v. Wade"

Although the exercises just reported represent the impact of legalizing abortion in the early 1970s, the estimated effects can be applied to today's environment to gauge the potential impact of a reversal of *Roe v. Wade*. Obviously the passage of time makes such an exercise purely hypothetical; for instance, birth control technology and availability have changed since then, making it easier to avoid an unwanted pregnancy in the first place. Nevertheless, such a simulation may at least be able to provide some sort of indication of what one might expect to happen to birth rates in response.[7]

The first question that needs to be addressed is the extent to which abortion would be made illegal if *Roe* was reversed. To provide an upper bound on the estimated effect of this policy change, I initially assume that a reversal of *Roe* through, say, a constitutional amendment leads to abortion being outlawed nationwide. We can use the results of the previous analysis based on a comparison between repeal states and very distant nonrepeal states to inform this question. In that application, women were assumed to be unable to travel from those distant nonrepeal states to repeal states to obtain an abortion, just as if abortion were illegal nationwide. The results of that analysis indicated that abortion legalization reduced births by 10.8 percent (see table 5.2). One might assume that if abortion were made illegal again that births would then increase by 10.8 percent. We could apply this estimate to the current level of births, roughly 4 million per year, to estimate the impact of a national ban on the procedure. Based on these statistics, we might expect births to rise by 432,000 per year.

This estimate is likely to be considerably overstated, however, if *Roe* were overturned by a subsequent Supreme Court decision that gave states the ability to set their own policies in this regard; then some states would ban the procedure and others would not. Therefore, abortion availability would be restricted in those locations where it was prohibited, but women in those locations would be able to travel to obtain an abortion elsewhere. Clearly, the extent of the impact of these changes would depend upon the number of states that maintained the legal status of abortion. It is impossible to know this or even the extent to which travel would occur between states.

We could gauge the impact, however, based upon the cross-state variation in policies that existed in the early 1970s. Then, abortion was legal in New York, California, Washington, Alaska, and Hawaii and, with the traveling that occurred for women to obtain abortions (although there was probably little travel to the latter two states), births still fell by 4.1 percent in those states relative to the rest of the country. If *Roe* were reversed and abortion remained legal in just those five states, then births in the remainder of the country might rise by 4.1 percent.[8] Roughly 3 million of the 4 million annual births take place in these other states, and so combining these estimates indicates that perhaps 123,000 additional births might occur per year. If more states maintain the legality of abortion, travel would be even more common and the estimated impact on the number of births would be smaller than this.

As I indicated earlier, all of these figures are predicated on the conditions that existed in the early 1970s and they do not incorporate changes like improved contraceptive methods and access, among other things. Although one should interpret these results with a great deal of caution, they are useful in providing a frame of reference regarding the possible magnitude of the impact of any such policy change.

The Impact on Adoptions

The results from the preceding section suggest that the legalization of abortion in the early 1970s had a sizeable impact on fertility at the time. This finding largely coincides with the theoretical predictions made in chapter

3. There, we saw that if the cost of abortion fell below the cost of an unwanted birth, then women would choose to abort. The legalization of abortion represents a tremendous reduction in its cost and one could imagine that the new cost fell below the cost of an unwanted birth for many women, leading to the reduction in births actually witnessed in response.

Nevertheless, the evidence presented so far only addresses the reduction in all births and does not distinguish between those that are wanted and unwanted. Evidence regarding the impact on unwanted births could provide additional support for the predictions of the model. Unfortunately, no direct observations of wanted and unwanted births are available, so indirect methods are required to assess this issue. To that end, in this section I consider the impact of abortion legalization on adoptions, which are certainly correlated with unwanted births.[9]

In theory, quasi-experimental methods could be employed to assess the impact of abortion legalization on adoptions in much the same manner as that implemented earlier. If legalization reduced unwanted births, then adoptions should have declined beginning in 1971 in repeal states and then declined beginning in 1974 (or soon thereafter) in nonrepeal states. The difference in adoption rates between the two sets of states should follow the same pattern as the bottom panel of figure 5.2, where the dip in the difference in adoption rates would occur during the period in which abortion was legal in some states, but not others.

In practice, however, adoption data for conducting such an exercise is available only through 1975, since the federal agency that collected it was disbanded in 1976.[10] Since the estimated birth effects reported earlier show a slow bounce back in the 1974–1975 period, it is unlikely that we would be able to observe the second half of the treatment effect in this application. Moreover, even during the years in which adoption data are available, it does not exist for every state in every year. Data from New York are noticeably absent throughout the period, and data from California exist only through 1971, just one year following abortion legalization there. Therefore, our ability to assess the impact of abortion legalization on the rate of adoption is seriously limited. Certainly without data reported consistently for at least a subset of repeal and other states, it does not make sense to construct figures like those reported earlier in this chapter to assess the impact of legalization on adoption.

Nevertheless, quasi-experimental methods that are incorporated into regression models may still provide some useful evidence in this regard. In their econometric analysis of these data, Bitler and Zavodny (2002) conclude that the adoption rate for white women (adoptions per 1,000 women of childbearing age) declined by 34 percent in response to abortion legalization. No statistically significant impact is observed for blacks. Aggregate results are not presented, but since whites represent the vast majority of the population, the overall effect must have been large as well. Although the data limitations highlighted earlier reduce the reliance one should place on these findings, they shed some light on an important question.

To provide some context to Bitler and Zavodny's findings, we can compare the estimated impact on adoptions to the estimated impact on births. This provides an indication of the number of births prevented that would have otherwise led to an adoption. Before making such a comparison, however, some discrepancies in data and methods need to be resolved in estimates of the reduction in births and adoptions. Therefore I have reestimated models comparable to those used to construct estimates in table 5.2 for both births and adoptions for white women.[11] The main difference that needs to be resolved is that Bitler and Zavodny do not have data for every state and every year, so similar data restrictions need to be imposed in the analysis of births.[12] After imposing these conditions, the results of this analysis indicate that abortion legalization reduced the birth rate for white women by 9 percent and the adoption rate for white women by 32 percent.[13]

These figures can be used to estimate the extent to which averted births to white women would have otherwise led to an adoption had abortion not been legalized. In 1970, the birth rate for white women stood at 81.5 births per 1,000 women in repeal states. If the birth rate fell by 9 percent, then 7.3 fewer births per 1,000 white women would have occurred. If adoption rates fell by 32 percent in these states in response to abortion legalization, then there would have been 1.8 fewer adoptions based on a baseline rate of 5.5 adoptions per 1,000 women of childbearing age in repeal states in 1970. This means that about one-quarter of those white children who would have been born had abortion been illegal would have been put up for adoption. One should be somewhat circumspect in drawing firm conclusions from this statistic, however, because of the data limitations underlying its construction.

The Impact on Pregnancies

So far, this chapter has largely focused upon the prediction that a large reduction in the cost of abortion would lower that cost below that of an unwanted birth at least for some women, resulting in fewer such births. But our model also indicates that if these abortion costs fell considerably below that of an unwanted birth for some women, then pregnancies would be predicted to increase as well. Since the costs that we are dealing with here are only conceptual and cannot be explicitly measured, it is impossible to determine a priori whether or not any pregnancy effect should have been expected. Empirical evidence is needed to address this question.

Yet past research has been limited in its ability to examine the impact of abortion legalization on pregnancies largely because of the lack of reliable data prior to its legalization. In fact, without such data, earlier studies examining the impact of abortion legalization have frequently simply assumed that there was no effect on the likelihood of pregnancy (cf. Tietze 1973; Sklar and Berkov 1974; Quick 1978). Therefore, even thirty years after abortion was legalized we know little about its impact on this dimension.

In this section, I report the results of such an analysis, examining the extent to which the increased use of abortion following its legalization in the early 1970s resulted from an increase in pregnancies. To overcome the limitations of abortion data, I apply quasi-experimental methods comparable to those used earlier in the chapter to data from a national sample of women who provided retrospective reports of past pregnancies and their outcomes a decade or more after abortion was legalized.

The validity of the results of this exercise rests heavily on two assumptions. First, I assume that the passage of time facilitates a more accurate enumeration of abortions and pregnancies in the era before it was legal. Contemporaneous self-reports of illegal abortions certainly would have been vastly understated. But women who had such abortions may have become more willing retrospectively to report it after legal abortion became more firmly established and the stigma associated with the activity diminished (at least somewhat). Second, to the extent that women in the retrospective survey were still reluctant to declare a past pregnancy that resulted in an abortion (legal or otherwise), I assume that any differences in the rate of under-reporting between quasi-control and treatment groups is constant over time. In other words, I am assuming that the fraction of women who obtained illegal abortions, but were unwilling to report doing so retrospectively, did not differ between repeal and Roe states. The credibility of these assumptions along with the implications if they were violated also will be discussed.

Data and Methods

This analysis will utilize quasi-experimental methods comparable to those used in past work and will take advantage of retrospective data reported in Cycles 3 and 4 of the National Survey of Family Growth (NSFG), conducted in 1982 and 1988. These surveys interviewed 7,969 and 8,450 women between the ages of 15 and 44 in 1982 and 1988, respectively.[14] A crucial aspect of these surveys for the present analysis is that they contain complete pregnancy histories for every woman. These pregnancy histories can be employed to determine women's behavior over the sample period of particular interest for this study, 1965 to 1980.

Within the context of a quasi-experiment, I examine the extent to which differences in fertility patterns emerge between early legalization states and the rest of the country during the period in which abortion laws differed.[15] Since I am able to date pregnancies by the date of conception in these data, this period would be between 1970 and 1972, not the 1971 to 1973 period upon which we focused earlier in the chapter. Any difference that does emerge should disappear in the period that follows, when the legal status of abortion was uniform nationwide. The findings reported earlier in the chapter indicate we already know that this pattern exists for births, but this analysis extends the exercise to abortions, fetal losses, and pregnancies.

The quasi-experimental nature of this exercise helps address a number of potential problems in this analysis. First, the nature of the data employed here leads to an age composition of the sample, which changes in each year of the analysis. For instance, only women between the ages 32 to 44 in the 1982 NSFG survey and 38 to 44 in the 1988 survey could contribute information regarding their behavior in 1965, when they would have been 15 to 27 and 15 to 21, respectively. Each year, the age range increases until by 1980 I have information regarding women's behavior at ages 15 to 42 from the 1982 survey and 15 to 36 from the 1988 survey. As long as the age profile between repeal and other states is similar, however, any impact of changing age composition on fertility behavior will be "differenced out."

A similar issue arises with the under-reporting of abortion and pregnancy in these surveys, which may have changed before and after abortion was legalized. Within the quasi-experiment, only changes that occur across states and over time can introduce bias into the analysis. Therefore, I need to maintain the assumption that any changes that take place in the level of under-reporting of abortion do so uniformly across states. I have tested this assumption for the 1973 to 1980 period, over which abortion rates can be calculated from the NSFG and compared to abortion rate data collected by the Alan Guttmacher Institute, which is regarded as the most accurate abortion data available. Over this time period rates of under-reporting in early legalization and other states are not significantly different from each other.

But rates of under-reporting still may have differed across states before 1973. For example, the stigma associated with reporting an abortion may be negatively correlated with the legal status of abortion in the state. Therefore, the level of abortion and pregnancy reporting may have risen differentially across states consistent with the difference in the timing of legal abortion across states. One plausible alternative would be that women in all states changed their reporting behavior once abortion was legalized in the first set of states. Women who obtained an illegal abortion may have been among the most likely to under-report their behavior and its incidence should have dropped dramatically once abortion was legalized either locally or even with some travel cost. Suggestive evidence supporting the latter interpretation will be described later.

Although the quasi-experimental framework helps address certain limitations of this analysis that would otherwise exist, it also narrows the range of questions that I am able to address. In particular, this method identifies only effects that differed between pseudo-control and -treatment group states. Any impact that had universal effects will go undetected in this framework. For instance, abortion legalization reduced births in repeal states in the early 1970s, but it also reduced births in other states that are nearby (albeit to a lesser extent) because women could travel. We observed this behavior in the results reported earlier, comparing births in nonrepeal states that differed by their distance to a repeal state. A similar problem exists here, but would also apply to other pregnancy outcomes. In the earlier analysis of birth rates using *Vital Statistics* data, I was able to distinguish states by their distance to repeal states to assess this issue. Unfortunately, there are too few observations in the NSFG to undertake a similar approach here and obtain estimates with any sort of precision.

Because of this problem it is impossible to gauge the impact of abortion legalization on the total number of abortions performed. Such an estimate would be very valuable because it could help us identify the number of illegal abortions performed before abortion was legalized. If we knew the overall increase in its use and we knew how many abortions were performed following legalization, we could combine these two estimates to determine the number of abortions performed before legalization. The methods utilized here do not allow us to do this since we can detect only the difference in abortion rates between repeal and nonrepeal states, not the overall increase in abortions.

Similarly, this analysis cannot determine with certainty whether or not the overall level of pregnancies rose in response to abortion legalization, just whether a gap emerged between the two sets of states in the early 1970s. It is possible that contraceptive behavior and / or sexual activity may have changed in nonrepeal states as well beginning in 1970 since women would have known they had the option of travel to obtain an abortion. To the extent that any increase in pregnancies in nonrepeal states matched those in repeal states, no pregnancy effect would be observed in this analysis. Although one could not rule out a pregnancy effect if no gap emerges between the two sets of states, such a finding would certainly lead one to believe that any effect in this dimension was not that large.

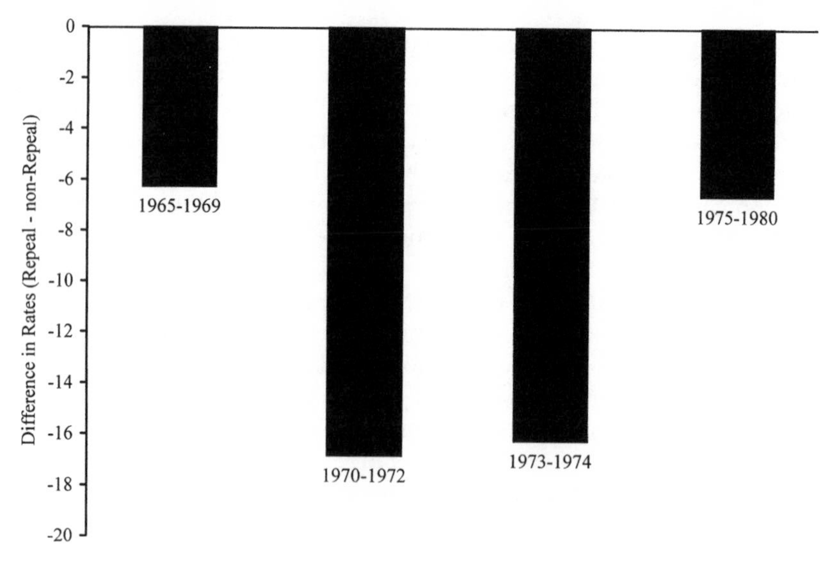

FIGURE 5.7. Impact of Abortion Legalization on Birth Rates Using NSFG Data. *Source*: Author's calculations.

Results

Figure 5.7 through figure 5.10 present differences over time between repeal and other states in the rate of births, abortions, fetal losses, and pregnancies. In these figures, years are aggregated into subperiods (1965 to 1969, 1970 to 1972, 1973 to 1974, and 1975 to 1980) because the small sample sizes make single-year comparisons rather difficult. These groupings reflect a baseline period in which there is no difference in laws, the period in which laws differed across states, a transition period, and then a final period in which the differential impact of legalization at different times should have dissipated. These figures are also somewhat different than those reported earlier in the chapter because I report the level difference in rates rather than the percentage change. Although the latter was easier to interpret regarding birth rates earlier in the chapter, using percentage changes in this case would obfuscate the results. This is because the likelihood of reported abortion prior to legalization is so low that percentage differences in this outcome across states can significantly magnify what are really very small differences in behavior. To be consistent throughout this analysis, I have chosen to report all outcomes, not just abortions, in level differences.

Figure 5.7 represents the impact of legalization on the birth rate using these data. The general pattern in this figure is comparable to that reported earlier in the chapter. Birth rates fell dramatically in repeal states

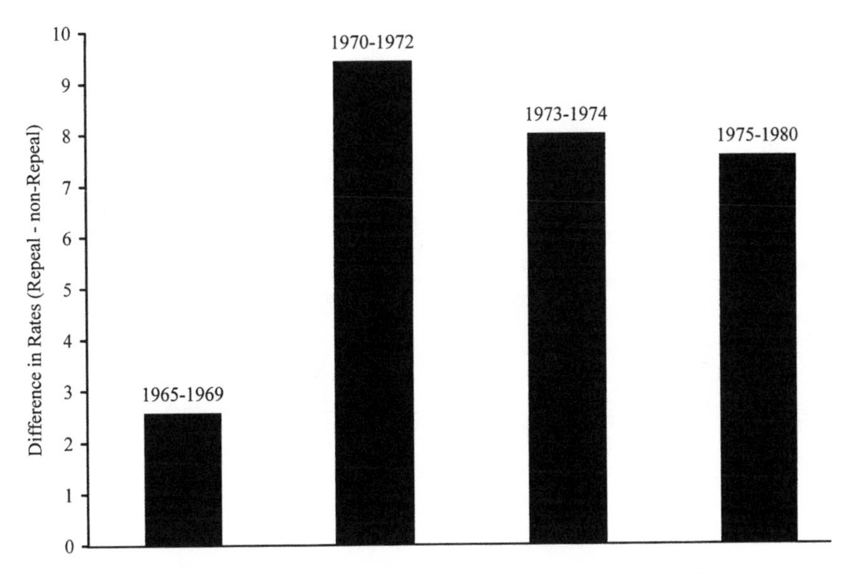

FIGURE 5.8. Impact of Abortion Legalization on Abortion Rates Using NSFG Data. *Source*: Author's calculations.

relative to other states during the 1970–72 period relative to the earlier period. This difference reverts back to its original level over the 1975–80 period. Both comparisons provide support for a causal impact of abortion legalization on birth rates on the order of 10 births per 1,000 women. The sample birth rate in the NSFG for 1970 was 118 births per 1,000 women, so a reduction of 10 births per 1,000 would represent roughly an 8.5 percent decline. Previous evidence shows the difference in the 1973–74 transition period to be between those that immediately precede and follow it, but the level of imprecision in these data is sufficient to prevent ruling out such a pattern.

Figure 5.8 presents similar comparisons for abortion rates. Here, as one would expect, reported abortions did become considerably more common among women in repeal states relative to other states in the period in which the laws differed across states. This rate rose by about 7 abortions per 1,000 women in those states in response to its legalization compared to other states. This finding provides a prima facie indication that the difference in pregnancies was relatively unaffected by the legalization of abortion since the impact on births is close to the negative value of the impact on abortions. Any remaining difference may be attributable to randomly generated differences in fetal losses across states. These outcomes will be explored subsequently.

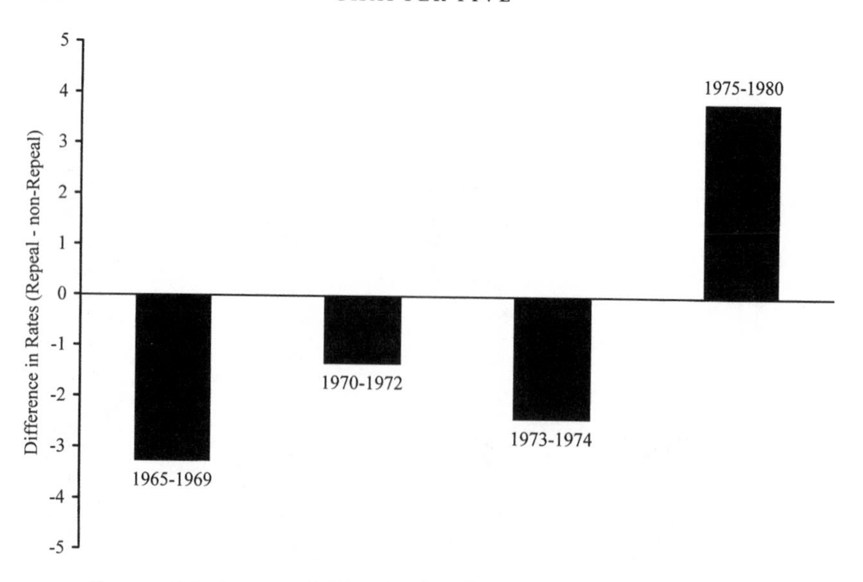

FIGURE 5.9. Impact of Abortion Legalization on Fetal Loss Rates Using NSFG Data. *Source*: Author's calculations.

Another interesting result apparent in this figure is that the difference in abortion rates that appears following the initial legalization of abortion in repeal states in 1970 dissipated very little after abortion was legalized in the remainder of the country. The reason for this is that abortion rates did indeed increase in the other states, but they continued to rise in the repeal states as well through the latter part of the decade despite the relatively small change in the legal environment over this period. This could be consistent either with greater demand for abortion services or greater access to abortion after legalization in repeal states. It is impossible to distinguish between these two hypotheses with the available data.

The impact of legalization on fetal losses is shown in figure 5.9. Here we see that there was little change in fetal loss rates in the 1965–74 period, which would indicate that abortion legalization had no obvious effect here. The slight reduction in fetal losses in repeal states relative to nonrepeal states that took place in the 1970–72 period, which cannot be distinguished from random variation in this outcome, explains the discrepancy between the reduction in births and the increase in abortions between the two sets of states in the period if pregnancies were unaffected. In this figure as well, the pattern for the late 1970s is somewhat surprising in that it shows fetal losses increased a great deal in repeal states compared to nonrepeal states. This finding potentially contradicts the view that fetal

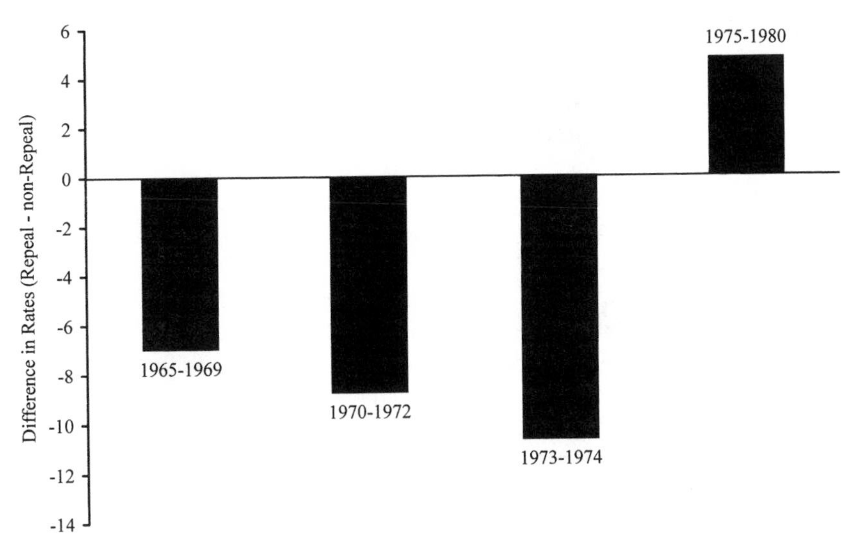

FIGURE 5.10. Impact of Abortion Legalization on Pregnancy Rates Using NSFG Data. *Source*: Author's calculations.

losses are attributable to biology and signify a random event. I will return to this anomaly shortly.

Figure 5.10 examines the impact of changes in abortion laws on pregnancies directly. Here there is little evidence of an impact of the initial legalization on pregnancies since the difference between groups of states was relatively stable between the 1965–69 and 1970–72 periods. This suggests that all the additional abortions performed in repeal states following early legalization represented births that otherwise would have taken place but would have been unwanted. No pregnancy effect is evident here. This evidence is consistent with the previous three figures, which has to be the case since reported pregnancies have to result in a birth, abortion, or fetal loss.

On the other hand, pregnancies in repeal states jumped dramatically over the 1975–80 period relative to the 1965–69 baseline period, increasing by about 12 pregnancies per 1,000 women. But these additional pregnancies did not lead to any additional births, as witnessed in figure 5.7. In that figure, the difference in births in the late 1970s is shown to revert back to the pattern exhibited in the 1960s. Figures 5.8 and 5.9 show that these additional pregnancies in repeal states between the 1965–69 and the 1975–80 periods can be roughly equally split into additional abortions and fetal losses. Although the impact on fetal losses seems large, one possible explanation for this is that women who have abortions report them as fetal losses instead. Alternatively, those women who are more likely to become pregnant under legal abortion may also be more likely to miscarry if pregnant.

The fact that both abortions and pregnancies increased in repeal states relative to nonrepeal states in the late 1970s, with no concomitant reduction in births, provides the first evidence that additional abortions do not have to result in fewer births, and may result from changes in pregnancy behavior. One hypothesis for the increase in pregnancies is the greater access to abortion in repeal states in the late 1970s. Evidence to support this was provided in table 5.3. It would be unwarranted, however, to draw a causal connection here since there is no exogenous change in abortion availability. Nevertheless, these results do open that possibility, which will be further explored in the subsequent chapter.

These results also may be used to address the assumption made earlier that the rate of under-reporting in abortions was not affected differentially across states by its legalization. Suppose that the under-reporting of abortion fell in the repeal states around 1970, but not in the other states until 1973. If so, reported pregnancies would be expected to rise around 1970 in the repeal states and no evidence of this is found in the results.

What does appear to have happened is that reported pregnancies rose universally in the 1970–72 period that does not appear in a difference-in-differences framework. Evidence supporting this is the noticeable nationwide increase in reported pregnancies relative to the pre-1970 trend in these data. This may reflect the nationwide reduction in the use of illegal abortion as soon as it was legalized in a few states. If the pregnancies that would have resulted in illegal abortions would have also gone unreported, but then were reported once they could be aborted legally (at least somewhere in the United States), then we would observe results like this. On the other hand, nationwide pregnancies actually may have risen somewhat in response to legal abortion in a few states. It is impossible to distinguish between these alternatives using the available data.

All of the results described here have also been validated in regression models that hold constant personal characteristics (race / ethnicity, mother's education, religion, and a complete age profile) as well as fixed effects for the time period of the pregnancy (to control for national trends in outcomes) and whether the respondent lived in an early repeal state (to control for time-invariant differences in outcomes across state categories). Since these regression results are not elsewhere published, I have included them here in table A.1. Although the results are somewhat imprecise, all the differences reported to be meaningful here are statistically significant at the 10 percent level or lower, at least when reasonable restrictions are imposed.[16] The magnitude of the estimated effects is also similar to those described earlier.

Summary of Findings

The legalization of abortion in the early 1970s clearly had very dramatic implications for women's fertility. I have provided strong evidence indicating that it reduced the birth rate for women overall and in many different demographic groups. The impact was particularly large for teens and women 35 to 44, nonwhites, and unmarried women. Evidence from adoption data further supports the proposition that the births that did not occur represented those that would have been unwanted. I also did not find any evidence indicating that abortion legalization increased pregnancies, suggesting that sexual activity and / or contraceptive intensity may not have been significantly affected. Each additional abortion largely replaced one (presumably) unwanted birth.

On the other hand, once abortion had become established as a legal procedure, increases in its use may have been related to a greater incidence of pregnancy. Evidence for this is apparent in the fact that subsequent increases in abortion in repeal states several years after it had been legalized represented more pregnancies, but no fewer births. One limitation in drawing this conclusion is that it is unclear why abortion rates continued to rise in repeal states relative to other states in the late 1970s. No exogenous differential change in its cost is obvious over this period leaving open the possibility that some other factor led to both the increased use of abortion along with the increase in pregnancies. Nevertheless, the evidence presented here certainly suggests that pregnancy and abortion may move together once abortion becomes a legal and reasonably accessible option. This possibility will be explored in subsequent chapters.

TABLE A.1.
Estimates of the Impact of Abortion Legalization on Pregnancy Outcomes
(coefficients multiplied by 1,000—standard errors in parentheses)

	Births			*NSFG Abortions*	*NSFG Pregnancies*		*NSFG Fetal Losses*	
	Vital Statistics (age 15–34)	*NSFG unrestricted*	*NSFG restricted Repeal* (1975–80) = 0*	*unrestricted*	*unrestricted*	restricted *Repeal* (1970–72) = Repeal* (1973–74) = 0*	*unrestricted*	restricted *Repeal* (1970–72) = Repeal* (1973–74) = 0*
Repeal* (1970–72)	–6.64 (1.34)	–12.59 (8.53)	–11.36 (6.45)	6.83 (2.86)	–4.11 (9.47)	—	1.65 (3.69)	—
Repeal* (1973–74)	–1.53 (1.57)	–12.78 (9.08)	–11.55 (6.18)	5.40 (2.75)	–6.98 (10.64)	—	0.40 (4.17)	— —
Repeal* (1975–80)	1.57 (1.46)	–1.72 (7.73)	— —	5.13 (1.95)	10.21 (9.10)	13.34 (6.57)	6.80 (3.62)	6.13 (2.49)
Sample Size	816	142,777	142,777	142,777	142,777	142,777	142,777	142,777

Note: Estimates using *Vital Statistics* data in column 1 are obtained from population-weighted regression models of the aggregate level of the birth rate for 15– to 34–year–old women by state and is otherwise comparable to the models reported in Levine et al. (1999). It includes state and year fixed effects along with a vector of other state characteristics. Estimates in the remaining columns are obtained from weighted linear probability models where the dependent variable is a discrete variable indicating whether the relevant outcome occurred in a particular year for each woman in the sample. The following covariates are also included: period-fixed effects (1970–72, 1973–74, and 1975–80), a repeal state-fixed effect, indicators of race /ethnicity, indicators for specific religion, and array of exact age indicators, the level of education of a respondent's mother, and an indicator for the year in which the survey was completed. Reported standard errors are corrected for heteroskedasticity and an arbitrary covariance structure between time periods for the same woman.

Chapter Six

THE IMPACT OF RESTRICTIONS ON ABORTION ACCESS

SINCE THE *Roe v. Wade* decision in January of 1973, the main sources of change in abortion policy have been attempts at the state level to impose moderate restrictions on abortion access, as documented in chapter 2. The ability of states to impose such restrictions was provided in the *Roe* decision itself, which legalized abortion but still recognized that states have some rights to regulate the procedure. It was reaffirmed in *Planned Parenthood of Southeastern Pennsylvania v. Casey* (1992), which established a standard whereby restrictions would be allowed as long as they did not impose an "undue burden" on women. The main forms of restrictions that states have been allowed to impose include Medicaid funding restrictions, parental involvement laws, and mandatory delay laws. This chapter will examine the empirical evidence regarding the impact of these restrictions on women's behavior.

In addition, this chapter will also consider the impact of changes in provider availability. The legal right to have an abortion may be far less significant if a woman does not have access to a provider willing to perform the procedure. Although the ability to travel to obtain a legal abortion is always possible if no abortion provider is available locally, the need to do so increases its cost in much the same way as a legal restriction. The empirical issues are not quite the same, as I will describe subsequently, but the predicted impact is similar, and so I will consider both sets of issues in this chapter.

The theoretical models presented in chapter 3, along with the assumptions imposed there, indicate that these forms of limits on abortion access may not have the opposite effect (of smaller magnitude) of the legalization of abortion itself. Those models indicated that a reduction in the cost of abortion that placed its cost below that of an unwanted birth would reduce the occurrence of unwanted births, but that further reductions in its cost mainly modify the likelihood of pregnancies. The fact that the cost of an abortion or an unwanted birth differs across women makes it difficult to specify an exact theoretical prediction regarding the impact of changes in abortion access. But I assumed that abortion legalization would lower the cost of an abortion below that of an unwanted birth, at least for most women, so that it may substantially reduce unwanted births. Evidence to this effect was reported in the preceding chapter.

Within a legal abortion environment, however, I had also assumed that the relatively minor changes in abortion access brought about by legal restrictions or provider availability do not increase abortion's cost above the threshold of the cost of unwanted births for many women. Therefore, the main impact of the policy change would be to reduce the likelihood of a pregnancy. Moreover, more sophisticated models also predicted the possibility of a counterintuitive birth effect: an increase in the cost of abortion from a relatively low level may actually reduce the likelihood of giving birth. This could occur because the reduction in pregnancies may occur among some women who otherwise may have chosen to given birth had they gotten pregnant. I do not emphasize this possibility in later discussions because support for it is not that strong, but some of the results presented are consistent with this prediction.

This chapter will review the empirical evidence evaluating the implications regarding moderate restrictions on abortion access. Initially, I present a methodological discussion that describes the way in which the issues addressed by research on abortion restrictions differ from those regarding abortion legalization. The next two sections of the chapter will review the evidence to date. Initially, I will review earlier work, which was more limited in terms of its methodology and in the questions it asked. Beyond some methodological limitations, this earlier work is also prone to consider the impact of restricted access on abortion prevalence only, largely ignoring the potential impact on pregnancies or births. After that I will review more recent work that expands the outcome measures employed and addresses many of the methodological limitations of the earlier work. This review will largely describe the results of regression analyses that are based upon quasi-experimental methods. Following this, I will present a few specific examples where quasi-experimental methods can be applied directly in a graphical format to help illustrate and provide some intuition for the types of results found in the literature.

Quasi-Experiments and Abortion Restrictions

As in chapter 5, this discussion will largely utilize a quasi-experimental framework for describing the impact of changes in abortion access on women's fertility outcomes. Although the underlying methods reported here are similar to those described regarding the impact of abortion legalization, there are some important differences. The main concern with any quasi-experimental design is the extent to which the exercise replicates the idea of a controlled experiment, where treatment and control groups are randomly assigned. Regarding abortion legalization, states that opted to repeal their abortion bans were not randomly selected, but one could argue that the specific timing of the law change was random. Therefore, as long as the response was reasonably well timed to the introduction of the law change, we may conclude that the impact of legalization was causal. The Supreme Court's decision in *Roe v. Wade* would also likely reflect an exogenous change in abortion policy in the remaining states since at least its specific timing was unexpected. Moreover, the combination of the two successive experiments provided the opportunity to evaluate further whether the response was causal since any predicted gap in women's behavior between states following the initial repeal laws was expected to reverse itself following *Roe v. Wade*. For the most part, the evidence reported in the previous chapter followed these patterns, suggesting that the law changes directly caused the behavioral responses.

But the quasi-experiments that relate to changes in abortion access do not necessarily share all of these features. First, it is often more difficult to find discrete breaks in policy at a particular point in time for a large number of states. With legalization, states could easily be categorized into repeal states or Roe states and within these groups abortion was legalized in 1970 and 1973, respectively. But the process by which changes in abortion access come into being does not always lead to such natural categories. Restrictions are typically adopted when a particularly aggressive state (or set of states) passes a law that is beyond standards previously approved by the Supreme Court. The law is instantly challenged, usually at both the state and federal levels, with injunctions imposed, and some years later a decision is handed down either affirming or denying the state's ability to institute the restriction. For some states, a U.S. Supreme Court decision settles the issue and the restriction is imposed. In other states, additional court challenges at the state level follow, delaying its imposition. Still other states wait until the legal issue is resolved and then decide whether or not to impose the restriction in some year subsequent to the final court decision. Therefore, the timing of a restriction does not necessarily occur at the same point in all states that adopt it. This process makes it difficult to directly apply simple quasi-experimental methods that enable us to graph changes over time in outcomes between treatment and control groups to look for the effect of the policy change, like I did in the last chapter.

Under these circumstances, researchers generally apply two approaches. First, regression-based models are commonly used that simulate a quasi-experimental design. They relate a particular outcome to indicators of exposure to the restriction along with state- and year-specific fixed effects. These models are described in chapter 4, but their main attribute is that their results can be interpreted within the same quasi-experimental framework as the more descriptive approaches used earlier. Nevertheless, these methods are less transparent. Second, researchers sometimes adopt a case study approach, comparing outcomes over time in a state or subset of states in which abortion access was restricted, to outcomes over time in a set of carefully chosen control states in which no restriction occurred.

The process that leads to abortion restrictions at the state level also calls into question whether or not the policy change was truly random. For those states in which the legal change was a direct result of a court's decision, at least the timing of the change is exogenous in much the same way as it was with abortion legalization. But the same argument cannot be made for those states that do not implement the change until sometime after the court's decision. It is difficult to tell whether or not those states were responding to the court's decision itself or other changes that may have been taking place within the state at about the same time that may be related to the behavioral outcomes considered. If it is the latter, quasi-experimental methods will provide inappropriate inferences (cf. Besley and Case 2000).

Moreover, an analysis of abortion restrictions cannot easily take advantage of a reverse experiment, which the process of abortion legalization offered. In that case, any difference in outcomes that emerged between repeal states and Roe states after 1970 was expected to diminish after 1973, providing a stronger test of causality. The process by which abortion restrictions have been imposed across states does not offer such an opportunity, taking away a valuable validation tool.

On the other hand, an analysis of limits on abortion access can take advantage of other features exclusive to them to help determine whether any estimated impact truly represents causality. For instance, some forms of restrictions are binding only on certain segments of the population. Parental involvement laws affect only minors. Medicaid funding restrictions affect only women in low-income households. One way to assess further whether the impact of these restrictions is causal is to examine whether the policies are estimated to have a differential effect on the target population. Some of the research reported in this chapter has used this approach as well.

An analysis of provider availability brings with it other limitations. Here it is more difficult to claim that changes in the availability of abortion providers can be viewed as a random event. It is possible that doctors' decisions to offer abortion services may depend upon their own geographic preferences, their training in medical school, or the like, and would be independent of women's fertility outcomes. If so, then differences in women's access to abortion services where they live could be considered randomly assigned to them and differences in their fertility outcomes could be determined and attributed to the differential access.

Alternatively, providers could locate in areas where the demand for their services is high. If so, differences in provider availability among women would not be random, but would be a function of the women's own behavior. In other words, provider availability is determined by both supply- and demand-side factors; only variations brought about by the supply side can be considered exogenous to women's behavior. Under these circumstances, the application of quasi-experimental methods cannot provide estimates of the causal impact of changes in provider availability, so other methods will have to be adopted. I will later discuss the methods that researchers have employed to address this.

Early Research

Before presenting the results of more recent research that utilizes a quasi-experimental framework to evaluate the impact of changes in abortion access, I review earlier evidence to provide some background on the evolution of the literature. As in the previous chapter regarding abortion legalization, this review is intended to provide an overview of this development and is not intended to be exhaustive. The studies described here are summarized in table 6.1.

When economic analysis was first introduced to study the issue of abortion, the primary focus was on determining the relationship between the demand for abortion and alternative measures of its cost. Standard economic reasoning tells us that demand curves slope downward, so an increase in the "price" of obtaining an abortion should lead to a reduction in the demand for abortion services. Therefore, if the number of abortion providers falls, if travel distance to the nearest provider increases, or if government regulations make it more difficult to obtain an abortion, the number of abortions demanded should fall.

Within this literature, Deyak and Smith (1976) represent the first attempt to estimate an abortion demand model. They use data on abortions in New York State and treat the travel distance to obtain a legal abortion as a proxy measure for its price. Shelton et al. (1976) provide a similar empirical analysis using data from Georgia. Both papers report a strongly negative relationship between travel distance and abortion prevalence, suggesting there is a downward sloping demand curve for abortions. Other studies estimating abortion demand models have relied on other sources of variation in "prices," such as the number of abortion providers and the observed price of abortion (Singh 1986; Joyce 1988; Medoff 1988; Garbacz 1990; Lundberg and Plotnick 1990; Rothstein 1992; Lundberg and Plotnick 1995). These studies typically examine the relationship between abortions as a share of "pregnancies" (abortions plus births)

TABLE 6.1.
Summary of Early Research Studies Examining the Relationship between Abortion Access and Abortion Demand

Paper	*Access Measure*	*Data*	*Methodology*	*Main Findings*
Deyak and Smith (1976)	travel distance to obtain an abortion	*Vital Statistics* data from upstate New York	Estimates the relationship between abortions performed and travel distance from women's place of residence.	negative relationship between travel distance and demand for abortion
Shelton et al. (1976)	travel distance to obtain an abortion	*Vital Statistics* data from Georgia	Estimates the relationship between the abortion ratio and the travel distance between county seat and Atlanta.	negative relationship between travel distance and demand for abortion
Trussell et al. (1980)	Medicaid funding restrictions	Various sources	Compares trends in Ohio and Georgia, which stopped funding abortions, with Michigan, which continued funding.	Abortions fell and births were unaffected in Ohio and Georgia compared to Michigan.
Singh (1986)	Medicaid funding restrictions, and number of abortion providers	1980 data from Alan Guttmacher Institute, Centers for Disease Control, and other sources	Estimates OLS models relating abortion rate/ratio to abortion access.	positive relationship between abortion access measures and demand for abortions
Cartoof and Klerman (1988)	parental involvement laws	*Vital Statistics* data from Massachusetts and surrounding states	Examines the impact of the 1981 Mass. parental involvement law using a pre-post comparison design. Data from neighboring states capture the impact of travel.	In-state abortions fell, but out-of-state abortions rose, resulting in no change in total number of abortions.
Medoff (1988)	price of abortion, Medicaid funding restrictions	Alan Guttmacher Institute data for 1980 and other sources	Estimates two-stage least squares models relating abortion rate in-state to average price of abortion.	negative relationship between abortion price and demand

TABLE 6.1. (*cont'd*)

Paper	*Access Measure*	*Data*	*Methodology*	*Main Findings*
Joyce (1988)	Medicaid receipt and number of abortion providers, Medicaid restrictions	*Vital Statistics* data from New York City in 1984	Uses logit models relating decision to abort among pregnant women to access measures.	Women eligible for Medicaid are less likely to abort, and the number of providers in women's neighborhoods is unrelated to pregnancy outcome.
Lundberg and Plotnick (1990 and 1995)	number of abortion providers, Medicaid funding restrictions	National Longitudinal Survey of Youth (1979–86)	Uses nested logit model incorporating sequential decision-making of pregnancy, abortion, and marriage; abortion access measures are restricted to affect abortion only.	Abortion availability is positively related and Medicaid funding is negatively related to abortion.
Garbacz (1990)	price of abortion, Medicaid funding restrictions	Alan Guttmacher Institute data for 1982	Estimates OLS models relating abortion rate in state to average price of abortion and status of Medicaid funding.	negative relationship between the price of abortion and demand for abortions
Rothstein (1992)	price of abortion, Medicaid funding restrictions	Alan Guttmacher Institute data for 1985 and other sources	Estimate OLS models relating abortion rate in state to average price of abortion.	negative relationship between abortion price and demand
Henshaw (1995b)	parental involvement laws	*Vital Statistics* data for Mississippi and surrounding states	Examines the impact of the 1993 Miss. parental involvement law using a pre-post comparison design. Data from neighboring states capture the impact of travel.	In-state abortions fell, but out-of-state abortions rose, resulting in no change in total number of abortions.

to one of these price-related measures and find the expected negative relationship.[1] The results of these studies tend to support a downward sloping demand curve for abortions.

Government regulations can also affect the price of abortion, and the policies that have been most extensively studied include Medicaid funding restrictions and parental involvement laws. Both policies make obtaining an abortion more difficult, increasing its price. Many of the previously cited papers regarding abortion prices and availability also include measures of Medicaid funding restrictions, and Cartoof and Klerman (1986) and Henshaw (1995b) address parental involvement laws. All find a negative relationship between funding restrictions and abortions. However, Cartoof and Klerman find that a parental involvement law in Massachusetts had no effect on teenage women's behavior because so many traveled to neighboring states; Henshaw comes to a similar conclusion based on Mississippi's parental involvement law.

These early statistical efforts, however, were somewhat limited in terms of methodology and scope. In terms of methodology, the studies that examined provider availability and other forms of the price of an abortion neglected to recognize that prices are determined by the behavior of those who supply abortion services and those who demand them.[2] Therefore, one cannot treat the prices faced by women as being randomly assigned to them since their behavior helps determine it. Moreover the data employed in these analyses often represented a single cross-section of the population. Therefore, prices differ only across different locations at a point in time, and may simply proxy other location-specific factors that affect abortion demand. Finally, an important shortcoming of this early research is its virtually exclusive focus on the abortion decisions of pregnant women, ignoring the implications of abortion policy on the likelihood of pregnancy.

Despite the limitations of much of the work in this early literature, some of it does set the stage for the types of analyses conducted more recently. For instance, the Shelton et al. (1976) paper described earlier also examined changes in abortion prevalence when abortion clinics opened in two small cities outside Atlanta and found that the procedure increased disproportionately for the residents of surrounding counties. Although the decision for those clinics to open in those locations may have depended upon women's demand for abortion services, the specific timing of the sharp increase in abortions immediately following the opening of the clinics suggests that distance to a provider was having a causal effect.

Trussell et al. (1980) also set the stage for more recent work in two dimensions. This paper considers the impact of Medicaid funding restrictions imposed in two states by comparing changes in abortion and birth rates in those states to a third state with no law change. One important strength of the paper is that it implicitly utilizes a quasi-experimental approach for a small subset of states. Its estimates are based on changes over time within states, which implicitly control for time-invariant differences across states, and it uses a third state as a comparison, which provides a counterfactual that adjusts for trends in behavior. Moreover, by examining both abortions and births, one can determine the impact on pregnancies (assuming the rate of spontaneous abortions is unaffected). The authors find that the funding restrictions were associated with a significant decline in abortion rates. Importantly, they also find that births were largely unaffected, which means that pregnancies had to fall.[3] A further discussion of similar evidence from other studies will be provided subsequently within the context of more recent research.

More Recent Evidence

The limitations of this earlier research have been largely addressed in more recent work. First, most of the recent papers examine the impact of policy *changes* that arguably provide exogenous, discontinuous, variation in women's access to abortion and are less likely to be the result of women's behavior itself. Second, these changes are then studied in a quasi-experimental framework in which changes in the likelihood of abortion among women in a treatment group, who are subject to the sudden policy change, are compared to women in a control group whose policy environment has been unaffected. As long as the policy change was unrelated to changes in the demand for abortion services among the residents in those locations, it provides a means to more accurately estimate the impact of the change in some form of abortion access on abortion demand. Finally, recent research has extended the range of outcomes being analyzed to consider birth and pregnancy outcomes in addition to abortions. Table 6.2 summarizes this research, distinguishing between those studies that still focus exclusively on abortion demand and those that consider other outcomes as well.

Medicaid Funding Restrictions

One of the policy changes most frequently analyzed is Medicaid funding restrictions. Studies that examine this policy include Blank et al. (1996), Currie et al. (1996), Haas-Wilson (1996), Levine et al. (1996), Haas-Wilson (1997), Cook et al. (1999), and Bitler and Zavodny (2001).[4] Most of these papers use data for all women to determine whether a policy that only affects lower-income women has any impact, making it more difficult to find much of an effect.[5] Still, most estimate a negative relationship between Medicaid funding restrictions and abortion rates in most specifications. Taken as a whole, the evidence indicates that Medicaid funding restrictions lower the abortion rate by perhaps 3 to 5 percent. Levine et al. (1996) also find that the impact of Medicaid funding restrictions is concentrated on the low-income population, as one would expect.

Some of these studies also examine the impact of these funding restrictions on births as well (cf. Levine et al. 1996; Matthews et al., 1997;

TABLE 6.2.
Summary of More Recent Research Studies Examining the Impact of Changes in Abortion Access on Abortions, Births, and Pregnancies

Paper	*Type of Access*	*Data*	*Methodology*	*Main Findings*
Studies Examining Abortion Outcome Only				
Althaus and Henshaw (1994)	mandatory delay	aggregated data from state *Vital Statistics* records	Examines the deviation from predicted level of monthly abortion rates following law change in Mississippi.	Finds a reduction in abortions in the months following implementation of delay law.
Blank et al. (1996)	Medicaid funding restrictions, parental involvement laws, and provider availability	state-level data from 1974 to 1988	regression models including state and year fixed effects; instrumental variables to control for endogeneity of providers	negative effect of Medicaid restrictions, no effect of parental involvement laws, and positive effect of provider availability
Currie (1996)	Medicaid funding restrictions	Microdata from the National Longitudinal Survey of Youth	Compares outcomes across states that have Medicaid funding restrictions in effect to those states in which policy has been enjoined by a court decision.	Funding restrictions are negatively related to the abortion decision.
Haas-Wilson (1996)	Medicaid funding and parental involvement laws	state-level data 1978–1990	regression models including state and year fixed effects	Medicaid funding restrictions and parental involvement laws are negatively related to abortion demand among teens.
Bitler and Zavodny (2001)	parental involvement laws, Medicaid funding, and mandatory delay	state-level data from 1974 to 1997	regression models with state and year fixed effects and state-specific trends in some specifications	Finds some evidence of a reduction in abortions in response to parental consent laws.

Haas-Wilson, 1997; and Cook et al. 1999). Assuming fetal losses are unaffected by such policy changes, evidence regarding births and abortions has direct implications regarding the impact on pregnancies. In addition, Kane and Staiger (1996) examine the impact on teen birth rates, but do not also consider the impact on abortion rates because of data limitations.

TABLE 6.2. (*cont'd*)

Paper	*Type of Access*	*Data*	*Methodology*	*Main Findings*
Studies Also Examining Other Outcomes				
Rogers et al. (1991)	parental involvement laws	individual *Vital Statistics* data	case study of 1981 Minnesota parental involvement law; pre-post comparison for teens aged 15 to 17 and comparison to older teens and other women	Abortion rates fell for minors, but there was no impact on birth rates.
Ohsfeldt and Gohmann (1994)	parental involvement laws	state-level data for 1984, 1985, and 1988	regression models of the ratio of abortions and pregnancies of 15–17 year olds to older women as a function of parental involvement law	Both abortion rates and pregnancy rates of 15–17 year olds fell in relation to older women in response to parental involvement law.
Joyce and Kaestner (1996)	parental involvement laws	individual *Vital Statistics* data from each state	case study of 1989/90 parental involvement laws in Tennessee and South Carolina; comparisons of minors within state to older teens and to women in Virginia	Finds no effect of policy on abortions or births.
Kane and Staiger (1996)	distance to an abortion provider,Medicaid funding restrictions, parental involvement laws	1973–88 county-level *Vital Statistics* data	regression models including county and year fixed effects along with quasi-experimental techniques based on changes in distance for women in some counties	Teen birth rate rises when travel distance to an abortion provider falls or when Medicaid funding restrictions are imposed.
Levine et al. (1996)	Medicaid funding	state-level data from 1977 to 1990, and microdata from the NLSY	OLS models including state and year fixed effects and, in some specifications, state-specific trends	Medicaid funding restrictions reduce abortion rate and either have no effect or reduce births. Evidence from microdata indicates that effect is concentrated among low-income women.

TABLE 6.2. (*cont'd*)

Paper	*Type of Access*	*Data*	*Methodology*	*Main Findings*
Studies Also Examining Other Outcomes				
Matthews et al. (1997)	Medicaid funding, parental involvement laws	state-level data from 1978–88	OLS models including state and year fixed effects and, in some specifications, state-specific trends	Medicaid funding restrictions and parental consent laws either reduce the abortion rate and birth rate or have no significant effect on either outcome.
Haas-Wilson (1997)	Medicaid funding, family planning subsidies, parental involvement	state-level data from 1978 to 1992	OLS models including state and year fixed effects	Government policies are not significantly related to abortions or births.
Joyce et al. (1997)	mandatory delay	individual *Vital Statistics* data from each state	case study of 1992 Mississippi law with pre-post comparisons and comparisons to Georgia and South Carolina	Finds strong evidence that abortions fell, but only weak evidence that births increased.
Ellertson (1997)	parental involvement laws	counts of abortions and births from *Vital Statistics* data in each state	comparison of minors to young nonminors before and after law change in Minnesota, Indiana, and Missouri	In-state abortion rates to minors fell, but may be attributable to increased travel out-of-state. No evidence of change in births.
Cook et al. (1999)	Medicaid funding restrictions	individual *Vital Statistics* data from North Carolina	case study of North Carolina Medicaid funding policies in which annual lump sum allocation sometimes runs out	Abortions decline and births increase in response to funding restrictions.
Levine (2003)	parental involvement laws, mandatory delay	state-level data 1985–96 from various sources and Cycles IV and V (1988 and 1992) of the National Survey of Family Growth	regression models including state and year fixed effects and, in some specifications, state-specific trends; additional regression models of sexual activity and contraceptive use including state and year fixed effects	Parental involvement laws reduce the likelihood of abortion for teens but not older women, but have no effect on births. Evidence from microdata indicates reduction in pregnancies brought about by increased use of contraception.

Of these studies, only Cook et al. (1999) provide any evidence that births rise. Yet the experiment being studied in this paper is fundamentally different from those in the other analyses, which would lead one to predict a different response. These authors examine an unusual program in North Carolina in which the state Medicaid program had a fixed annual budget for funding abortions. Thus, in some years, women on Medicaid who needed abortions late in the year were unable to obtain Medicaid funding. They found that the number of abortions fell in these months, and the subsequent birth rate rose. The key difference between this policy and other policies that have been studied is that women did not know that the price of abortion would be high *at the time they became pregnant.* Thus, one might expect no effect of these Medicaid funding cuts on pregnancy and, as a result, a rise in the birth rate.

None of the other studies cited finds a positive impact on births. In fact, some of these studies (Kane and Staiger 1996; Levine, et al. 1996; and Matthews et al., 1997) find some evidence that births may actually decline in response, although the support for this effect is not that strong. Based on all the available evidence in this regard, one could conclude that a standard Medicaid funding restriction (i.e., one that is not like the North Carolina policy) does not appear to increase the birth rate. Since the weight of the evidence also indicates that the abortion rate declines in response, one could also conclude that pregnancies decline as well.

Parental Involvement Laws

Among more recent studies, considerable research effort has also explored the impact of parental involvement laws on the behavior of teens. Beyond the standard problems encountered by all studies regarding abortion access, described earlier, research examining parental consent laws has to address some additional issues. First, minors represent a very small share of women of childbearing age (or even of abortion recipients—see table 2.4), and so studies that use aggregate data have very little chance of finding any effect. Second, a parental involvement law may be more likely to lead a pregnant teen to cross a state line to obtain an abortion in a nearby location where there is no such law. This problem does not exist for Medicaid funding, since the neighboring state would not cover the bill either. Traveling across state lines is a problem because the best source of abortion data, which is the Alan Guttmacher Institute (AGI), is mainly available by state of occurrence, not state of residence, as described in chapter 2.[6]

Studies in this area that address the impact on the demand for abortion include Rogers et al. (1991), Ohsfeldt and Gohmann (1994); Blank et al.

(1996), Haas-Wilson (1996), Joyce and Kaestner (1996), Matthews et al. (1997), Haas-Wilson (1997), Ellertson (1997), Bitler and Zavodny (2001), and Levine (2003). The evidence provided in this literature is less robust across papers, but some of the discrepancies may be attributable to several differences among them. First, some of this research uses data on abortions by state of occurrence rather than state of residence (cf. Rogers et al. 1991; Haas-Wilson 1996; and Ellertson 1997), and so their findings that parental consent laws reduced abortion rates cannot rule out the possibility of cross-state travel. Other research uses data for all women of childbearing age rather than just teens because these studies represent broader efforts to understand the determinants of abortion (cf. Blank et al. 1996; Matthews et al., 1997; Haas-Wilson, 1997; Bitler and Zavodny 2001); as such it is not surprising that they are less likely to find an effect of parental involvement laws that affect only those under age 18. Still other work has employed a case study approach where it may not be surprising that the results differ from one case to the next (cf. Rogers et al. 1991; Joyce and Kaestner 1996). Both the studies by Ohsfeldt and Gohmann (1994) and Levine (2003) use national data on abortions to minors that adjust somewhat for cross-state travel and use nonminors as within-state control groups; both find that abortions to minors declined in response to the enactment of parental involvement laws. The estimated effect in both of these papers is quite large as well, indicating that the imposition of a parental involvement law reduces the abortion rate of minors by 10 to 20 percent.

This literature has addressed the impact on both births and pregnancies as well. Although the evidence here is somewhat weaker that abortions fell in response to parental involvement laws, to the extent that they did decline there is no evidence of a concomitant increase in births. Ohsfledt and Gohmann (1994) estimated the impact on pregnancies in models analogous to those for abortions and found that pregnancies to minors relative to nonminors declined as well in response to parental involvement laws. They did not directly estimate a model of the birth rate, however. Kane and Staiger (1996) examined the impact on births directly and found that teen births certainly did not increase, and may have even declined in response. Levine (2003) finds no effect on births either, which indicates that pregnancies must have declined. In fact, that paper goes one step further and explores the impact of parental involvement laws on minors' sexual activity and contraceptive use. Although the data employed are somewhat limited there, the paper finds that contraceptive use increased significantly among minors, but not among older women, when states enacted and enforced parental involvement laws; no pattern in sexual activity was detected.[7]

Mandatory Delay

Much less attention has been paid to the effect of mandatory delay laws, probably because they have only begun to be enforced since the 1992 Supreme Court's *Casey* decision (see chapter 2). Preliminary evidence obtained very shortly after the implementation of such a law in Mississippi indicates that abortions declined after it went into effect (Althaus and Henshaw 1994). This conclusion was based upon the deviation in monthly abortion rates from a simplistic projection of its predicted value. But Joyce et al. (1997) introduce more sophisticated methods in their analysis of the same Mississippi law change. That research utilized a quasi-experimental design, comparing outcomes over time between Mississippi (the treatment group) and Georgia and South Carolina, which had no law change (the control group). Moreover, their data enabled them to determine whether abortions performed on state residents were conducted in-state or out-of-state. The results in that paper indicate that abortions fell in Mississippi relative to Georgia and South Carolina following the law change, suggesting that the law reduced abortion demand. Although women did become more likely to travel out of state to obtain abortions, they still aborted less frequently.

But Joyce et al. (1997) do not find consistent results regarding births. Apparently, births rose in Mississippi relative to South Carolina, but not relative to Georgia. Careful inspection of the data (as I will report subsequently) seems to indicate that some change took place in South Carolina that led to the differential there, not in Mississippi. Based on this evidence, it would be difficult to conclude that births rose as a result.

Beyond the two case studies in Mississippi, Bitler and Zavodny (2001) and Levine (2003) consider the impact of state-level mandatory delay laws more broadly in their analyses of statewide patterns of abortions and births. The results of these studies do not indicate any significant effect when these laws are introduced. Over the sample period considered in those papers, however, only a handful of relatively small states had instituted such laws, which may explain the absence of any findings. Based on all the available evidence in this regard, it is probably too soon to draw strong conclusions regarding the impact of mandatory delay laws on behavior.

Provider Availability

Several of the studies previously referenced also include measures of the availability of abortion providers in a woman's area of residence. Many of them, however, do not address the fundamental problem that abortion availability is determined both by providers' willingness to offer the procedure in the area as well as residents' demands for it (i.e., both supply-

and demand-side factors). These studies routinely find that provider availability is correlated with the abortion rate, but it is impossible to tell if women responded to the change in availability or whether the availability responded to women's behavior. Therefore, the primary contributions of these studies are their analyses of state-level abortion policies, which is how I have listed them in table 6.2.

Two important exceptions do exist here, however, that recognize this problem and have introduced methods to resolve it. In one example, Blank et al. (1996) employ an "instrumental variables" approach in their analysis of the determinants of abortion rates. Rather than relate outcomes to some measure of provider availability in a woman's location, they predict the level of provider availability using some factor unrelated to these outcomes. For instance, the greater supply of medical services in general is likely to result in more abortion providers regardless of women's behavior. Blank et al. predict the number of abortion providers in a location based on the number of non-obstetricians and gynecologists and the number of hospitals in the area (which would represent what are called the instrumental variables). This predicted value could then be effectively used to examine the relationship between abortion providers and fertility outcomes since these outcomes are unlikely to have much influence on the prediction. The results indicate that the number of abortion providers in an area does increase demand for abortion services.

Kane and Staiger (1996) provide another example of research that takes into consideration the locational decisions of abortion providers in their analysis of teen birth rates. One of the factors that they consider in explaining changes in teen births is travel distance to the county of the nearest abortion provider. Travel distance may provide a good indicator of abortion access since it is less likely to be influenced by the characteristics of the residents of a certain area, particularly for those women with no provider in their own county and for those women experiencing a change in travel distance. In a number of different specifications, Kane and Staiger find that, if anything, teen birth rates fall when travel distance rises. Although no abortion data are presented in this paper that can be used to verify that these changes had any impact on abortion rates, to the extent that they did reduce abortions, pregnancies had to have fallen.

Quasi-Experimental Examples

As I described earlier in the chapter, the institutional features that lead to restrictions on abortion access tend not to be conducive to a direct, quasi-experimental analysis of the data. To use the types of graphical techniques employed in the previous chapter, one needs the treatment to occur simultaneously so that behavioral outcomes over time can be compared between control and treatment groups. With the types of restrictions examined here, this has not been the case as access tends to be restricted in different places at different times. Although econometric techniques that simulate this quasi-experimental approach can be, and have been, utilized to circumvent this problem, the findings from such studies may be less transparent.

But in a few instances, researchers have been able to take advantage of institutional features that make these graphical techniques available; this section of the chapter will present them. The three examples presented here include an analysis of Medicaid funding restrictions from Levine et al. (1996), an analysis of a mandatory delay law implemented in Mississippi from Joyce et al. (1997), and an analysis of altered travel distance to an abortion provider from Kane and Staiger (1996). Each study captures a different way in which abortion access may be restricted, providing independent evidence regarding their impact. These examples should help provide some intuition for the econometric results presented earlier.

Medicaid Funding Restrictions

Levine et al. (1996) examine the impact of Medicaid funding restrictions on abortions, births, and "pregnancies" (where the latter is defined to be the sum of the first two). As I described in chapter 2, these restrictions originated from the Hyde Amendment, which prohibited the use of federal Medicaid funds to pay for abortions. It was originally passed in 1976, but court challenges left the status of the law unclear until the U.S. Supreme Court ruled on it in 1981 in *Harris v. McRae*, which upheld its legality. The Hyde Amendment does not preclude states from providing their own funds to pay for abortion, however; after it was initially passed, some states chose to cover the procedure and others did not. But the court challenges in the period before 1981 left the status of the law unclear. A woman making fertility decisions would have had difficulty incorporating this uncertainty into her decision-making process. By 1981, however, the status of the law became clear; since many states had previously chosen not to cover the procedure, a number of them instituted strong, enforceable funding restrictions virtually immediately following the Supreme Court's decision.

In Levine et al. (1996) one component of the analysis takes direct advantage of this institutional history to divide states into control and treatment groups. The treatment group represents women in those states that instituted Medicaid funding restrictions in 1981. The control group represents women in states that never imposed such restrictions over the entire period considered in their analysis, which was 1977 to 1988. Women who lived in the few states that implemented restrictions after 1981 or stopped

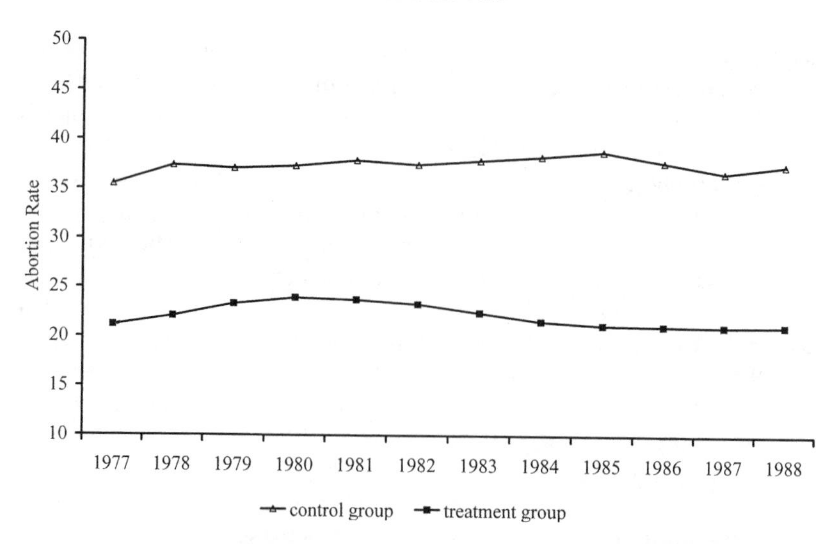

FIGURE 6.1. Impact of Medicaid Funding Restrictions on the Abortion Rate. *Source*: Reprinted from Levine, Phillip, B., Amy Trainor, and David J. Zimmerman. "The Effect of State Medicaid Funding Restrictions on Pregnancy, Abortion, and Births." *Journal of Health Economics* 15: 555–78, copyright 1996, with permission from Elsevier. *Note*: Data points for 1983 and 1986 represent linear averages from the earlier and following years because abortion data are not available in those years.

enforcing their restriction after initially implementing it in 1981 were omitted from this part of their analysis.

Their results are replicated in figures 6.1 through 6.3. These figures represent time-series patterns in the rates of abortions, births, and pregnancies, respectively, in control and treatment group states, where a rate reflects the number of occurrences of an outcome per 1,000 women of childbearing age (15 to 44).[8] The first observation to make regarding figure 6.1 is that the abortion rates in control and treatment group states were at very different levels in 1977, but these differences are taken into account in a quasi-experimental framework by examining changes within sets of states over time. Through 1980, abortion rates were rising slightly in treatment group states and perhaps in control group states as well. In control group states, the abortion rate then continued to remain reasonably constant throughout the remainder of the sample period. In treatment group states, however, the abortion rate fell somewhat in the period just following 1981 and then remained at a lower level through the rest of the period. The drop in abortion rates just following the law change that occurred in treatment group states, but not in control group states,

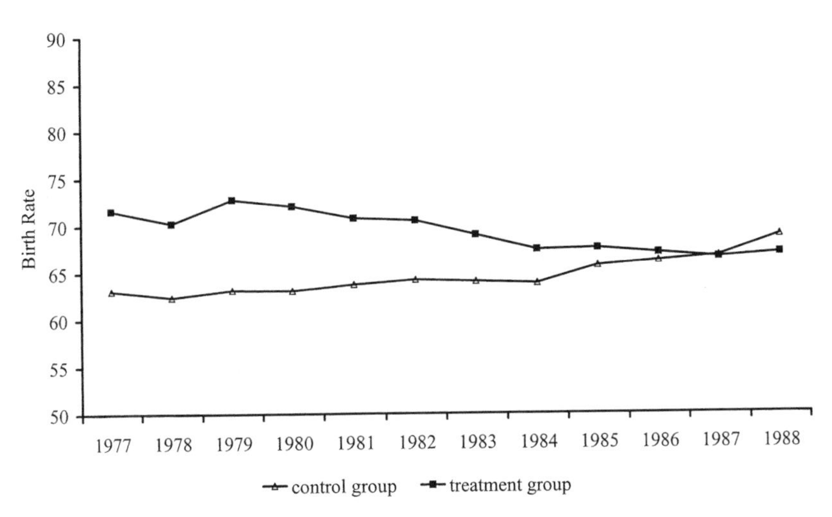

FIGURE 6.2. Impact of Medicaid Funding Restrictions on the Birth Rate. *Source*: Reprinted from Levine, Phillip, B., Amy Trainor, and David J. Zimmerman. "The Effect of State Medicaid Funding Restrictions on Pregnancy, Abortion, and Births," *Journal of Health Economics* 15: 555–78, copyright 1996, with permission from Elsevier. *Note*: Data points for 1983 and 1986 represent linear averages from the earlier and following years because abortion data are not available in those years.

represents the treatment effect. It suggests that Medicaid funding restrictions reduced the frequency of abortions.

The impact on births in the two sets of states is presented in figure 6.2. Through 1980, the birth rate in the two sets of states is reasonably constant, although somewhat noisy in control group states. But after that, the birth rate falls continuously in treatment group states and rises slightly in control group states, which indicates a relative fall in birth rates in the former. One could conclude that this represents a treatment effect suggesting that funding restrictions reduced the birth rate. On the other hand, we do not observe the emergence of a discrete break just after 1981 in the two sets of states; but rather we see two trends that are drifting, and these differential trends explain the relative reduction in treatment state births. Based on this evidence, it is difficult to conclude that there was a definitive treatment effect that led to a reduction in births when Medicaid funding restrictions were imposed. On the other hand, there is no evidence that births rose in response.

Combining these two effects, if funding restrictions reduced the abortion rate but did not increase the birth rate, then pregnancy rates must have fallen. This is the conclusion one would draw from figure 6.3. Here

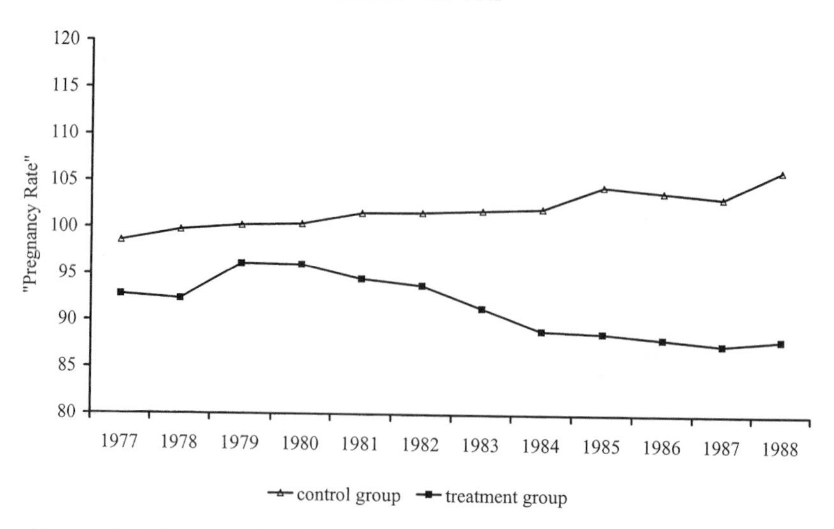

FIGURE 6.3. Impact of Medicaid Funding Restrictions on "Pregnancy Rate." *Source*: Reprinted from Levine, Phillip B., Amy Trainor, and David J. Zimmerman. "The Effect of State Medicaid Funding Restrictions on Pregnancy, Abortion, and Births," *Journal of Health Economics* 15: 555–78, copyright 1996, with permission from Elsevier. *Note*: Data points for 1983 and 1986 represent linear averages from the earlier and following years because abortion data are not available in those years.

we see that pregnancies are trending slightly higher in both groups of states through 1981 and continue to do so in control group states. But pregnancy rates decline following 1981 in treatment group states, and this would reflect a treatment effect.

Mandatory Delay Laws

Case studies often present examples that fit quite nicely into a direct, quasi-experimental analysis since they identify a policy change in a particular location and then they generally choose similar nearby states to act as a control group. Comparing trends in the two sets of states before and after the date of the policy change provides a quasi-experimental estimate of its impact.

Joyce et al. (1997) provide a typical example of this approach. In this study, the authors examine the introduction of a mandatory delay law in the state of Mississippi in August of 1992. They chose both Georgia and South Carolina to act as control groups in their analysis because these two states had similar abortion policies with the exception of mandatory delay throughout the period under study, 1989 to 1994. In addition, abortion data by state of residence, not state of occurrence, are available for

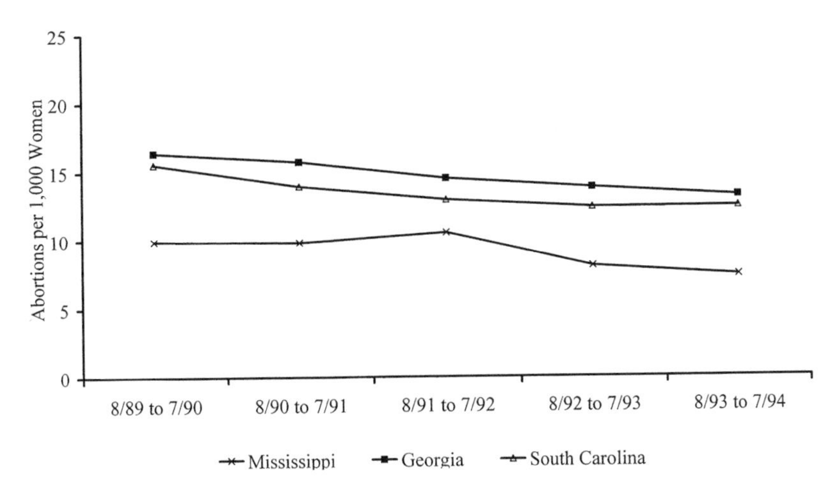

FIGURE 6.4. Impact of Mississippi's Mandatory Delay Law on Abortions to Whites. *Source*: Reprinted from Joyce, Theodore, Stanley K. Henshaw, and J. D. Shatrud. 1997. "The Impact of Mississippi's Mandatory Delay Law on Abortions and Births." *Journal of the American Medical Association* 278 (8): 653–58, copyright 1997, with permission from the American Medical Association.

all three states on a monthly basis and are utilized in their analysis. This prevents the problems that are associated with out-of-state travel to get an abortion that may result if one state imposes a restriction and the others do not. They compare abortion and birth rates in the two sets of states both before and after the law change to determine whether the restriction had any impact.

Figures 6.4 and 6.5 present the results of their analysis.[9] In that paper, results are presented separately for whites and nonwhites and, in some models, for teens and nonteens by race as well. Since the purpose of this exercise is largely illustrative, I report only the results for all whites and direct the reader to that paper for more detail. Since these authors have access to monthly data, they examine outcomes in periods that are based on the exact timing of the law change, which occurred in August of 1992. Therefore, in their analysis of abortions, they report annual abortion rates in the August to July period over time. They do the same with births up through the period of the law change, but the impact of that change should not take place until perhaps several months afterward, since time passes between the abortion decision and a birth outcome.

The evidence provided in figure 6.4 suggests that the mandatory delay law in Mississippi did reduce resident abortion rates for white women. The abortion rate was declining slightly in Georgia and South Carolina throughout the sample period and exhibits no break from this trend

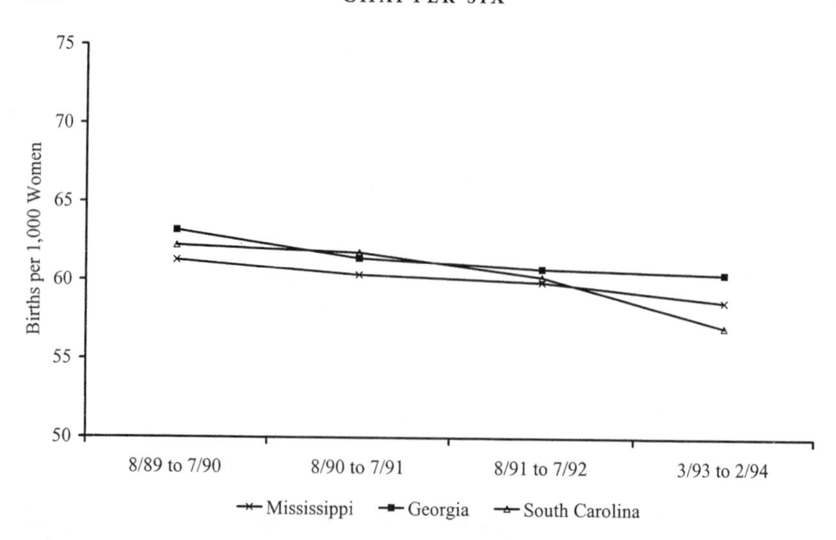

FIGURE 6.5. Impact of Mississippi's Mandatory Delay Law on Births to Whites. *Source*: Reprinted from Joyce, Theodore, Stanley K. Henshaw, and J. D. Shatrud. 1997. "The Impact of Mississippi's Mandatory Delay Law on Abortions and Births." *Journal of the American Medical Association* 278 (8): 653–58, copyright 1997, with permission from the American Medical Association.

around the time of the law change. In Mississippi, abortion rates were rising slightly in the period before the law change, but then they took a noticeable drop after the delay law was implemented. This evidence suggests that the treatment itself led to the decline in abortion rates. Since the abortion data represent abortions by state of residence, out-migration to obtain an abortion cannot explain the findings in this figure.

On the other hand, the evidence regarding births in figure 6.5 does not support much of an impact of the mandatory delay law in Mississippi for white women. In fact, birth rates in Mississippi and Georgia are virtually perfectly parallel throughout the period. In South Carolina, there is a noticeable drop in birth rates in 1993/1994. In a difference-in-differences framework, if just Mississippi and South Carolina were being compared, then one would conclude that birth rates in Mississippi rose relative to South Carolina following the law change and one may be tempted to conclude that this impact was causal. Closer inspection of the data based on this figure, which includes the Mississippi/Georgia comparison, would probably lead one to conclude that the law did not have an impact on birth rates in Mississippi, but that some spurious change in births to South Carolina happened to take place in that year. This is one of the limitations of a case-study methodology. In analyses that examine all states at once, those spurious changes in states tend to average out, so that they do not have an undue influence on the results.

Overall, the results of this quasi-experiment indicate that abortions among white women fell in response to the mandatory delay law in Mississippi, but there is no strong evidence of any increase in births. Again, this would lead one to conclude that pregnancy behavior was affected so that the reduction in abortions came about in response to a reduction in pregnancies.

Travel Distance to an Abortion Provider

Quasi-experiments that address provider availability are hard to come by since changes in availability are driven by market forces. Therefore, it is difficult to know whether these changes are related to abortion demand itself. Since the key to a good quasi-experiment is something that resembles random assignment, it is hard to find good examples where these methods are applicable.

Kane and Staiger (1996) present an application where such methods are actually quite informative. These authors focus on the distance that a woman would be required to travel to locate an abortion provider. Since travel distance may depend upon the demand for abortion in the area, one may hold suspect a simple relationship suggesting that greater travel distance is negatively related to the likelihood of abortion. But in part of their analysis, Kane and Staiger consider instances in which relatively large differences in travel distance emerge between one year and the next. Specifically, they consider trends in teen birth rates in those counties in which the distance to the nearest abortion provider changed by 50 miles or more between successive years. One would think that these counties represent examples in which an abortion provider opened where there had been none nearby or in which a provider closed and there were no others nearby.

Although a clinic opening or closing could easily be related to abortion demand, Kane and Staiger track year-to-year changes in teen birth rates in those areas. If birth rates shift instantaneously in a significant way at the time of the opening / closing, then it would be hard to argue that changes in demand led to the event. One would think that such changes in behavior would be of a longer-run nature if it were going to provide the impetus for a change in the provider's behavior. Therefore, the immediate response in births brought about by a large change in travel distance would likely indicate that the change in travel distance had a causal impact.

Figures 6.6 and 6.7 present the results of their analysis.[10] The patterns in figure 6.6, in particular, are striking. This figure represents what happens when distance to an abortion provider shrinks dramatically, as when a local provider opens in a county that did not have one before. The

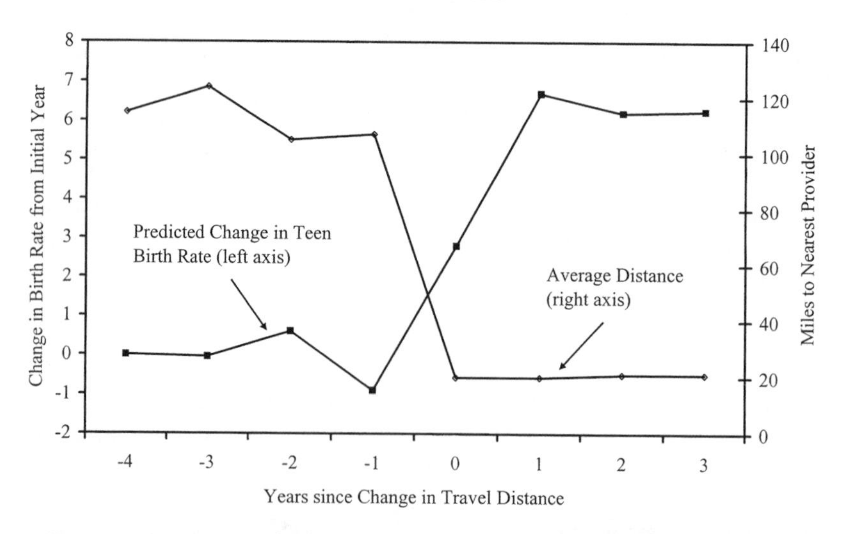

FIGURE 6.6. Impact of Abortion Provider Opening Nearby on Teen Birth Rates. *Source*: Reprinted from Thomas J. Kane and Douglas Staiger. 1996. "Teen Motherhood and Abortion Access." *Quarterly Journal of Economics* 111 (2): 467–506, copyright 1996, with permission from the President and Fellows of Harvard College and the Massachusetts Institute of Technology.

average distance to a provider shrinks by about 100 miles for women in these counties. At precisely the same time, the birth rate takes a sudden jump upward. This rules out the possibility that greater utilization of abortion services was eliminating unwanted births. In fact, it is consistent with a model where abortion provides a form of insurance from uncertainty and, if it is available at low cost, leads to more pregnancies. Those pregnancies in which positive information is obtained ex-post then result in additional births.

The results shown in figure 6.7 are more difficult to interpret, however. In this figure, women in these counties experienced a 60 or so mile increase in the distance they had to travel to obtain an abortion. Here there is no indication that births were affected at all and may have just been trending upward in these locations regardless of the change in abortion access. It is clear, however, that the main increase in births took place before the change in abortion access, indicating that births did not increase in response to this change.

We need to keep in mind some important limitations from this analysis. First, a county that experiences a change such as this is likely to be rural, with a relatively small population. Therefore, one may expect the results to be somewhat imprecise and potentially unrepresentative of aggregate behavior. Second, no evidence is available at the county level that can be

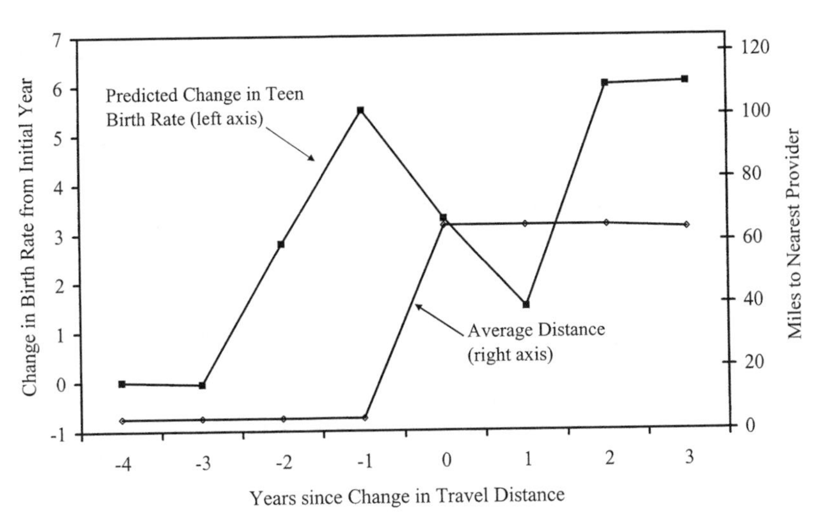

FIGURE 6.7. Impact of Nearby Abortion Provider Closing on Teen Birth Rates. *Source*: Reprinted from Thomas J. Kane and Douglas Staiger. 1996. "Teen Motherhood and Abortion Access." *Quarterly Journal of Economics* 111 (2): 467–506, copyright 1996, with permission from the President and Fellows of Harvard College and the Massachusetts Institute of Technology.

used to identify whether the change in abortion access had any impact on the abortion rate. Nevertheless, the application is an interesting one and the results are consistent with other econometric analyses in this paper. Even a cautious interpretation of the findings in this paper, including this quasi-experimental evidence, suggests that greater travel distance does not result in more births.

Overview and Interpretation

In this chapter, I have reviewed the literature examining the impact of Medicaid funding restrictions, parental involvement laws, mandatory delay laws, and the availability of abortion providers in one's area. This literature provides virtually no evidence that births rise when abortion access is restricted in one of these ways, despite the fact that abortions do seem to become less likely. The combination of these findings on abortions and births suggests that relatively minor restrictions on abortion access lead to fewer pregnancies. Any reduction in abortions is brought about because fewer of the women who would have had an abortion get pregnant. Unfortunately, the relative lack of data regarding sexual activity and contraception has made it difficult to test the obvious implications for these behaviors, although one study (Levine 2002) has found some supporting evidence in this regard for minors when parental involvement laws are introduced.

The results presented in this chapter along with those from chapter 5 are consistent with the predictions of economic models of abortion. Without the insights of these models, one may have expected that relatively minor restrictions on abortion access would have had the opposite effect from abortion legalization, albeit of smaller magnitude. In the preceding chapter, I presented evidence indicating that births fell in response to abortion legalization as women who otherwise would have had unwanted births aborted their pregnancies instead. This suggests that a future ban on its legal practice would lead to more unwanted births. Less severe restrictions, according to this view, would then be predicted to lead to a smaller increase in unwanted births. But the evidence presented in this chapter provides no support for that proposition.

Two caveats are in order, however, in this interpretation of the findings from the past research reviewed here. First, the evidence generally supports the proposition that abortion restrictions reduce the likelihood of abortion, but this evidence is not universal. Some estimates from some econometric specifications do not find a statistically significant impact of abortion restrictions on the likelihood of abortion. One could combine this with a reasonable reading of the evidence that abortion restrictions may not have any impact on births. Taken together, this would yield perhaps the most cautious interpretation of this evidence that these restrictions have no impact at all.

A second caveat regarding this interpretation of the available evidence is that it ignores the potential problems caused by aggregation. The evidence suggests that births do not increase in response to restrictions on abortion access. But this is the average effect aggregated over all women. It could be the case that some groups of women respond to a restriction by increasing contraceptive intensity and / or reducing sexual activity in a way that reduces their likelihood of getting pregnant and giving birth. It could also be that some other women will respond to such changes in access by choosing to give birth to an unwanted pregnancy (which they would do if the cost of abortion rose above the cost of the unwanted birth in an economic model). But the latter group of women may be balanced by the former group so that when they are all grouped together in an econometric analysis we do not observe the increase in births for this group. Although we cannot dismiss this possibility, we would still be able to conclude that this behavioral response would not be that large because otherwise it would appear in aggregated results.

Chapter Seven

ABORTION POLICY IN AN INTERNATIONAL PERSPECTIVE

THE TREATMENT of abortion policy presented to this point has focused exclusively on the United States. I have presented a brief history of changes in abortion access in the United States as a whole and in each of the states over the past several decades and provided a number of statistics describing the use of abortion services in this country. I have also presented empirical evidence designed to examine the impact of changes in U.S. abortion policy on fertility outcomes. This evidence was interpreted within the framework of an economic model. But economic models do not attempt to explain behavior in just one country; one should be able to extend their predictions to women more broadly in response to changes in abortion policy.

To that end, this chapter will examine abortion policies in some other countries and women's behavioral responses to policy changes. I will begin by describing the policies in place in different countries, focusing on Europe, Canada, and Japan, and discussing how these policies have changed over time. Then I will briefly present some international comparisons regarding the use of abortion in these countries along with the United States. This discussion is designed to present the institutional features of abortion in an international context in much the same way that I covered them in the United States in chapter 2. Data limitations across countries, however, limit the extent to which international comparisons can be made.

The remainder of the chapter will provide empirical evidence of the behavioral responses observed when abortion policies change in other countries. This analysis will focus almost exclusively on the countries of Eastern Europe because this is the region that has undertaken the most extensive changes in abortion policy that can be examined, as described later. Quasi-experimental techniques like those used extensively elsewhere in this book will be used here as well. In this case, however, treatment and control groups are comprised of countries rather than states.

Quasi-experimental methods applied to an international framework can help alleviate the difficulties that often plague cross-country comparisons. Analysts sometimes point to differences in the institutional environments across countries in one regard or another and argue that those differences explain some important outcomes. A critic could easily argue that underlying differences in "culture," or some other broad and largely unobservable feature of countries, is really the driving force behind differences in behavior. In a quasi-experimental framework, however, these factors would represent long-standing differences across countries that would not influence the estimated impact of the policy. This is because estimates are based on changes in outcomes within countries that implement some policy change, thereby eliminating this country-specific effect. A comparison with changes in other countries over time that had no such change enables us to control for year-specific factors that influenced all countries at the same time. In this manner, the typical problems encountered by cross-country comparisons are substantially alleviated here. Nevertheless, methodological issues do remain and will be discussed subsequently.

International Abortion Policies and Prevalence

Types of Abortion Policies

Abortion policies in the countries considered in this analysis run the gamut from those in which it is illegal except to save the life of the mother to those in which it is available upon request with no restrictions and completely paid for by the government. Table 7.1 presents a brief description of the abortion policies in all European countries, differentiated between east and west by their status as formerly Communist states, along with Canada and Japan.[1]

One complication in presenting such information is that there have been several changes in the lines drawn between countries over the past couple of decades, making it difficult to provide constant definitions of what a country is. The Soviet Union split into separate republics, Czechoslovakia became the Czech and Slovak Republics, and Germany reunified. In all cases, I treat the smallest level of aggregation for these countries to provide a consistent treatment throughout their history. For instance, the former German Democratic Republic and the former Federal Republic of Germany are always treated as two separate units of analysis in this study. Data for Germany after reunification has been obtained separately for the two regions. In addition, I consider only the republics of the former Soviet Union that reside in Europe in this analysis.

Many of these countries changed their abortion policies over the past several decades and these changes are indicated here. Beyond a brief description of the main provisions of their abortion laws, table 7.1 also lists whether or not these countries enforce mandatory delay laws, parental involvement laws, and whether the government provides a large subsidy

TABLE 7.1.
Brief Description of Abortion Policies in Europe, Canada, and Japan*

Country	*Years Legalized*	*Description*	*Category*	*Mandatory Delay*	*Large Subsidy*	*Parental Involvement*
Western Europe						
Austria	1974–present	Legal upon request in the first 12 weeks of pregnancy following medical consultation.	Upon Request	No	No	No
Belgium	before 1991**	Prohibited except to save the life of the mother.	Life	NA	NA	NA
	1991–present	Legal in the first 12 weeks of pregnancy following mandatory counseling and a 6-day waiting period.	Upon Request	Yes	No	No
Denmark	1973–present	Legal in the first 12 weeks of pregnancy. Women must be informed of the risks and alternatives.	Upon Request	Yes	Yes	Yes
Finland	1970–present	Legal in the first 12 weeks of pregnancy upon the approval of two physicians. Women must be informed of the risks of the procedure and provided with information about contraception following it.	Medical/ Social	Yes	Yes	No
France	1975–present	Legal in the first 10 weeks of pregnancy following mandatory counseling and a 1-week waiting period.	Upon Request	Yes	Yes	Yes
Germany (former FRG)	1976–94	Circumstances limited to rape or incest, maternal health, or social or emotional distress.	Medical/ Social	Yes	Yes	No

TABLE 7.1. (*cont'd*)

Country	*Years Legalized*	*Description*	*Category*	*Mandatory Delay*	*Large Subsidy*	*Parental Involvement*
Germany (*cont'd*)	1995–present	Legal in the first 12 weeks of pregnancy after mandatory counseling and a 3-day waiting period.	Upon Request	Yes	Yes	No
Greece	1978–86**	Legal in the first 12 weeks of pregnancy to protect the mother's physical or mental health only.	Physical/ Mental Health	NA	NA	NA
	1986–present	Legal upon request in the first 12 weeks of pregnancy.	Upon Request	No	Yes	Yes
Ireland	unknown origin through present	Abortion is strictly prohibited except to save the life of the mother.	Life	No	No	No
Italy	1978–present	Legal in the first 90 days of pregnancy subject to mandatory counseling, a 1-week waiting period, and physician approval.	Medical/ Social	Yes	Yes	Yes
Netherlands	before 1981**	Legal only to save the mother's life.	Life	NA	NA	NA
	1981-present	Legal on demand after a 5-day waiting period with no formal gestational limit.	Upon Request	Yes	Yes	Yes
Norway	1979–present	Legal in the first 12 weeks of pregnancy. Women must be informed of the risks and alternatives.	Upon Request	No	Yes	Yes
Portugal	before 1984	Abortion was strictly prohibited except to save the life of the mother.	Life	NA	NA	NA
	1984–present	Legal under limited circumstances (rape, maternal health, fetal deformities) after a 3-day waiting period.	Physical/ Mental Health	NA	NA	NA

TABLE 7.1. (*cont'd*)

Country	*Years Legalized*	*Description*	*Category*	*Mandatory Delay*	*Large Subsidy*	*Parental Involvement*
Spain	before 1985	Abortion was strictly prohibited except to save the life of the mother.	Life	NA	NA	NA
	1985-present	Legal under limited circumstances (rape, maternal health, fetal deformities).	Physical/ Mental Health	NA	NA	NA
Sweden	1975–present	Legal in the first 18 weeks of pregnancy.	Upon Request	No	Yes	No
Switzerland	1942–present	Legal only if a woman's life or (physical or mental) health is threatened.	Physical/ Mental Health	NA	NA	NA
United Kingdom (excluding N. Ireland)	1967–present	Legal in the first 24 weeks of pregnancy for social and medical reasons upon the approval of two physicians.	Medical/ Social	No	Yes	Yes
Eastern Europe						
Albania	before 1992	Legal for limited medical reasons only.	Medical	NA	NA	NA
	1992–present	Legal upon request in first 12 weeks of pregnancy.	Upon Request	No	No	No
Bulgaria	1973–89	Legal for medical reasons only or upon request in the first 10 weeks of pregnancy for certain categories of women, like those with three or more children.	Medical/ Social	Yes	No	No
	1990–present	Legal upon request in the first 12 weeks of pregnancy.	Upon Request	No	No	No
Czech Republic	1957–86	Legal for maternal health or social reasons in the first 12 weeks of pregnancy.	Medical/ Social	No	Yes	No

TABLE 7.1. (*cont'd*)

Country	*Years Legalized*	*Description*	*Category*	*Mandatory Delay*	*Large Subsidy*	*Parental Involvement*
Czech Republic (*cont'd*)	1987–present	Legal in the first 12 weeks of pregnancy upon request.	Upon Request	No	No	Yes
Germany (former GDR)	1972–94	Legal upon request in the first 12 weeks of pregnancy.	Upon Request	No	Yes	No
	1995–present	Legal in the first 12 weeks of pregnancy after mandatory counseling and a 3-day waiting period. Procedure is subsidized in majority of cases.	Upon Request	Yes	Yes	No
Hungary	1973–92	Legal in the first 12 weeks of pregnancy on social grounds only for unmarried women, older women, and women with 3 or more children.	Medical/ Social	No	Yes	No
	1993–present	Legal in the first 12 weeks of pregnancy after counseling and a 3-day waiting period.	Upon Request	Yes	No	Yes
Poland	1956–92	Legal in the first 12 weeks of pregnancy for medical and social reasons.	Medical/ Social	No	Yes	Yes
	1993–present	Legal only when the pregnancy threatens the mother's life or health, in cases of rape/incest, or in cases of fetal defects.	Medical	NA	NA	NA
Romania	1966–89	Legal in very limited circumstances (threat to mother's life, rape, very large family, etc.).	Medical	NA	NA	NA

TABLE 7.1. (*cont'd*)

Country	*Years Legalized*	*Description*	*Category*	*Mandatory Delay*	*Large Subsidy*	*Parental Involvement*
Romania (*cont'd*)	1990–present	Legal upon request in the first 12 weeks of pregnancy.	Upon Request	No	No	No
Slovak Republic	1957–86	Legal for maternal health or social reasons in the first 12 weeks of pregnancy.	Medical/ Social	No	Yes	No
	1987–present	Legal in the first 12 weeks of pregnancy upon request.	Upon Request	No	No	Yes
Former Soviet Republics						
Belarus	1955–present	Legal upon request in the first 12 weeks of pregnancy.	Upon Request	No	Yes	No
Estonia	1955–91	Legal upon request in the first 12 weeks of pregnancy.	Upon Request	No	Yes	No
	1992–present	Idem.	Upon Request	No	No	No
Latvia	1955–91	Legal upon request in the first 12 weeks of pregnancy.	Upon Request	No	Yes	No
	1992–present	Idem.	Upon Request	No	No	Yes
Lithuania	1955–91	Legal upon request in the first 12 weeks of pregnancy.	Upon Request	No	Yes	No
	1992–present	Idem.	Upon Request	No	No	No
Moldova	1955–present	Legal upon request in the first 12 weeks of pregnancy.	Upon Request	No	Yes	No
Russian Federation	1955–present	Legal upon request in the first 12 weeks of pregnancy.	Upon Request	No	Yes	No
Ukraine	1955–present	Legal upon request in the first 12 weeks of pregnancy.	Upon Request	No	Yes	No

TABLE 7.1. (*cont'd*)

Country	*Years Legalized*	*Description*	*Category*	*Mandatory Delay*	*Large Subsidy*	*Parental Involvement*
Other Countries						
Canada	1969–88	Legal upon the approval of a committee if pregnancy affects life or health of woman.	Medical/ Social	No	Yes	No
	1988–present	Legal upon request with no formal gestational limits.	Upon Request	No	Yes	No
Japan	1949–present	Legal for maternal health or social reasons in the first 22 weeks of pregnancy.	Medical/ Social	No	No	No

Notes:
* See note 1 in this chapter for sources.
** Abortions were openly performed in at least some regions of the country in the period prior to broad legalization.

to pay for the procedure. One of the columns in this table indicates the "category" in which the country's abortion law fits. I create four such categories here.[2] "Life" represents those countries that allow an abortion only to save the life of the mother; these are the countries with the most restrictive laws. Other countries are categorized as "physical / mental health," and in these countries women are also allowed to have an abortion if the mother's physical or mental health may be harmed by the birth of a child. The third category is labeled "medical / social." In these countries women are able to obtain an abortion for any medical reason or for social reasons, like they cannot afford to have another child. In these countries, women typically need to present their case to a tribunal or other sort of body asking for permission to have an abortion. Although these committees often are very likely to grant a request under a wide array of possible scenarios, just the act of having to seek permission inflicts an additional cost on women seeking an abortion in these countries. Other countries allow abortion "on request" and they are labeled accordingly in the table.

It is important to recognize, however, that women in countries who can get an abortion on request may still face hurdles they need to overcome before obtaining the procedure. For instance, women in Germany are subject to a three-day waiting period and must be presented with information regarding the alternatives to abortion, like adoption and the available social services should the woman decide to keep the baby. Therefore, the label "on request" does not mean that abortion access is completely unrestricted in those countries. It just means that a woman who wants to get an abortion can get one as long as she is persistent in her request. On the other hand, some of the on-request countries, like Denmark and Sweden, do have virtually unrestricted abortion access.

Policies in Western Europe, Japan, and Canada

A comparison of current abortion policies in the developed countries considered here (i.e., those in Western Europe, Canada, and Japan) to those in the United States suggests that U.S. policies are among the more liberal. This conclusion is based on the legal status of abortion in these countries and not necessarily on the way in which these laws are enforced or on other practical distinctions. On this basis, Denmark and Sweden have more liberal policies, but most other countries do not. Belgium, France, Germany, and the Netherlands all have significant waiting periods, and abortions in the United Kingdom and Italy require physician approval. Ireland, Portugal, and Spain along with Switzerland have the most restrictive laws.

In addition, some of these developed countries legalized abortion well after the 1973 *Roe v. Wade* decision did so in the United States. Abortion was largely illegal in the Netherlands through 1981, Greece through 1986, and Belgium through 1991. Although the procedure was offered openly in these countries prior to its legalization, one would imagine that its illegal status still limited abortion services. Abortion in Canada was available upon the approval of a hospital committee through 1988, but then became available upon request after that. Spain and Portugal also liberalized their abortion laws in the mid-1980s, but their liberalization still left significant restrictions on abortion access.

The former Federal Republic of Germany relaxed its abortion law as well in 1993. In fact, abortion policy in Germany was one of the more contentious issues involved in the 1990 German reunification (Dorbritz and Fleischhacker 1999). The parties were deadlocked on this issue, and so they decided to leave different laws in place in the two regions until the end of 1992, upon which time agreement would need to be reached on a new national policy. By that time, a new law had been passed, legalizing abortion upon request after a mandatory waiting period and mandatory counseling, but that law was challenged in the courts and ruled unconstitutional in 1993. By 1995, legislation was approved that modified the 1992 law to make it consistent with this ruling, particularly the provisions that the mandatory counseling offered to abortion patients must be geared toward preserving the life of the fetus. These changes in Germany and those described previously reflect the only ones that occurred in the developed countries over the past few decades.

The history of family planning policy in Japan is interesting despite the fact that its abortion policy has remained unchanged for about fifty years. Following World War II, Japan was among the first countries to adopt liberal abortion policies, making the procedure available for a broad range of medical or social reasons well into the second trimester of pregnancy. But Japan was very conservative in its introduction of the birth control pill, which was approved for use in the United States in 1960 (Goldin and Katz 2002). In 1998, the Japanese Ministry of Health and Welfare chose to defer approval once again until further study could be conducted (Norgren 2001). Yet the following year, the same ministry moved very quickly to approve the use of Viagra, which treats erectile dysfunction, relying only on evidence from other countries. The political fallout from this apparent contradiction in treatment led to the hasty approval of the birth control pill in Japan in 1999. But for fifty years, abortion was broadly available while the birth control pill was not.

Among the developed countries in which abortion is not severely restricted (i.e., those in which abortion is available upon request or for medical or social reasons), some countries also maintain additional restrictions on abortion access similar to those in the United States. For instance, half of the countries in this group also impose mandatory delay. Half of these countries also require minors to involve their parents in some way. The main difference between many of these countries and the United States is that most of them provide large subsidies to pay for the procedure, which is consistent with the universal nature of health insurance in many of them.

Abortion Policies in Eastern Europe

As we currently stand, abortion policy in Eastern Europe is generally more liberal than it is in Western countries. With the exception of Poland, abortion is available upon request in every Eastern European country. But this stability did not always exist. During the Soviet era there was a great deal of variability across these countries. In the Soviet Union, as well as in each of its former republics since its breakup, abortion had been readily available for decades. But some of the satellite countries had adopted pro-natalist policies that had restricted or virtually ruled out the availability of abortion. These countries include Albania, Romania, Bulgaria, Czechoslovakia, and Hungary. During the political turmoil in these countries beginning in the late 1980s, they each reformed their policies, instituting laws in which abortion was available upon request. In Albania, Romania, and Bulgaria, these changes took place in conjunction with the political upheaval brought about by the collapse of the Soviet Union around 1990. In what became the Czech and Slovak Republics (1987) as well as in Hungary (1993), however, the timing did not coincide with political change.

Only in Poland did the political changes that took place in this era allow that country to impose substantive restrictions on abortion access. There, the downfall of communism allowed the Catholic Church to regain its importance in this heavily Catholic country. According to Titkow (1999), "after 1989 it became increasingly difficult to gain access to legal abortion, especially in state hospitals" (p. 174). By 1993, formal legislation had been enacted outlawing abortion except in circumstances in which the mother's health or her life is in jeopardy, or in cases of rape/incest or fetal defect.

Additionally, recall that German reunification was hindered by the difference between the liberal laws in the former German Democratic Republic and the moderate laws in place in the Federal Republic of Germany. The resolution of this dispute included provisions like a waiting period and mandatory counseling, which represented new restrictions that had not existed in the GDR. But abortion is still available on request in the eastern regions, despite the additional hurdles that were imposed. Since the Alan Guttmacher Institute currently categorizes all of Germany as a country in which abortion is available upon request, I do so here as well. By this standard, abortion access has not changed in the eastern regions.

The Prevalence of Abortion

Figure 7.1 displays the abortion rate (the number of abortions per 1,000 women of childbearing age) in a number of selected countries. The data necessary to create this figure were obtained from Alan Guttmacher Institute (1999), and the countries chosen represent a sampling of those who have been determined to have accurate counts of the number of abortions performed. The range in abortion rates among these countries is striking. In Germany only 7.6 abortions per 1,000 women of childbearing age (or 0.76 percent) were performed in 1996, which is about one-seventh the rate in Bulgaria in that year. Yet other countries have abortion rates that are considerably higher than that in Bulgaria. The abortion rate was 68.4 in Russia in 1995 and 78.0 in Romania in the following year. But even these statistics are probably a bit low; they are not reported in figure 7.1 because those statistics are believed to be incomplete.

Comparisons of countries like Germany and Bulgaria, Romania, or Russia may be misleading, however, because access to contraception is very different between Eastern European and Western European countries. But large differences exist in the utilization of abortion even

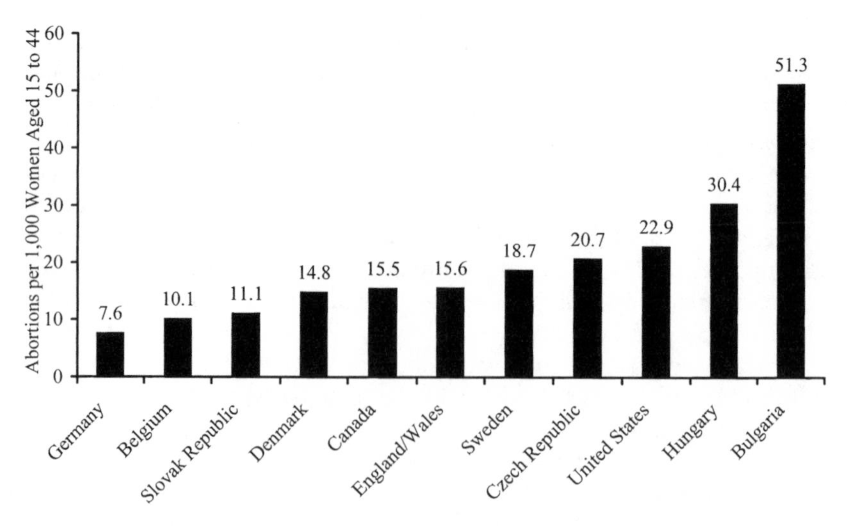

FIGURE 7.1. Abortion Rate in Selected Countries, 1995/1996.
Source: Alan Guttmacher Institute, 1999.

in the developed countries. The United States actually has the highest abortion rate reported here, at 22.9 abortions per 1,000 women of childbearing age in 1996, but Sweden was not far behind in that year with a rate of 18.7.

Looking across countries, it does not appear that there is a strong relationship between the type of abortion policy in place and the occurrence of abortion. For instance, all five of the countries with the highest abortion incidence have liberal abortion laws where abortion is available upon request. But Germany and Belgium also have abortion laws in which abortion is available upon request and they have the lowest abortion rates reported. In England/Wales, physician approval is required before an abortion can be performed, but the abortion rate in this country is in the middle of the distribution, with a rate of just over 15 abortions per 1,000 women of childbearing age. Clearly, the stringency of a country's abortion law is not the only determinant of the abortion rate. This fact reinforces the need to control for other differences across countries that may affect this outcome in an econometric analysis.

A similar comparison across countries, but for teens, is provided in figure 7.2. In general, high abortion rate countries have high teen abortion rates as well. Hungary and Bulgaria have among the highest abortion rates for both groups, and Germany and Belgium are at the bottom for both groups. However, some interesting differences exist. For instance, the teen abortion rate in the United States is very high by international standards. It is about the same level as that in Bulgaria and Hungary.

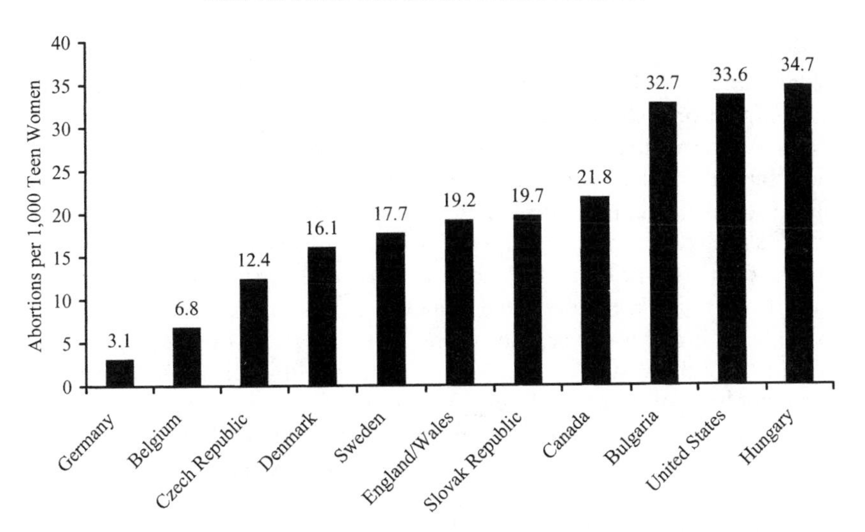

FIGURE 7.2. Teen Abortion Rate in Selected Countries, 1995/1996.
Source: Alan Guttmacher Institute, 1999.

Although the abortion rate for all women in the United States is high in the rankings, it is still considerably below these other countries in its absolute level. The same is not true for teens.

The Impact of Changes in Abortion Policy

In the preceding section, I described the current status of abortion law in Europe, Canada, and Japan, and highlighted the changes that have taken place in those locations over the past several decades. These changes may be employed within a quasi-experimental framework to evaluate their impact on women's fertility outcomes. This section will report the results of such an exercise, focusing mainly on Eastern Europe, relying on the data generated in Levine and Staiger (forthcoming) as well as on some of the results from that analysis. I will also present a comparison of trends in Canada relative to the United States to examine the impact of Canada's legalization of abortion in 1988.

An analysis of Eastern Europe provides valuable evidence because that region has undergone a number of dramatic policy changes over the past two decades. Albania, Romania, Bulgaria, the Czech and Slovak Republics, and Hungary moved to legalize abortion from regimes in which abortion was either severely or moderately restricted. Poland represents the sole country that moved in the opposite direction, imposing stringent restrictions on abortion access when its policy had been only somewhat restricted previously. The number of policy changes ("experiments") available makes Eastern Europe a valuable laboratory in which to study the impact of such changes.

In Western European countries, the changes in abortion policy were less significant than those in the East, making them less useful to study. For instance, Belgium, Greece, and the Netherlands legalized abortion in the past two decades, but the procedure had been practiced openly in those countries prior to legalization. Moreover, in Portugal and Spain, abortion policy was liberalized somewhat, but still remains very restrictive. Data limitations also inhibit the ability to study the impact of abortion policy in Western Europe since countries in which abortion is not broadly legal do not have complete counts of abortion available.

The methods employed here are similar to those used in the remainder of the book. Initially, I will report the results of an econometric analysis that incorporates the quasi-experimental framework into the context of a regression analysis. In other words, I will report the results of regression models that examine the relationship between abortion policy and abortions, pregnancies, and births in models that include country and year fixed effects, along with other covariates. The specific details of the data and the econometric analysis are reported in Levine and Staiger (forthcoming).

These results are useful for clearly summarizing the overall impact of abortion policy on these outcomes, but they are not always that intuitive. Therefore, I will also present a series of case studies, examining individual examples of changes in abortion policy by comparing a country that changed its policy to a relevant control group. In addition to reporting these case studies for some Eastern European countries, I will also present a similar exercise comparing Canada, which relaxed its abortion laws in 1988, to the United States.

Past Evidence from Earlier Changes in Policy

Before moving on to these quasi-experimental exercises, I first briefly report some of the evidence from early research that has looked at the impact of past changes in abortion policy in Eastern Europe, focusing on Frejka (1983).[3] This paper takes advantage of a number of changes in abortion policy that took place in some of these countries in the 1950s and 1960s. In the mid-1950s, most Soviet satellite countries adopted liberal abortion laws that mimicked those introduced in the Soviet Union itself over this period.[4] But in the following decade or so, Czechoslovakia, Hungary, Bulgaria, and Romania introduced restrictive abortion policies.

Frejka (1983) tracks the impact of these changes in abortion policy by simply presenting time-series patterns in births and abortions within each Eastern European country over the 1950 to 1980 period. Some of the time-series patterns are striking, particularly in Romania. In that country, legal abortions skyrocketed following the legalization of the procedure there. The statistic he presents is the "total abortion rate," which represents the number of abortions a woman would have over her entire childbearing years if she had the age-specific abortion rates of women alive at a particular time. In the mid-1960s, Frejka reports that the total abortion rate in Romania rose to well over 7 abortions per woman over the childbearing years. When restrictions were imposed in 1966, the legal total abortion rate dropped instantly and precipitously, although one cannot tell how accurate these statistics were when legal abortion access was highly restricted.

The impact of these trends in abortions is noticeable in the birth rate as well. During the period of rapidly rising abortions, births fell in response, conceivably as unwanted births were prevented. The total fertility rate, which represents the number of births a woman would have over her entire childbearing years if she had the age-specific birth rates of women alive at a particular time, fell from over three in the mid-1950s to less than two in the mid-1960s. Immediately after abortion was severely restricted, however, the total fertility rate jumped back over three, suggesting that unwanted births were taking place again. But within just a couple of years, the birth rate fell rapidly again, down to a level of perhaps 2.3. This rapid decline in births is consistent with either increased use of contraception or the rapid emergence of a large market for illegal abortions.

Results from Regression Models

The outcomes that I will consider in this analysis are the abortion rate, the birth rate, and the "pregnancy rate," which is defined as the sum of the abortion and birth rates. In each case, the rate reflects the number of occurrences of the outcome per 1,000 women of childbearing age. All of the analyses of abortions and pregnancies will utilize only those countries in which the abortion data has been judged to be virtually complete by the Alan Guttmacher Institute (1999). One difficulty in doing so is that no country in which abortion is highly restricted can have abortion data that is virtually complete, so it is impossible to estimate the impact of changing such a policy on the abortion rate and, therefore, the pregnancy rate.

Using the experiments available in Eastern Europe, Levine and Staiger (forthcoming) have estimated the impact of moving from a regime where abortion is available upon request to one in which abortion is available for medical or social reasons or to one in which abortion is available only if the mother's life, or her physical or mental health, is at stake. These categories can roughly be thought of as liberal, moderate, and restrictive abortion policies. Given the economic model of abortion along with the types of assumptions made previously in this book, we would predict that moving from a liberal abortion policy to a moderate one would reduce the abortion rate and have little effect on the birth rate. But moving to a restrictive policy is likely to increase the birth rate, as women will have little choice other than to give birth to a child that will be unwanted. These predictions can be examined based on the changes in abortion policy that took place in Eastern Europe. In fact, one advantage of this research is that it can estimate both types of effects within the same model. The evidence from the United States explores both types of changes separately.

The specific details of the econometric procedures employed in Levine and Staiger (forthcoming) are beyond the scope of the discussion here; the interested reader is directed to that source for more information. But briefly, the authors estimate regression models where each of the outcomes considered here is included as the dependent variable in a regression model where the key independent variable is the type of abortion policy in place in each Eastern European country and year between 1980 and 1997. Additional control variables are included in these regressions, including demographic and macroeconomic factors. Importantly, state and year fixed effects are always included, which enable us to interpret the results as in a quasi-experiment, and in some specifications state-specific linear trends are included as well.

One limitation with a quasi-experiment in this context is that there were a tremendous number of social, economic, and cultural changes taking place in these countries over this period as a result of the turmoil that occurred when the Soviet Union collapsed. If other changes taking place within a particular country were responsible for the change in abortion laws, then the quasi-experimental framework would be invalid. The treatment could no longer be considered to be randomly assigned. However, to the extent that these other changes taking place were doing so uniformly across control and treatment countries, then we would be able to control for them with year fixed effects. Another reason, why this problem may not be so severe is that some of the changes that took place did not correspond to the immediate political problems faced within a country. For instance, the Czech and Slovak Republics liberalized their abortion laws a few years before the downfall of the Soviet Union. Hungary did so afterward. Therefore, one should keep in mind that the potential for problems in the quasi-experiment exist, but that they do not obviously invalidate the exercise.

The results of this analysis are supportive of the predictions of an economic model. Levine and Staiger find that severe restrictions on abortion access have a large impact on fertility. Imposing such restrictions increases the birth rate by perhaps 10 percent. This evidence is consistent with that examining the impact of the legalization of abortion in the United States, once one takes the possibility of travel into account (see chapter 4). Different effects emerge when a country moves from a world where abortion is available upon request to one in which abortion is moderately restricted. The results indicate that imposing these moderate restrictions reduced the abortion rate by about 25 percent. On the other hand, this analysis also shows that there is no statistically significant rise in birth rates in response to these restrictions. Combining these two effects suggests that the impact on abortions is brought about by a change in the likelihood of pregnancies, which are estimated to decline by about 10 percent in response. The remainder of the chapter is intended to provide case studies of some of the changes that took place in Eastern Europe (as well as in Canada) to help illustrate these results.

The Romanian Experience

During the Communist era, the Romanian government had in place extremely strong pro-natalist policies (Baban 1999). Contraception was outlawed. Families that did not have children were taxed. Women were required to obtain annual medical checkups to verify their reproductive health. Not only was abortion outlawed in virtually all circumstances, but the state police vigorously enforced the law by routinely investigating obstetricians and gynecologists to make sure that no such procedures were taking place. Yet illegal abortions under considerably adverse circumstances were rampant.

As a result of these repressive policies and their consequences, on the first day following the overthrow of the communist regime at the very end of 1989, Romania reversed these policies (Baban 1999). In particular, beginning on January 1, 1990, abortion became legally available upon request. Since abortion policy in Romania used to be so highly restrictive, I am unable to evaluate the impact of this change on the frequency of abortion because of data limitations. I can examine the impact on fertility, however. Based upon earlier discussions I would predict that births would fall substantially as a result, since unwanted births could now be prevented.

It is important to recognize, however, that this change in abortion policy in Romania occurred at the same time as the change in the political leadership in that country. The correlation between the political turmoil and the change in abortion policy at that time does make it more difficult to identify the specific impact of the abortion policy alone. In a quasi-experimental context, this means that it is important to pick control groups that were also experiencing similar political troubles. Although the turmoil may not have been identical, it may reduce a lot of the time-specific factors that affected both sets of countries and it is the best that can be done under the circumstances. In light of this, I use for this exercise the European republics

FIGURE 7.3. Impact of Abortion Legalization in Romania on Birth Rates. *Source*: Author's calculations. *Note*: The percentage differences are normalized so that their values equal zero in 1989.

of the former Soviet Union as a control group. Abortion policy has not changed in the former Soviet Union, nor in the republics that emerged from it after its collapse, for the past several decades; over the period abortion has always been available upon request.

The results of this analysis are presented in figure 7.3. In this figure, I display the percentage difference in birth rates between Romania and the republics of the former Soviet Union in the period just before and just after abortion was legalized in Romania. Through the 1980s one can see that the gap was growing; this resulted from an increasing birth rate in Romania that was not matched in the European republics in the Soviet Union. Since abortion was legalized on January 1, 1990, one may have expected to see births begin to decline by the second half of that year and then by more than that in the following year because of the full year of exposure. This is precisely the pattern that is observed in figure 7.3. It shows that births fell relative to the former Soviet Republics by about 11 percent in 1990 an then an additional 6 percent in 1991, representing a total decline of about 17 percent. The difference stabilized after that. This quasi-experimental exercise strongly suggests that legalization of abortion in Romania had a dramatic causal impact on the fertility behavior of the women in that country.

One other issue that has been raised regarding the legalization of abortion in Romania is its impact on maternal mortality. The rate of risky illegal abortions performed in Romania prior to legalization in 1990 was high, and there were a large number of reported deaths to women as a

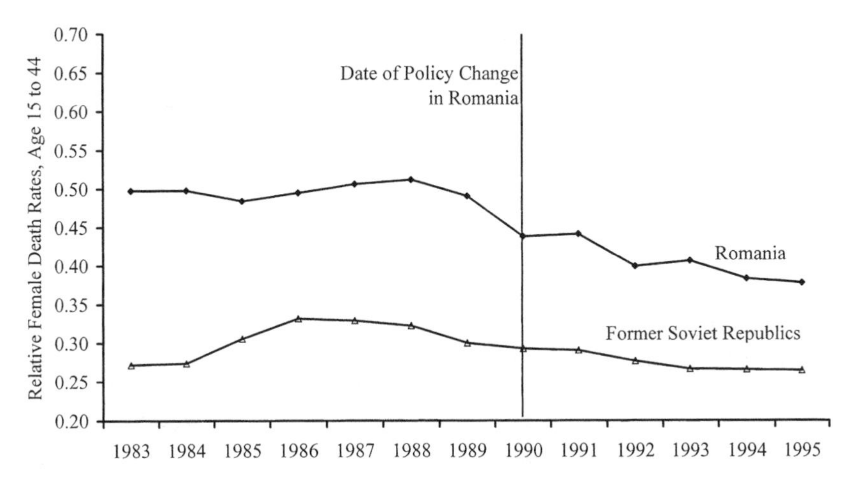

FIGURE 7.4. Impact of Abortion Legalization in Romania on Maternal Mortality. *Source*: Author's calculations. *Note*: The relative female death rate is the ratio of the female death rate to the male death rate for men and women in this age group. These rates have been normalized so that they equal zero in 1989.

result of such a procedure. Baban (1999) reports that about 500 to 600 maternal deaths were recorded each year in Romania during the 1970s and 1980s. That level plummeted to 263 in 1990, 183 in 1991, and all the way down to 95 by 1996, which clearly suggests that abortion legalization significantly improved maternal health.

But maternal mortality is a difficult concept to measure, and these statistics do not take advantage of a control group to detect whether any other changes were taking place at this time. Here, I replicate the quasi-experimental exercise conducted earlier for births, but employ a different indicator of maternal mortality as the outcome. The outcome considered represents the ratio of female deaths to male deaths among those aged 15 to 44. These mortality statistics are likely to be much more reliable and incorporating men as a base can help assess general trends in medical treatment within each group. We would still expect this ratio to decline by more in Romania than in the former Soviet Republics if abortion legalization reduced the likelihood of dangerous illegal abortions.

Unfortunately, a straightforward quasi-experimental plot like that in figure 7.3 regarding births made it difficult to draw strong conclusions. Instead, in figure 7.4, I have simply plotted the trends in this relative female-to-male mortality ratio to illustrate the impact of legalization. In Romania, the relative mortality ratio held steady at about 0.5 throughout the 1980s. Starting in 1990, the first year in which abortion was legalized in that country, female deaths declined considerably relative to men, falling to a ratio of about 0.4 by 1992 and holding reasonably steady since then. The specific timing of the decline in that country at exactly the point when abortion was legalized certainly implies that abortion legalization significantly reduced the incidence of risky illegal abortions and the mortality that sometimes resulted from them.

On the other hand, the female-to-male mortality ratio had been declining steadily since 1986 in the former Soviet republics. In a quasi-experimental framework, the decline in the former Soviet republics makes it more difficult to identify what really happened. If we looked only at the pattern in Romania, relative female mortality is roughly constant through 1989 and then noticeably declines following the 1990 policy change. One would interpret this as a treatment effect. But unrelated factors led relative female mortality to begin declining in the former Soviet republics a few years earlier than that. If we look at the post-1990 difference in relative female mortality between Romania and the former Soviet republics, it would not seem like there was much of an impact of the Romanian policy change. At such times, statistical analysis requires some artistic ability trying to interpret exactly what is happening. It would be my interpretation that abortion legalization did indeed reduce the mortality associated with illegal abortions in Romania, but alternative interpretations certainly are possible based upon this evidence.

The Polish Experience

Polish abortion policy moved in the opposite direction of that in Romania in the early 1990s. Abortion was available with moderate restrictions in Poland through the 1980s, and then became severely restricted officially in March of 1993. But Titkow (1999) reports that the legal crackdown on abortion in 1993 followed severe de facto restrictions that began earlier than that, perhaps as early as 1990. Therefore, one might predict that unwanted births would have become more likely in Poland after these restrictions were imposed. The former republics of the Soviet Union provide a reasonable control group for Poland as well, so we can compare fertility trends in the two sets of countries over time to determine whether this prediction is valid in Poland's case.

The evidence presented in figure 7.5 suggests that births did indeed increase in Poland relative to the former Soviet republics, following Poland's restrictions. Throughout the 1980s, births in Poland were falling continuously in relationship to the former Soviet republics. But that trend reversed itself in 1990 and 1991 as Polish births jumped by about 10 percent relative to the comparison group. Because of the distinction between the de facto policy change and the official legal change in the rules governing abortion access, it is difficult definitively to assign causality to

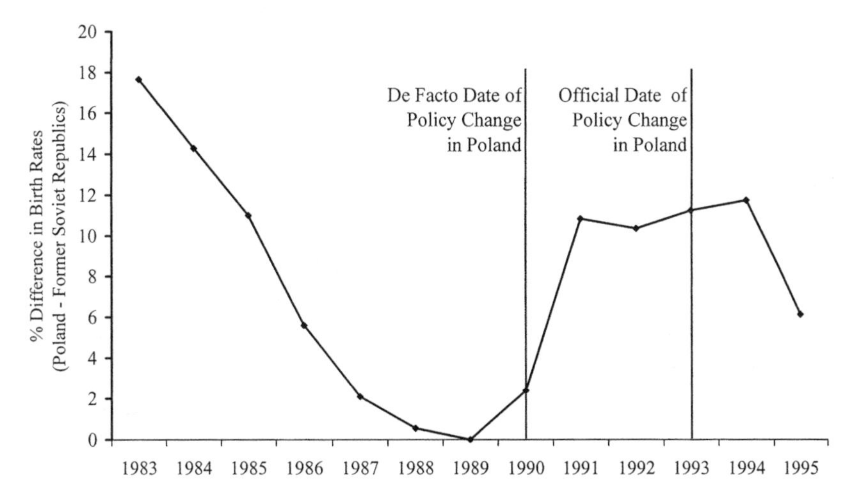

FIGURE 7.5. Impact of Abortion Prohibition in Poland on Birth Rates. *Source*: Author's calculations. *Note*: The percentage difference has been normalized so that it equals zero in 1989. See Titkow (1999) for de facto date of policy change.

the rule changes here, but these results strongly suggest that the imposition of severe abortion restrictions significantly increased the birth rate.

The Bulgarian Experience

The past two examples provide an indication of changes either away from or toward very restrictive abortion policies. Bulgaria provides us with different information since abortion was moderately restricted through the 1980s, but then changed its policies so that abortion became legal upon request in February of 1990 (Vassilev 1999). This case provides two advantages relative to the earlier examples. First, since abortion was not highly restricted in the period prior to the change, abortion data are available from that point so we can examine the impact of the change on the likelihood of abortion. Second, the predicted impact of this change in policy is also different than that in response to the change in Poland or Romania. If the cost of abortion was already below that of an unwanted birth before the law change, at least for many Bulgarian women, then further liberalization is likely to lead to more abortions through more pregnancies; births will not fall.

The evidence provided in figures 7.6 and 7.7 support these predictions. In both of these diagrams, the European republics of the former Soviet Union are used as a control group as they have been in the earlier analyses of Poland and Bulgaria. Figure 7.6 presents the percentage difference in

FIGURE 7.6. Impact of Abortion Legalization in Bulgaria on Abortion Rates. *Source*: Author's calculations. *Note*: The percentage difference has been normalized so that it equals zero in 1989.

the abortion rate between Bulgaria and the former Soviet republics in the period before and after Bulgaria's change in abortion policy. Throughout the 1980s, the difference in the rate of abortion in the two sets of countries is relatively constant. But in 1990, the year that abortion became available upon request, the abortion rate rose in Bulgaria relative to the former Soviet Union republics and remained higher throughout the early 1990s. On average, it would appear that abortion rates in Bulgaria rose by about 15 percent in response to the law change.

The impact on births is represented in figure 7.7. Throughout the 1980s, the relationship of births between Bulgaria and the former Soviet republics was reasonably constant. One could argue that births in Bulgaria were rising slowly relative to those in the former Soviet republics, but even so, this trend was not that large. Following the introduction of abortion upon request in Bulgaria in 1990, there is no noticeable drop in birth rates despite the fact that abortions rose. Although there is some year-to-year variation, overall it appears that births continued to follow their slow upward trend throughout the period with no break around the date of the policy change.

The Canadian Experience

All of the international analyses reported so far regarding the impact of changes in abortion policy have focused on the experiences of countries in Eastern Europe. But a change in Canadian abortion policy also took

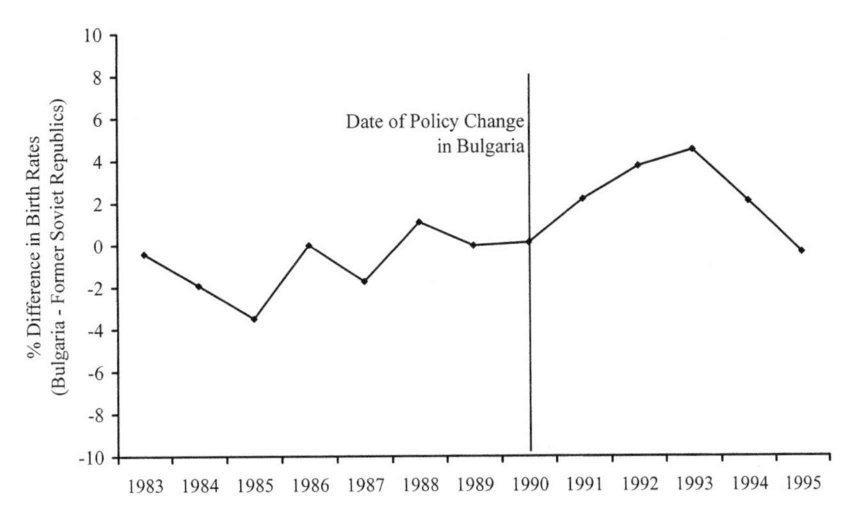

FIGURE 7.7. Impact of Abortion Legalization in Bulgaria on Birth Rates. *Source*: Author's calculations. *Note*: The percentage difference has been normalized so that it equals zero in 1989.

place recently and can be used to examine the behavioral responses to it. In Canada, a 1969 law required that an abortion could be performed only if it were approved by a hospital committee (Muldoon 1991). The committee could approve the procedure for a broad range of therapeutic reasons. But in January of 1988, the Supreme Court of Canada ruled in *R. v. Mogentaler* that the 1969 law was unconstitutional, and abortion became available upon request. Although subsequent legislative attempts have been made to restrict the procedure, they have not been successful.

In a quasi-experimental framework, the United States represents a suitable control group for Canada over this period. Although some states did institute relatively minor restrictions on abortion access throughout the 1980s and 1990s, no national policy changes took place around the time of the 1988 Canadian Supreme Court decision. Figures 7.8 and 7.9 present the results of a comparison of the difference in abortion and birth rates, respectively, between these two countries. Through the 1980s, the difference in abortion rates between the United States and Canada was fairly stable. Rates in the United States were higher, but the differential did not change much over this period. Following the 1988 Canadian Supreme Court decision, however, Canadian abortion rates began to increase considerably relative to those in the United States over the next several years before the difference stabilized. The Canadian abortion rate is still lower than that in the United States, but the differential is much smaller than it used to be.[5] Between 1988 and 1996, Canadian abortion rates rose over

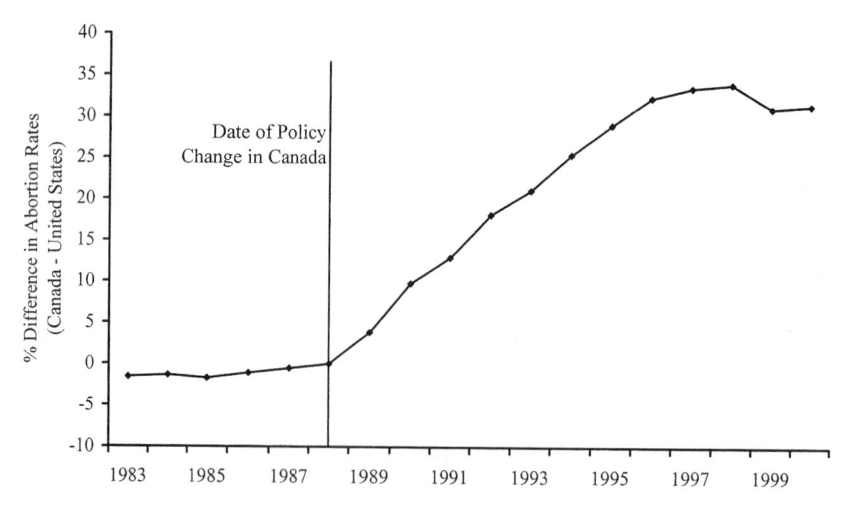

FIGURE 7.8. Impact of Abortion Legalization in Canada on Abortion Rates. *Source*: Author's calculations. *Note*: The percentage difference has been normalized so that it equals zero in 1988.

30 percent relative to those in the United States. Although this evidence does seem to indicate that it took some time for the market for abortion to evolve in Canada, it also seems to point to the fact that the law change had a causal influence on the prevalence of abortion there.

Yet there is little evidence that this increase in Canadian abortions brought about by making it available upon request in that country led to any reduction in the birth rate. Figure 7.9 displays a comparable figure for births. Through much of the 1980s, the birth rate in Canada was declining slowly relative to that in the United States. That relative decline took a pause in the first half of the 1990s, the same period in which abortion rates were rising, before continuing in the second half of the 1990s. The increased incidence of abortion in Canada in response to a relaxing of their abortion law certainly did not lead to fewer births.

Overview of the Evidence

In this chapter, I have provided an evaluation of the impact of changes in abortion policy that have taken place over the past two decades, focusing mainly on Eastern Europe, but also examining behavioral responses in Canada. The evidence here based on cross-country comparisons over time is generally consistent with that found in the United States, which relies on cross-state comparisons over time. In both cases, we find that a severely

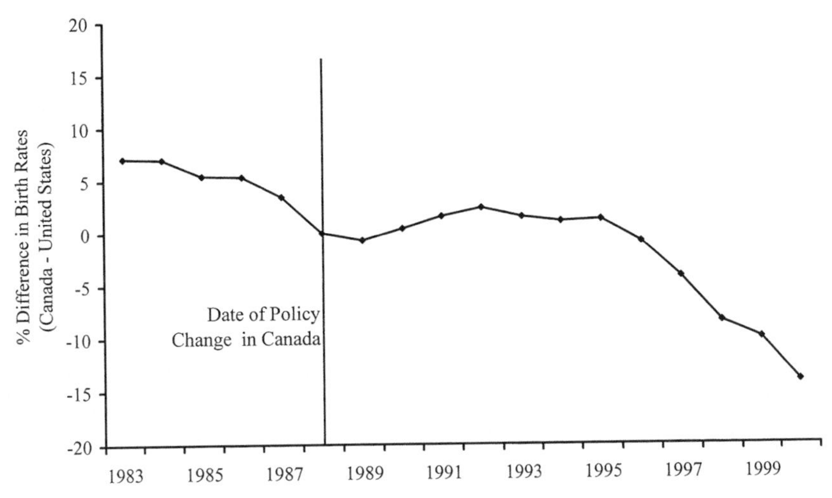

FIGURE 7.9. Impact of Abortion Legalization in Canada on Birth Rates. *Source*: Author's calculation. *Note*: The percentage difference has been normalized so that it equals zero in 1988.

restricted abortion environment leads women to give birth to children who are presumably unwanted. On the other hand, more moderate restrictions do not appear to increase the birth rate. Women do abort less (more) when these sorts of restrictions are imposed (lifted), but we do not see that women give birth more often. Overall, on the basis of the many quasi-experiments conducted and reported in this analysis, all support these dichotomous findings: legalizing abortion reduces births whereas moderate restrictions on abortion within a legal abortion environment reduce pregnancies.

Chapter Eight

UNFINISHED BUSINESS

ALTHOUGH OUR KNOWLEDGE regarding the impact of abortion policy has grown extensively, there remain a number of important unanswered questions. The material presented so far has focused on its impact on abortions, births, and pregnancies. These may be the primary outcomes that one would consider, but they are not the only relevant ones. The purpose of this chapter is to explore some of these additional outcomes, as well as some other relevant issues regarding abortion. These topics are covered here largely because we know considerably less about them, but I will still present what the issues are, what we know about them, and what is left to be answered.

The additional outcomes that I will consider are marriage, children's outcomes, and lifecycle outcomes for women. Abortion policy has direct implications for marriage because fertility and marriage decisions are often interconnected. Since I have shown that major changes in abortion policy have consequences for a woman's fertility, one may suspect that it has implications for marriage as well. Major changes in abortion policy that alter the number of children born may also affect the subsequent characteristics of a birth cohort. When, say, abortion was legalized in the United States, evidence supports the proposition that it led to fewer births. But this leads to a question regarding the characteristics of those children born compared to those who would have been born otherwise. Are their outcomes different, and, if so, in what ways? Changes in abortion policy that influence a woman's decision to give birth may also have repercussions for the woman throughout her life. If access to legal abortion enables a woman to prevent an unwanted birth, she may decide to have an additional child at a subsequent date or not. A woman's ability to control her fertility better may affect other things as well, such as her educational attainment and labor market outcomes.

All of the additional topics described so far pertain to other outcomes that may occur in response to changes in abortion access that have not been addressed elsewhere in this book. However, the theoretical and empirical methods described earlier are useful to help analyze related policy questions as well. For instance, changes in welfare policy in general and welfare reform specifically have led some to be concerned about their impact on abortion and fertility. Welfare generosity can easily be incorporated into economic models of fertility and abortion; the predictions from these models provide some interesting insights and testable propositions. Although only limited evidence exists in this regard, I review it here.

I also address an additional set of topics in this chapter for which relatively little is known, but in which public interest is high. For instance, the introduction of RU-486, or Mifepristone, generated quite a bit of controversy and continues to do so. I will review what economic models would have predicted to occur upon the introduction of this new drug and what is known about its impact so far. The other major focus of debate regarding U.S. abortion policy lately has been "partial birth abortion." Although economics has little to say about this debate, I will describe what it can offer. The final issue that I will address is a comparison of the impact of imposing moderate restrictions on abortion relative to improving contraceptive technology as a means to reduce pregnancies. A careful examination of the impact of contraceptive technology on sexual activity, contraceptive use, and pregnancy outcomes is beyond the scope of this book. Without such a study my ability to answer definitively a question like the impact of improved contraception is severely limited, but it represents an important question that I will address as best as I am able within the framework of this book.

Abortion, Marriage, and Marital Births

Motivation

The main fact motivating the limited research that has taken place regarding the relationship between abortion policy and marriage is the dramatic increase in the percentage of births that take place outside of marriage in the United States. Figure 8.1 shows that for all women, but especially for teens, this statistic has risen considerably over the past half century. Only about 5 percent of births to all women were nonmarital in the 1950s, but this statistic stood at about one-third of all births in 1999. For teens, nonmarital births comprised about 14 percent of all births in the 1950s, but 79 percent more recently.

Moreover, Akerlof et al. (1996) report that what they call the "shotgun marriage rate" fell a great deal over the past several decades. This rate examines all first births that were conceived before marriage and considers the fraction of those that resulted in a marital birth. The most recent statistics available in this regard are provided by Bachu (1999) and are displayed in figure 8.2. In this figure, one can see that among women between the ages of 15 and 29 as well as those between 15 and 19, this so-called shotgun marriage rate stood steady at roughly 50 percent from the 1930s through the 1960s and even into the early 1970s. But by the

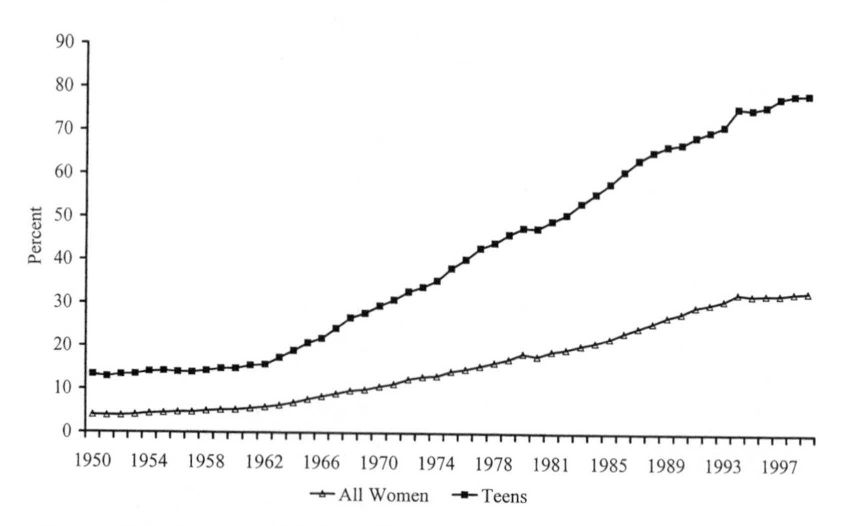

FIGURE 8.1. Percent of Births to Unmarried Women. *Source*: Ventura et al. (2000).

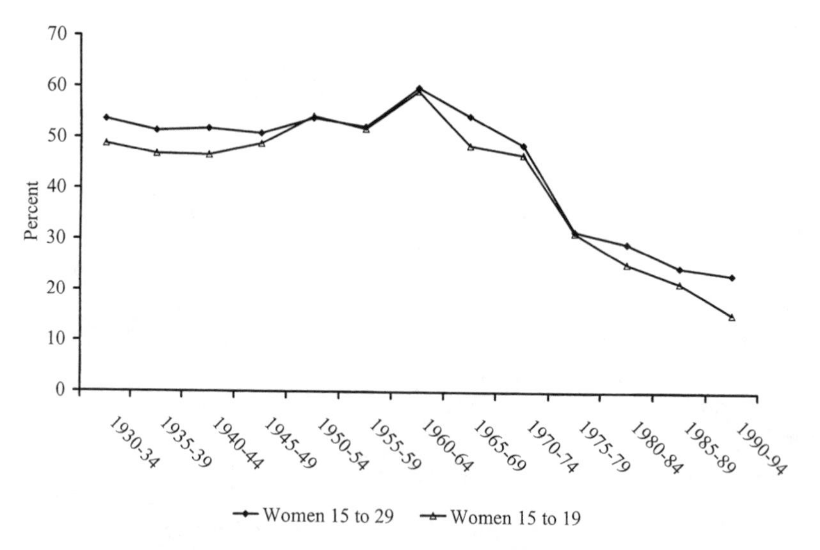

FIGURE 8.2. Percent of First Births Conceived Prior to Marriage and Born following Marriage. *Source*: Bachu (1999).

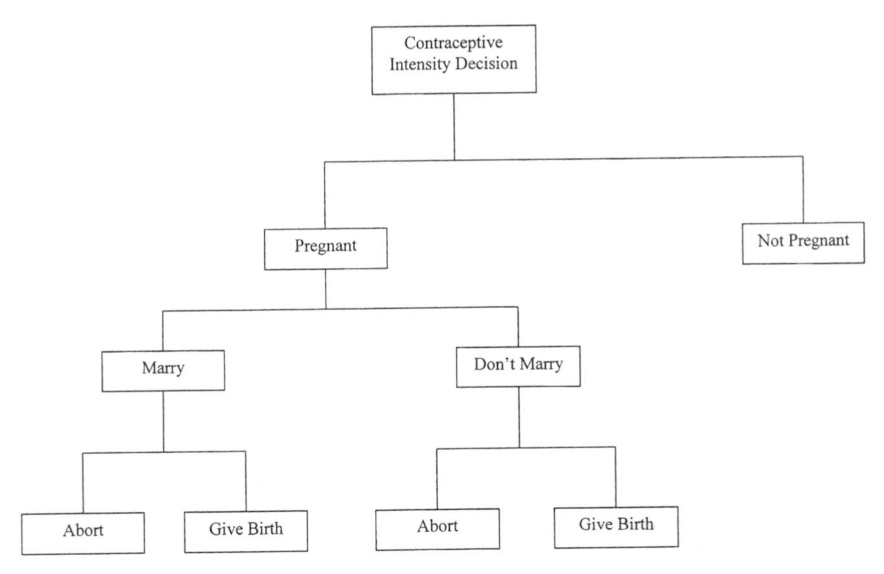

FIGURE 8.3. Abortion Decision Tree with Marriage.

late 1970s, this rate began to fall dramatically. It has fallen by more than half for women 15 to 29 and more than two-thirds for women 15 to 19 by the date of the most recent statistic, which represents the 1990 to 1994 period. At that time, 15 and 23 percent of first births to women 15 to 19 and to women 15 to 29, respectively, that were conceived before marriage resulted in a marital birth.

As a result, research in this area has focused on the impact of abortion policy on the marriage decision of women who have already become pregnant, especially teens. This focus simplifies the conceptual problem somewhat because the timing of the marriage decision, among all the other decisions that are made which lead to fertility, is not clear. Within the framework of a decision tree, like that presented in figure 8.3, the decision to marry may come before or after a pregnancy. But this research clearly places that decision after a pregnancy.

Models

Perhaps the two most influential papers in this area are Akerlof et al. (1996) and Kane and Staiger (1996). Both papers present theoretical models which recognize that the cost of abortion may affect a woman's (or man's) behavior well before the decision to abort or give birth. For instance, if parental consent is required before an unmarried teen can obtain an abortion (thus raising the cost), she may take actions that either reduce her probability of getting pregnant or increase the chances of marrying the child's father. Thus, the effects of a change in the cost of abortion can have quite unexpected effects on both marital and nonmarital births in these models as pregnancy and marital decisions are affected.

The Kane and Staiger (1996) model is very similar to the third model presented in chapter 3, labeled an "Extended Model of Abortion." In their model, women gain new information about the attractiveness of parenthood only after becoming pregnant, and the key piece of information that they focus on is the father's willingness to marry. In their model, reducing the cost of abortion reduces the cost of acquiring this information and encourages women to become pregnant even though many of these women will eventually choose to have an abortion. In other words, low-cost abortion allows these women to become pregnant in a risky situation, and then give birth only if things go well (e.g., the father agrees to marry). In their model, marriages can be affected if pregnancies are affected because every nonmarital pregnancy is associated with a probability that the man will marry the woman before the child is born. If there are more pregnancies, some of them will lead to a marriage and then a marital birth.

If the cost of an abortion is very high in this model and then falls below the threshold at which its cost is less than that of an unwanted birth, pregnancies that would have led to an unwanted birth will now be aborted. But a reduction in abortion costs of this magnitude would not be likely to lead to an increase in pregnancies in this model, so there would be no effect on marriages. Nevertheless, the only abortions that take place would occur to women who did not marry, so this change would reduce nonmarital births. On the other hand, if abortion costs continued to fall to the point where they are relatively inexpensive, then pregnancies would rise. This would occur because some women would take a chance on getting pregnant with the possibility that it will lead to a marriage and a wanted birth. Therefore, the increase in wanted births that would result from a further reduction in the cost of abortion means that there will be more marriages and more marital births.

The models presented by Akerlof, et al. (1996) have different predictions. This paper develops two models that are both intended to provide a potential explanation for the increase in nonmarital births over the past three decades, focusing on the impact brought about by abortion legalization, along with the greater availability of contraception at about that time. As in Kane and Staiger, both of the Akerlof et al. models focus on the decision to marry following a nonmarital pregnancy, and the uncertainty involved in this decision.

In one model, the increase in the availability of contraception and the legalization of abortion increases a woman's willingness to engage in sexual activity without a promise of marriage, particularly among those women who attach little psychological cost to having an abortion. For those women who would choose not to abort, competition from other women in seeking partners prevents them from seeking a promise of marriage before engaging in sexual activity. Therefore, abortion legalization would be predicted to reduce the likelihood of marriage in this model, although it would raise the likelihood of nonmarital births.

In a second model, Akerlof et al. consider the father's incentives to agree to marriage following a nonmarital pregnancy. The father is uncertain about the costs to the mother of a nonmarital birth, but is more likely to agree to marriage if he thinks these costs may be high. The availability of low-cost abortion limits the potential costs to the pregnant woman, and therefore may reduce the chance that the father will agree to marriage. Thus, with fewer fathers agreeing to marriage, marriages will decline and a larger fraction of births will be nonmarital after abortion legalization in this model as well.

The implications of the Kane and Staiger model and of both Akerlof et al. models conflict. The former predicts that marriage may be unaffected by abortion legalization, but nonmarital births will go down as those women who do not marry the father will abort. On the other hand, Akerlof et al. predict that abortion legalization will reduce the likelihood of marriage and increase nonmarital births. Furthermore, Kane and Staiger go on to predict that further reductions in the cost of abortion will lead to an increase in marriage and the marital birth rate. Akerlof et al. do not address the implications of further reductions in the cost of abortion.

One possible reconciliation of these two models considers the time frame within which the behavioral effects suggested in them might take place. Women may react more quickly in the Kane and Staiger model, since the behavioral response represents changes in the woman's own actions without regard to the broader social environment. In Akerlof et al., however, social norms need to change in response to the change in abortion policy, as competition among women or bargaining power between men and women are affected. Such responses are likely to be longer term in nature. In fact, the length of time in which a response may be expected in the Akerlof et al, models makes it difficult to test empirically. For instance, the quasi-experimental framework will attribute behavioral responses to the policy change only if the response takes place around the same time as the policy change. The behavioral responses suggested by Akerlof et al. are unlikely to be evident in such an exercise.

Empirical Evidence

The empirical literature has not addressed the direct impact of abortion policy on marriage as of yet. However, researchers have explored the empirical relationship between abortion and nonmarital childbearing. Since economic models of abortion and marriage also have implications for abortion and nonmarital childbearing, it may be possible to learn something about the former by reviewing the evidence regarding the latter.

The first piece of evidence that can be brought to bear on this question was presented in chapter 5. In that analysis, we saw that abortion legalization led to a decline in nonmarital fertility that was twice as great as that in marital fertility. This is relevant because it stands in sharp contrast to the predictions inherent in the Akerlof et al. models, which indicated that nonmarital fertility would indeed increase in response to abortion legalization. Again, the problem here may be the time horizon over which the policy is being evaluated. The quasi-experimental nature of that exercise is capable of detecting the instantaneous effect of abortion policy on marital and nonmarital fertility. But the mechanisms by which the Akerlof et al. models would alter fertility outcomes would be longer term in nature. Therefore, this piece of empirical evidence is not necessarily inconsistent with those models. On the other hand, the greater reduction in nonmarital births is consistent with the predictions of the Kane and Staiger model in response to a change in the legal status of abortion.

Similarly, the literature on the impact of relatively minor changes in abortion access that have occurred in the period since abortion was legalized can shed light on this question. Again, marriage is addressed only indirectly as it is incorporated in nonmarital fertility. The Kane and Staiger (1996) study, discussed in chapter 6, provides relevant empirical evidence. Their research indicated that relatively minor restrictions on abortion and reductions in provider availability were found actually to reduce the teen birth rate. Although extensions to marital and nonmarital fertility were not discussed earlier, it turns out that this reduction is concentrated among marital births, consistent with the predictions of their model.

Finally, Lichter et al. (1998) examines the impact of abortion policy on the prevalence of female-headed families.[1] This study uses Census data and examines the change in the fraction of female-headed families in each state between 1980 and 1990 brought about by changes in abortion access and abortion policies in the state. They find some evidence that those states in which abortion access declined and in which Medicaid funding restrictions or parental involvement laws were imposed experienced an increase in the fraction of families headed by women. There are some important limitations of this analysis, however. For instance, the authors include abortion access as an exogenous variable (a problem that I have discussed elsewhere in this book with respect to other analyses), and the model fails to assess the correspondence of the timing of the changes in outcomes to the changes in policy. Nevertheless, the implication that increases in the cost of abortion led to an increase in an outcome related to nonmarital fertility (that is, female-headed households) is not consistent with either model presented earlier or some previous research. Clearly more work is needed to understand how marriage, as well as fertility patterns by marital status, respond to changes in abortion policy.

Abortion and Selection

The legalization of abortion in the United States in the early 1970s led to a significant reduction in fertility, as reported in chapter 5. This means that a large number of children who otherwise would have been born were not, resulting in a birth cohort that was smaller than it would have been. There are two reasons why this reduction in the size of the birth cohort may have altered the outcomes of those children who were born relative to all of those who otherwise would have been born. First, smaller birth cohorts may have some advantages over larger birth cohorts. For instance, class sizes in school may be smaller, family sizes may be smaller, labor market outcomes may improve with less competition, and the like. Second, those children who were born may not have represented a random sample of all potential births. Those children who were aborted may have had differential outcomes had they been born compared to those who actually were born. Therefore, the characteristics of the birth cohort may have changed through this form of "selection" on who was born. It is not clear whether this selection would be "positive" or "negative." In other words, it is not clear a priori whether those children who were born were the ones with "better" or "worse" characteristics. The possibility of selection in either direction certainly exists.

Over the past decade or so, research has examined the possibility that abortion legalization altered the characteristics of those children born, and this research will be described here. As time has passed since the early 1970s and these children have aged, the outcomes that research can examine have expanded. We know more about their outcomes at younger ages because more time has been available to study them. For instance, more work has been able to examine the impact of abortion legalization on infant mortality since those children born in the early 1970s have lived much longer than a year. On the other hand, the adult outcomes for these children are just now being studied as the children born during that period are aging into adulthood. The discussion presented here will separately consider each of these outcomes, starting from those that occur at earlier ages and that we know more about and moving on to those at older ages where our knowledge is more limited.

Previous Evidence from Europe

Before moving on to a discussion of the impact of abortion legalization in the United States, I first review some earlier evidence available from Europe. The available evidence there is based on studies that followed children whose mothers had requested an abortion but whose requests were denied. The children born to these mothers therefore reflect those who otherwise would not have been born had abortion been available upon request. These studies generally obtain a comparison group of children, follow both groups over time, and compare outcomes. Any difference is attributed to the treatment of being born "unwanted," and any impact would be attributable to selection rather than cohort size since the number of children born under these circumstances is typically quite small.

These forms of quasi-experimental designs have been employed using data from members of the 1961 to 1963 birth cohort in Czechoslovakia and members of the 1939 to 1942 birth cohort in Sweden (Forssman and Thuwe 1971; David et al. 1988). Abortions were typically denied upon review of a psychiatric committee if the abortion would harm the mother's health, if the gestational age of the fetus was beyond some threshold, or if a previous abortion had been performed recently. An additional study compared members of the 1966 birth cohort in Finland ranked by their mother's reports of the extent to which the birth was wanted between the 24th and 28th week of pregnancy (David et al. 1988). In Sweden a birth that followed a denied abortion request was matched to the next birth that took place, a procedure that established treatment and control groups. In Czechoslovakia and Finland, the social and demographic characteristics of the child and family following a denied abortion or unwanted pregnancy were used to find a child with similar characteristics to use as a control group. In each case an extensive array of outcomes were compared between the two groups, including elements of social, emotional, and cognitive development, educational outcomes, criminal activity, and others.

Unfortunately, these methods do not establish comparison groups that are otherwise identical, lessening the importance of these studies. Moreover, the relatively small sizes of the samples included in these studies often made it difficult to obtain statistically significant differences between the two groups unless the difference was very large. Nevertheless, with these caveats in mind, we can still utilize these studies to learn something regarding the impact of being born under such circumstances.

These studies all found evidence indicating that children born as a result of unwanted pregnancies experienced significant disadvantages throughout their lives. Specifically with regard to the study in Prague, David et al. (1988) conclude, "All the differences noted were consistently in disfavor of the unwanted-pregnancy children. Over the years these differences widened and many that had not been statistically significant at age nine became so at age 16 or 21. While it is difficult to make individual predictions, there seems little doubt that, in the aggregate, unwantedness in early pregnancy has a not negligible effect on later development, influencing quality of life and casting a shadow on the next generation (21–22)."[2]

Abortion and Children's Well-Being in the United States

In the United States, considerable research has focused on the impact of changes in abortion access on infant health outcomes. It is largely based on some of the insights of Becker's (1981) work on the economics of fertility, which describes the trade-off between the number of children that a family has and the resources devoted to each child. Parents who have fewer children can spend more of their time and income on each of them. According to this view, the ability to limit family size to a desired level through contraception and the availability of abortion should enable families to improve the characteristics of those children born. This can be accomplished by, for instance, increasing prenatal care and exercising abortion to "select" healthier children.

Research in this area, which is summarized in table 8.1, has focused on the impact of changes in abortion access on neonatal and infant mortality (distinguished by a death in the first month or first year of life, respectively) along with the probability of low-birth weight. The first generation of research in this area used the geographic variation in the access to abortion (either the number of abortion providers or the abortion rate) to estimate abortion's impact on these outcomes (Grossman and Jacobowitz 1981; Corman and Grossman 1985; and Joyce 1987).[3] The evidence provided in these papers supports the notion that infant health improves with greater access to abortion. However, as I discussed in chapter 6 with regard to similar studies of the impact of changes in abortion access, the use of cross-sectional data in this context is troublesome because of the possibility that other factors associated with both infant health and abortion access may be correlated within a particular location. This makes it difficult to draw causal inferences from this sort of statistical analysis. In more recent work, Currie et al. (1996) have implemented methods that correct for this problem and find no impact of imposing a Medicaid funding restriction on children's birth weight.

One study, conducted by Gruber et al. (1999), has adopted quasi-experimental methods much like those described earlier in this book to examine the impact of abortion legalization on infant health (among other things, as described subsequently). Previously, I have provided evidence indicat-

TABLE 8.1.
Research Examining the Impact of Abortion Legalization on Children's Well-Being

Paper	*Outcome Measures*	*Measures of Access*	*Data*	*Methodology*	*Findings*
Corman and Grossman (1985)	neonatal mortality rate	number of abortion providers in county	1977 data from *Vital Statistics* and Alan Guttmacher Institute	Estimates the relationship between neonatal mortality rate in county and number of abortion providers in county.	Finds a negative relationship between neonatal mortality and number of abortion providers.
Grossman and Jacobowitz (1981)	neonatal mortality	average number of abortions in 1970–72 and whether abortion laws were liberalized in 1970	1970–72 *Vital Statistics* and Alan Guttmacher Institute	Estimates OLS models of the relationship between neonatal mortality rate in county and measures of abortion access.	Finds that both measures of abortion access are negatively correlated with neonatal mortality rate.
Joyce (1987)	neonatal mortality, birth weight, and gestational age	1976–78 average number of abortions in county	1976–78 *Vital Statistics* and Alan Guttmacher Institute	Estimates reduced form and structural models relating outcome measures to abortion rate.	Finds negative relationship between abortion rate and neonatal mortality rate that operates largely through abortion's effect on birth weight.
Currie et al. (1996)	birth weight	Medicaid funding restrictions	National Longitudinal Survey of Youth (1979)	Compares outcomes across states that have Medicaid funding restrictions in effect to those states in which policy has been enjoined by a court decision.	Finds no effect of restrictions on birth weight.
Gruber et al. (1999)	infant mortality, low birth weight, and child living arrangements	legal status of abortion	1980 U.S. Census	Uses difference-in-differences estimates based on timing of abortion legalization across states.	Abortion legalization led to a reduction in infant mortality, the percentage of children living in single-parent households, in a welfare household, and in poverty. There was no discernible impact on low birth weight.

ing that legalizing abortion in the early 1970s reduced births on the order of 5 to 10 percent. Those findings were obtained by comparing the difference in birth rates between states that legalized abortion in 1970 with a control group of states that did not, and then reversing the experiment in 1973 when those other states legalized abortion in response to the *Roe v. Wade* decision. This approach was illustrated in figure 5.1. The same approach can be used here with respect to the health outcomes of those children born in the two sets of states over this period.

When Gruber et al. implement this methodology, they find that abortion legalization did indeed lead to a significant reduction in infant mortality. These authors also derive methods to estimate what the infant mortality rate would have been for those children who were aborted following legalization relative to those who were born. They find that those children who otherwise would have been born were 40 percent more likely to die in the first year of life compared to those who were born. On the other hand, they find no evidence that abortion legalization had an impact on the likelihood that a child is born with low birth weight.

Gruber et al. (1999) also adopt a similar methodology and go on to explore the impact of abortion legalization on the subsequent living arrangements of children. The outcomes they consider are the likelihood that a child lives in a single-parent household, in a household headed by a welfare recipient, and whether the household is in poverty. To do this, they use data from the 1980 Census and compare these outcomes by the child's state and his or her age in 1980. Those children born between 1971 and 1973 would be 7 to 9 years old in 1980; these children represent those born at a time when abortion laws differed across states. Any difference that emerges in living arrangements between these children and children born earlier (i.e., those 10 or older in 1980) should disappear for children born following *Roe v. Wade* (i.e., those 6 or younger in 1980). This quasi-experimental approach mimics those adopted previously with regard to the impact of abortion legalization.

The results indicate that children's living circumstances were, in fact, affected by abortion legalization. Again, these authors also adopted methods that enabled them to compare the living circumstances of those children who were not born because abortion was legalized to those of the children who were born. They find that had these children been born, they would have been 60 percent more likely to live in a single-parent family, 50 percent more likely to live in poverty, and 45 percent more likely to live in a household headed by a welfare recipient.

One limitation of this strategy is that it is somewhat difficult to determine the extent to which any observed impact on children's outcomes is attributable to the reduction in cohort size or differential selection of the particular children who are born. Gruber et al. (1999) argue that their findings are largely driven by differential selection and not cohort size. They base this claim on the fact that their method focuses on the discrete changes in outcomes that occur across successive birth cohorts by state. To the extent that the reduction in cohort size improved the well-being of those children born, one would not expect such an effect to be discrete. For instance, if there are fewer 7-to-9 year olds in 1980 in some states, then children just older than that in those states would also be likely to benefit since more resources would be available within the household and the community to devote to them. This would lessen the effectiveness of the quasi-experimental design described earlier. Selection effects would only improve the well-being of those 7 to 9. Therefore, their ability to observe a treatment effect using this design is likely related to selection effects. Nevertheless, further research that addresses this claim more directly would be beneficial.

Abortion and Crime in the United States

The research presented so far shows that infant health, at least in the form of infant mortality, seems to improve when abortion access in enhanced. Children's living circumstances also seem to improve, but less research is available to confirm this conclusion. As the relevant birth-cohorts age, subsequent outcomes may also be addressed. Since these children were born in the early 1970s, the data necessary to assess infants' and children's outcomes have been available for some time. More recently, data has become available that has enabled some researchers to focus on adolescent outcomes. Young adult outcomes are still somewhat difficult to address because of data limitations. The relevant cohort is currently only about 30 years old, and there are often significant lags between the time when surveys are conducted and when they are made available for analysis.

The adolescent outcome that has received the most attention so far is that of crime. Criminal activity peaks for men in their late teens and early 20s, so any impact of abortion legalization on crime would have started taking place in the early 1990s. Donahue and Levitt (2001) use this premise in their research, which argues that legalizing abortion led to a significant decline in the crime rate. Evidence to this effect is presented in figure 8.4, which shows trends in the rate of violent and property crimes along with the murder rate since 1970. In all cases, the abortion rate rose through much of the 1980s and then began to decline around 1992, when those children affected by abortion legalization were in their late teens and early 20s.

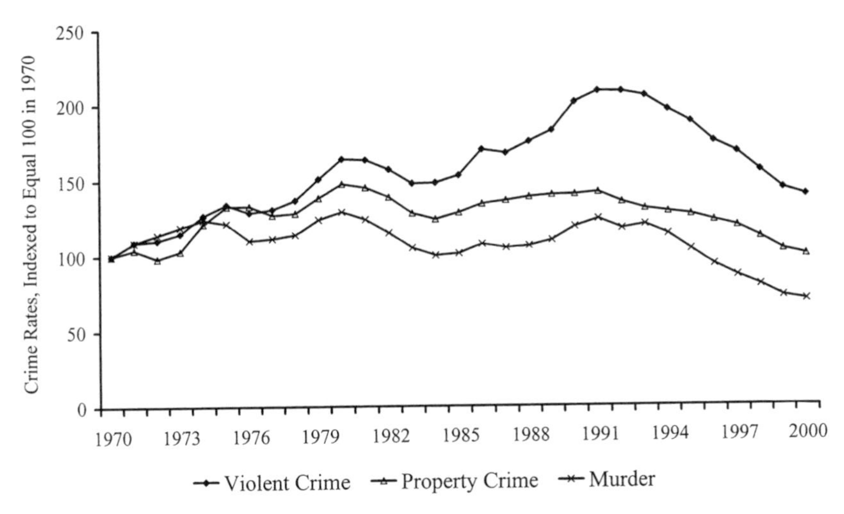

FIGURE 8.4. Trends in the United States Crime Rate, by Type of Crime. *Source*: Federal Bureau of Investigation (annual).

Donahue and Levitt provide a number of arguments supporting their hypothesis. Beyond the basic time-series trend presented in figure 8.4, they also argue that the crime rate in the five states legalizing abortion in 1970 (New York, California, Washington, Alaska, and Hawaii) began to fall earlier than that in the remainder of the country. They also show that the decrease in crime across states between 1985 and 1997 is correlated with the abortion rate in those states in the 1970s. Finally, these researchers examine the relationship between arrests by birth cohort and state with the abortion ratio (abortions as a fraction of births) in the arrestee's year of birth and state of residence. This approach is the closest to approximating the type of quasi-experiments that have been conducted in the past on related questions. In each case, Donahue and Levitt report that their results are consistent with the hypothesis that legalizing abortion reduced the crime rate. In fact, they argue that its legalization accounted for over half of the decline in crime.

The release of this study was met with a great deal of controversy, with considerable coverage in major news outlets as well as in academic circles. Critics pointed to ethical issues regarding the policy implications of the findings, while some economists highlighted methodological concerns regarding the analysis. The ethical questions are beyond the scope of this discussion, but limitations in the methodology that may call into question the accuracy of these findings are relevant here.

These limitations are expressed in Joyce (forthcoming), which is written as a response to the Donahue and Levitt paper. Joyce levies multiple methodological criticisms against Donahue and Levitt. First, he states that abortion data are not available for the period before abortion was legalized, so an analysis based upon changes in abortion rates that assigns a value of zero to those states and years in which abortion was illegal, as Donahue and Levitt do, imposes a great deal of measurement error into the analysis. Second, Joyce is concerned about the possibility that the crack epidemic, the timing of which varied across states, may have confounded Donahue and Levitt's analysis. Third, Joyce argues that much of the variation in the abortion ratio in each cohort's year of birth does not capture changes in the number of unwanted births that the Donahue and Levitt hypothesis requires. Specifically, since the increase in abortions in the aftermath of legalization may have resulted from additional pregnancies, it is not clear that unwanted births declined much in the middle and late 1970s. Instead, Joyce favors using the pure quasi-experimental exercise brought about by the law changes that are much more likely to have altered unwanted births. Joyce's analysis concludes that Donahue and Levitt's results are considerably overstated and, indeed, there may be no relationship at all between abortion and crime.

Donahue and Levitt (2003) have since written a rebuttal to Joyce arguing that his criticisms are misguided. Regarding measurement error, Donahue and Levitt argue that classic forms of measurement error introduce a downward bias in estimated effects, so the actual impact of abortion on crime would, in reality, be larger than they have estimated. Regarding the influence of crack, Donahue and Levitt indicate that the crack epidemic hit the repeal states of New York and California earlier and harder than the rest of the country, which would make it more difficult to find an impact of abortion and crime. Crack should have resulted in more crime in those states relative to the rest of the country during the period in which the early 1970s birth cohorts were coming of age. The fact that they are able to find an impact of abortion on crime despite this problem strengthens their findings, according to Donahue and Levitt. Finally, they argue that it is appropriate to use the variation in the abortion ratio across states through the late 1970s, rather than the pure quasi-experimental approach favored by Joyce, to assess the impact of abortion legalization. Abortion in repeal states was much more common throughout that period and represents the greater ability to reduce unwanted births in those states, according to these authors.

Based upon my reading of this literature, I believe the fundamental determinant of the strength of the original Donahue and Levitt study is the extent to which additional abortions in the middle and late 1970s led to more unwanted births. Since Donahue and Levitt's findings rely strongly on the variation across states in abortion in this period, their hypothesis that abortion reduces crime is empirically supported only if those additional abortions resulted in fewer unwanted births. Without a better understanding of the nature of those additional abortions, it is difficult to assess adequately the validity of the Donahue and Levitt hypothesis. Given the importance of this question, the controversy it has evoked, and the issues that remain regarding the true relationship between abortion and crime, additional study in this area is needed before we can draw firm conclusions.

Abortion and Subsequent Outcomes for Mothers

Beyond the impact of greater fertility control on children's well-being, the observed changes in childbearing in response to abortion legalization may have important implications for women's outcomes as well. A woman's fertility pattern over her childbearing years could alter her other life experiences. For instance, a woman who unintentionally becomes pregnant at, say, age 20 may choose to drop out of college if she were unable to abort the pregnancy. If that same birth could have occurred three years later, she may have graduated. Similarly, a 35-year-old woman who works and has two children already may choose to drop out of the labor market if an accidental pregnancy had to be carried to term. Although she may decide to re-enter the labor market at a later date, her subsequent career path may have been affected.

Abortion and Life Cycle Fertility

The fact that the introduction of legalized abortion led to an immediate drop in the birth rate does not necessarily indicate that women have fewer children over the rest of their childbearing years. If the births that did not occur were not "replaced" by additional births subsequently, then women would experience a net reduction in lifetime fertility. In this case, the short-run impacts on birth rates estimated in Levine et al. (1999) represent long-run reductions in birth rates and completed fertility. But the ability to better control one's fertility may have simply led women to delay births to a preferred date. In this case, abortion legalization would have no long-run affect on completed fertility. Obviously both could have occurred to some extent (i.e., the former for teens and the latter for older women), but the degree of the trade-off is unknown.

It is important to understand the extent to which each hypothesis is true because of their different implications for subsequent child outcomes. For instance, in response to the legalization of abortion, Gruber et al.

(1999) find improvements in child well-being and Donahue and Levitt (2001) report a reduction in crime when those children mature. One explanation for these findings is that those children who were born are differentially selected among those who would have been born if abortion had not been legal. But if births are just timed differently, then any selection effect would strongly depend upon whether children's outcomes are determined by the fixed characteristics of mothers or the age at which those mothers give birth. If it is the mother's fixed characteristics that matter, then the effects reported in Gruber et al. (1999) and Donahue and Levitt (2001) should diminish over time since the children those mothers would have had will eventually be born. If it is the age of the mother that matters, then even the delay will lead to lasting improvements in child well-being.

Analyses of the distinction between fertility timing and completed fertility can provide some insight. For example, much of the variation in birth rates over time in the United States, and particularly the baby boom and subsequent bust, is the result of changes in timing of births rather than changes in completed fertility (cf. Hotz et al. 1997). Differences in the timing of fertility across demographic groups over time can account for differences in their fertility patterns (cf. Chen and Morgan 1991; Rindfuss et al. 1996; Morgan et al. 1999; Martin 2000). In addition, some studies of the fertility process have found a key role of economic factors, and especially a woman's wage, in determining the timing of first birth (Heckman and Walker 1990; Hotz and Miller 1988). Heckman and Walker (1990), in particular, found that the strongest effects of economic variables were through the timing of first birth. But none of this work has carefully analyzed the direct impact of fertility control itself in this process. Unfortunately, no work of which I am aware has examined the impact of abortion legalization on both completed fertility and birth timing; this question deserves further study.

Abortion and Mother's Subsequent Outcomes

The ability to better control one's fertility may also affect other outcomes for women, including education and employment.[4] In fact, trends in educational and labor market outcomes over the past few decades, displayed in figure 8.5, are consistent with the proposition that the legalization of abortion helped propel women's educational and employment opportunities. Unfortunately, based on this evidence it is difficult to distinguish the impact of abortion legalization from other ongoing trends that may have started decades beforehand.

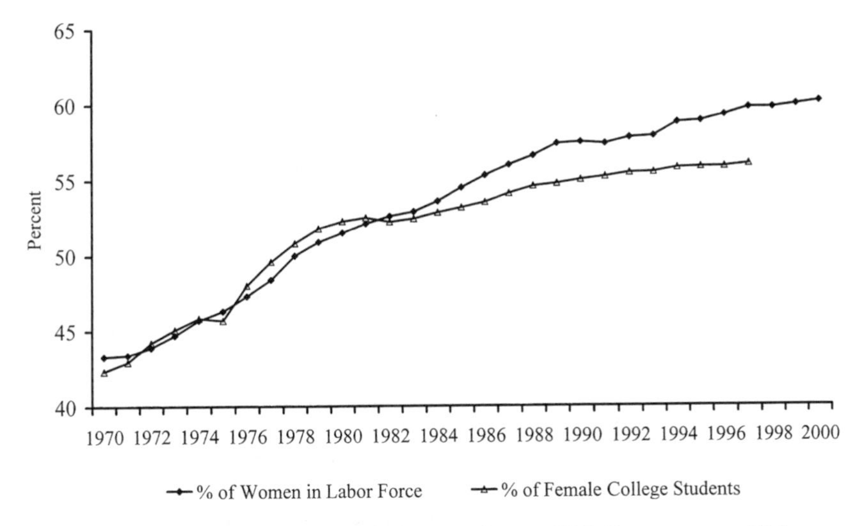

FIGURE 8.5. Trends in Women's Outcomes. *Source*: U.S. Department of Education (2001), and U.S. Bureau of Labor Statistics (2003).

Although little past research has attempted to estimate the impact of abortion legalization itself on women's subsequent outcomes, a great deal of work has focused on the impact of fertility more generally on these outcomes. This literature is plagued with problems of assessing causality. A careful test of this relationship would require exogenous variation in the ability to control one's own fertility and evidence that women's outcomes are altered in response to such changes. Previous research largely has not cleared this hurdle.

Much of this literature has focused on the relationship between teen and nonmarital childbearing on mothers' subsequent outcomes (cf. Maynard 1997; Wu and Wolfe 2001). But women who give birth, say, as teens have characteristics that may be very different from women who delay childbirth, and many of these differences are likely to be unobservable to the researcher. Although there have been some significant advances in this area in recent years (cf. Geronimus and Korenman 1992; Bronars and Grogger 1993; Hotz et al. 1997), it would be premature to draw any definitive conclusions based upon this evidence.

Only Angrist and Evans (1999) directly address the fertility control brought about by abortion legalization itself to examine the impact on subsequent outcomes for women. This study examines the influence of reduced teen fertility attributable to abortion legalization on educational outcomes and employment status of women. They find weak support for the notion that these outcomes are improved for black women when teen fertility is reduced as a result of legal abortion. But this work is limited to the role of childbearing as a teen rather than fertility patterns over the entire life cycle and examines only a subset of important outcomes for mothers. Additional work in this area is needed to settle this question.

Welfare and Abortion

Motivation

Prior to this chapter, this book has exclusively focused on the impact of abortion policy on fertility outcomes; so far this chapter has extended those outcomes to consider those for children and other outcomes for women. But other public policies clearly have the potential to affect these same outcomes through mechanisms similar to those presented here. For example, welfare generosity may influence abortion and other fertility decisions, which could then potentially alter any of the other outcomes considered in this book. I will therefore discuss what is known about the relationship between welfare and abortion here.

The linkage between welfare policy and abortion gained considerable prominence during the debates surrounding welfare reform legislation that was enacted in 1996. That law included social goals that went beyond direct measures of the self-sufficiency of potential welfare recipients. The goals were to:

> 1. Provide assistance to needy families so that children may be cared for in their own homes or in the homes of relatives;
> 2. End the dependence of needy parents on government benefits by promoting job preparation, work, and marriage;
> 3. Prevent and reduce the incidence of out-of-wedlock pregnancies and establish annual numerical goals for preventing and reducing the incidence of these pregnancies; and
> 4. Encourage the formation and maintenance of two-parent families. (U.S. House of Representatives, Committee on Ways and Means, 2000)

The promotion of marriage, marital fertility, and two-parent families has obvious implications for fertility outcomes. In fact, the law also provided bonuses to the states with the greatest reduction in the rate of nonmarital fertility with accompanying reductions in the abortion rate.

One feature of welfare reforms that states adopted in the 1990s that is particularly relevant here is a policy called the family cap. Prior to welfare reform, states provided benefits to eligible families that depended upon their family size; the larger the family, the larger the benefit. Some had criticized this feature of the program on the basis that it provided an incentive for welfare recipients to have additional children. As a result, states began to implement a family cap, which means that a recipient's benefit levels are not increased if they have an additional child while on welfare. Partly as a result of this provision, many pro-life advocates widely criticized welfare reform, anticipating an increase in abortions. For instance, then-Cardinal Bernard Law of Boston said, "[W]e deplore the loss of life that would ensue from increased abortions due to the allowance of child exclusion clauses (i.e., a family cap) in the states' implementation of this federal legislation" (McCoy 1996).

Welfare, Abortion, and Economic Theory

The controversy surrounding abortion and welfare reform in general, and the family cap in particular, does not necessarily follow from the predictions one would obtain from economic models of fertility, like those described in chapter 3. The standard economic model of abortion presented in that chapter, and represented in figures 3.1 and 3.2, indicate that births necessarily will decline with a reduction in welfare generosity. That model is adapted to examine this impact in figure 8.6. Recall from the earlier discussion that in this model women choose to abort or give birth once pregnant, depending upon which one costs less. Based on that decision, a level of contraceptive intensity is chosen to equate the lesser of these costs to the marginal cost of pregnancy avoidance (the additional cost brought about by reducing the likelihood of getting pregnant). In this model, a reduction in welfare generosity is incorporated as an increase in the cost of giving birth.

In figure 8.6, I show that if the cost of birth rises above the cost of an abortion (Case I), then the primary outcome will be a substitution of abortion for birth. There will be some increase in contraceptive intensity as well, but only up until the point where abortion becomes less costly than birth. Although this is consistent with the prediction that abortions will rise, this finding requires the cost of an unwanted birth to jump over the cost of an abortion. If the cost of birth rises, but does not exceed the cost of abortion, as in Case II, then there will be no impact on abortions. Births will still fall, but only through an increase in contraceptive intensity, which would result in fewer pregnancies. Therefore, the standard economic model of abortion indicates that a reduction in welfare generosity will reduce pregnancies and births, but may not have an impact on abortions.

On the other hand, the extended model of abortion that was also presented in chapter 3 suggests that it is unclear how the rate of abortions would respond to a reduction in welfare generosity. In that model, new information regarding the wantedness of a birth arrives after a woman becomes pregnant. One of its implications was that if abortion were sufficiently low in cost (i.e., below the cost of an unwanted birth), then some

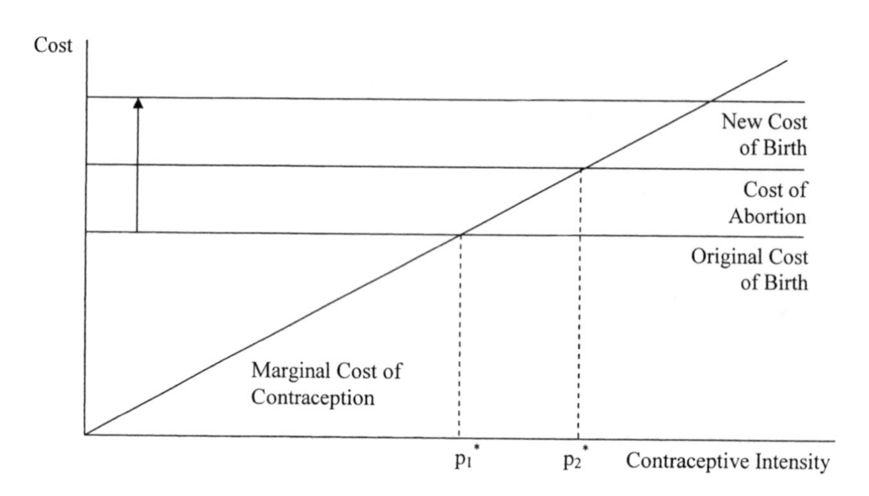

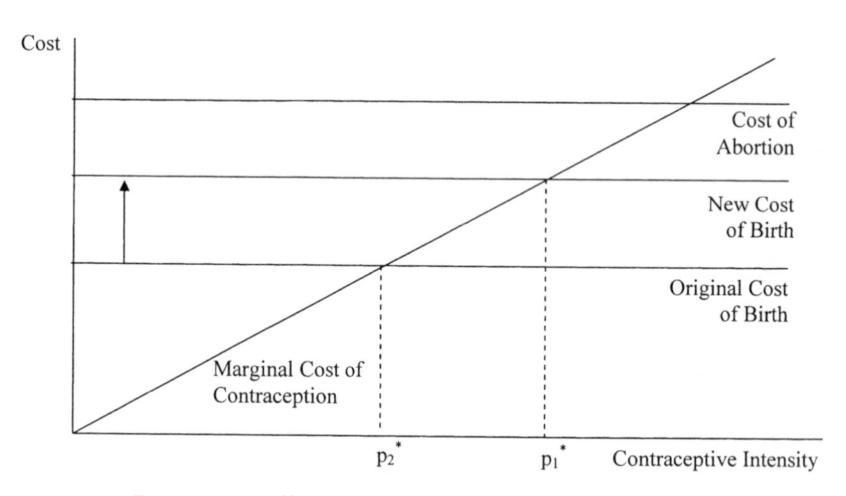

FIGURE 8.6. Effect of a Reduction in Welfare Generosity.

women may become pregnant to obtain the additional information that would be forthcoming at that point. She would then give birth if that information happened to be positive, but otherwise she would abort.

This model has offsetting predictions regarding the potential impact of a reduction in welfare generosity on abortions. In this model, women who become pregnant may now choose to abort rather than give birth in much the same way as they would in the standard model, so abortions may increase. On the other hand, the increased cost of giving birth brought about by a reduction in welfare generosity would also result in greater pregnancy avoidance and fewer pregnancies. But for some of those avoided pregnancies, negative information would have arrived had they occurred and those pregnancies would have resulted in an abortion. Those abortions no longer occur if welfare benefits are cut. Therefore, the overall impact on abortions depends upon which of these two offsetting effects is bigger; it is impossible to determine this a priori.

Therefore, the implications derived from economic models regarding the impact of a reduction in welfare generosity on abortion are unclear. In the standard model, abortions may either rise or remain unchanged. In the extended model, anything is possible depending on the magnitude of the offsetting effects that result. Either way, however, both have consistent predictions that pregnancies and births will fall in response.

Evidence

Despite the controversy regarding the potential impact of welfare reform on abortion and the theoretical ambiguity regarding its effect, little empirical evidence exists that can help us sort out this issue. The only studies of which I am aware that have focused specifically on welfare reform and abortion have been experimental in nature, with welfare recipients actually being assigned to control and treatment groups distinguished by whether or not they were subject to a family cap. These studies (Turturro et al. 1997; Camasso et al. 1999) were conducted in Arkansas and New Jersey in the early to mid-1990s. In both cases, the reported results suggested that abortions increased and pregnancies and births fell in response to the family cap.

Both studies have been subject to substantial criticism, however, that considerably lessens the impact of these findings (Kearney forthcoming). For instance, Loury (2000) reports that true random assignment was not practiced fully in the New Jersey experiment and that in both experiments many members of the control and treatment group did not know what policies applied to them. In addition, both analyses restricted their analysis to welfare recipients during a period in which welfare caseloads were falling rapidly. Therefore, it is difficult to tell if any observed effects are attributable to changes in fertility behavior or changes in welfare participation. Given the weaknesses inherent in these studies, it would be unwise to draw strong conclusions regarding the impact of welfare reform on abortions based on them.

Some past research has also examined the impact of welfare benefit levels on the incidence of abortion outside of the context of welfare reform. Klerman (1998) reviews this evidence but reports that many of these studies simply use the geographic variation in welfare benefits that occur at a point in time and relate that to the use of abortion. Such methods, as described previously in this book, are suspect because they do not account for long-standing and potentially unobserved differences across states that may also be related to both welfare generosity and the use of abortion. Among those studies that account for this problem (cf. Blank et al. 1996; Matthews et al. 1997), welfare benefit levels are not found to have a significant effect on abortion rates. Nevertheless, more evidence is needed here before we can draw strong conclusions.

Overall, our knowledge regarding the impact of welfare reform and welfare generosity is relatively limited. The theoretical ambiguity in predicting the impact of these changes in welfare policy makes it even more difficult to draw conclusions in this regard. Further research in this area would be very helpful.

Additional Topics

What can economic analysis tell us about some other controversial topics in abortion and fertility policy today? Here, I examine three issues: the introduction of RU-486 (Mifepristone), the prohibition of "partial birth abortion," and a comparison of abortion restrictions and improved contraceptive technology as methods to reduce unwanted pregnancies. Although economic models and empirical research have not advanced anywhere near the point where these topics can be addressed definitively, in this section I will provide some thoughts that may help inform the discussion somewhat.

The Impact of RU-486

A traditional abortion requires a woman to undergo an invasive surgical procedure that typically is performed in an advanced medical facility (usually an abortion clinic—see chapter 2). Although it is a very safe surgical procedure, it still can be physically difficult, requiring some time to recuperate, and may well be psychologically traumatic. More recently, an alternative to this procedure has become available that induces an abortion after taking a regiment of medications, which is referred to as a medical abortion. France was the first country to approve medical abortion in 1988 and the name of the drug was RU-486. Since then, the drug is still commonly referred to by that name, although currently its generic name is Mifepristone and its trade name is Mifeprex. As of September 2000, twenty-three countries have approved its use, including the United States (Jones and Henshaw 2002).

In the United States, Mifepristone may be used only to induce an abortion for pregnant women whose last menstrual period began no more than forty-nine days prior to taking the drug (U.S. Food and Drug Administration, Center for Drug Evaluation and Research, 2001). Therefore, medical abortions are available only for women who very recently became pregnant. The patient must go to a medical facility and take a dose of Mifepristone, which prevents the fertilized egg from attaching to the lining of the uterus. Two days later she must return to the facility and take another drug, Misoprostol, which stimulates uterine contractions and results in an outcome similar to a miscarriage. After about two weeks, the patient must return to her medical provider to confirm that the pregnancy has, indeed, been terminated. If not, surgical abortion may be recommended, although this option is relevant only in a small percentage of cases. The symptoms that result from this course of action include bleeding and cramping, which typically last from nine to sixteen days.

From the perspective of economics, the key question in determining what impact Mifepristone will have on fertility behavior is the cost of a medical abortion relative to that of a surgical one. The models presented earlier in this book provide a framework for evaluating how individuals would respond to a reduction in the cost of an abortion. Since we are considering the introduction of Mifepristone in a world in which abortion is generally available upon request (albeit with some restrictions), I will assume that a new, cheaper abortion procedure is likely to reduce the cost of abortion further below the cost of an unwanted birth for many women. I made a similar assumption earlier in the book regarding small changes in abortion costs brought about by abortion restrictions and found empirical support for this. Therefore, if medical abortion lowers the cost of abortion relative to that of a surgical procedure, then one would expect abortions to rise because pregnancies will rise as well; births will not go down.

This hypothesis is generated based on the assumption that medical abortion is less costly than a surgical abortion, but this proposition is not clear. Medical abortions do appear to offer certain advantages compared to surgical abortions that could be interpreted as a reduction in cost (recall that cost is used to represent all the negative aspects of the procedure and is not a monetary measure). One of the primary advantages to a medical abortion is the greater privacy that patients may feel. Trips to an abortion clinic may generate greater anxiety than to other medical providers, and part of the process of a medical abortion takes place at a woman's home. In addition, the procedure is less invasive and women who do not live close to an abortion provider may also benefit from this new alternative.

On the other hand, it does offer some disadvantages as well. The process can last perhaps two weeks, compared to a surgical abortion in which the process is completed very quickly. Besides the physical discomfort, this may cause greater emotional distress. It also requires three separate visits to the doctor rather than just one to a clinic. It is difficult to say a priori which procedure women view as less costly. Even for those women who view a medical abortion as less costly than a surgical one, it seems unlikely that the perceived cost reduction would be large. Thus, one might not necessarily expect the introduction of Mifepristone to have much of a behavioral effect at all.

It is too early to determine empirically the impact of Mifepristone in the United States since it was approved very recently. However, some evidence on the likelihood of its use is available for France, Great Britain, and Sweden (Jones and Henshaw 2002). In all locations, its use was reasonably uncommon soon after approval but has grown somewhat over time. In France and England / Wales only 8 and 11 percent of all abortions, respectively, are performed medically. In Sweden and Scotland its use is more common, representing 33 and 41 percent of all abortions, respectively.[5]

It is hard to say exactly what these statistics suggest regarding the impact of Mifepristone in the United States, but it is probably safe to conclude that its introduction does not represent a substantial methodological improvement in abortion procedures that would provide a significant cost savings to women.[6] Based on this limited evidence and the earlier discussion, I would conjecture that Mifepristone will not have much of a behavioral impact on the likelihood of pregnancies. But only the passage of time and further empirical inquiries will be able to validate this prediction.

"Partial Birth Abortion"

The debate regarding the abortion procedure that has been labeled partial birth abortion has been raging over the past several years. Legislation and legal battles at the state and federal levels about restricting it have taken place in much the same way as earlier fights over other abortion restrictions that have been addressed in this book, like Medicaid funding, parental involvement, and mandatory delay. A good deal of this book has been devoted to examining the impact of these earlier restrictions on women's behavior, so one might suspect that a similar analysis of partial birth abortion may be in order as well.

The term "partial birth abortion" is one that is not terribly well defined, but many relate it to the specific medical procedure known as intact dilation and extraction. This procedure is used only in abortions performed at relatively advanced stages of pregnancy. For example, a 1996 survey conducted by the Alan Guttmacher Institute of abortion providers indicates that the procedure is largely performed at gestations between 20 and 24 weeks (Henshaw 1998). Drawing upon provider responses regarding the frequency with which they perform this procedure, Henshaw concludes that about 650 of these procedures were conducted in 1996. The total number of abortions performed in 1996 was 1.4 million, and so partial birth abortion is extremely uncommon.[7]

Since the debate regarding restrictions on this procedure and their implementation has been so recent, it is impossible to conduct empirical examinations regarding their impact on individual behavior. Nevertheless, an economic model may indicate that restrictions on this one particular method of abortion would have little identifiable behavioral impact. The reason is that the procedure is so uncommon and takes place at such a late stage of gestation that it is difficult to believe that any change in its availability would have much influence on calculations regarding pregnancy, birth, or abortion. Economic models require women to incorporate various outcomes, along with the probability that they are likely to occur, in making decisions regarding these outcomes. The probability that she would get to a place where a so-called partial birth abortion would be necessary is so low that a ban on its availability would have a negligible impact on those calculations. Although this debate still has an important philosophical component that may deserve attention, economics does not have anything to contribute to it.

Abortion versus Contraception

In all of the analyses conducted so far in this book, contraceptive technology has been assumed to be fixed in theoretical models or held constant in statistical models. One of the conclusions resulting from these analyses is that relatively minor restrictions on abortion access within a legal abortion environment may lead to a reduction in pregnancies and abortions. The next chapter will provide a framework for evaluating the merits of using abortion policy to accomplish this goal. But if one sought to reduce these outcomes, a relevant question would be the relative value of doing so by imposing restrictions on abortion access or by other means, like improving contraceptive technology (which may include new methods, better distribution of existing methods, or greater education regarding the use and availability of existing methods).

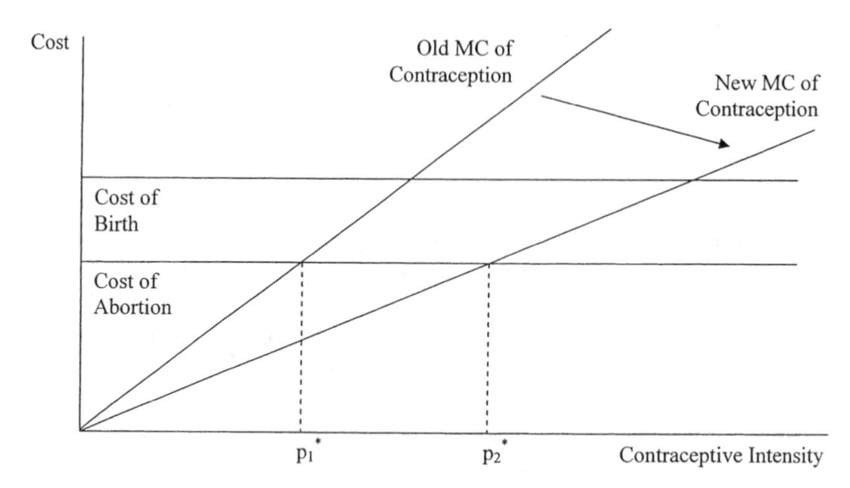

FIGURE 8.7. Effect of Improved Contraceptive Technology.

The models I have presented to examine the impact of changes in abortion costs can easily be modified to evaluate the impact of changes in contraceptive technology. In an economic model, improvements in contraceptive technology can be characterized by a reduction in the marginal cost of contraception. Recall that the marginal cost of contraception represents the increase in the cost of contraception brought about by reducing the likelihood of pregnancy by one percent. If the techniques available to avoid pregnancy improve, then we can characterize this by a reduction in the increment in cost associated with the same reduction in the likelihood of a pregnancy. This is just another way to say that the marginal cost of pregnancy avoidance declines with improved contraceptive technology. It becomes easier to avoid pregnancy with a given amount of effort.

Recall that in the standard model of abortion presented in chapter 3, women chose a level of contraceptive intensity at the point where its marginal cost just equals the cost of an unwanted birth or the cost of an abortion, whichever is lower. For present purposes I will assume that the cost of abortion is lower. In this framework, an improvement in contraceptive technology that reduces the marginal cost of contraception will increase the level of contraceptive intensity, reducing the likelihood of a pregnancy and an abortion. This implication can be seen in figure 8.7, where the fact that the marginal cost curve is now flatter reflects the improvement in technology. In this model, the impact of an improvement in contraceptive technology is the same as an increase in abortion costs.[8]

The question then becomes to what extent does the empirical evidence support these theoretical assertions. As I have shown in this book, the evidence indicates that the imposition of relatively minor abortion restrictions reduces the likelihood of abortions and pregnancies. To assess the impact of this approach relative to the impact of improving contraceptive technology would require empirical evidence on the latter. Such a review would need to evaluate the entire body of research, taking into consideration the methodological strengths and weaknesses of each piece, and to determine the extent to which strong conclusions can be drawn from it. If the conclusions are limited by the strength of the evidence, calls for additional research may be required. The scope of such a project is beyond that of this book, leaving unanswered the question of the relative efficacy of restricting abortion or improving contraception technology in order to reduce pregnancies. This topic is another one for which subsequent research would be beneficial.

Chapter Nine

SUMMARY AND IMPLICATIONS FOR ABORTION POLICY

THIS BOOK has investigated the impact of abortion policy on abortion, birth, and pregnancy along with other outcomes. In chapter 3, I presented successive theoretical economic models that build in complexity and address the potential impact of policy changes. The results of these models, along with the assumptions made there, indicate that restrictions on abortion access of different severity levels may have different effects on fertility outcomes. When very restrictive policies are relaxed, like those associated with abortion legalization, the main effect is a reduction in unwanted births brought about by an increase in the frequency of abortion. Pregnancies may increase as well, but this may be secondary in nature. On the other hand, when these policies are relaxed further, like making abortion available upon request with few restrictions, these models predict that abortions will increase more, but births are unlikely to fall further in response, and may even rise. The increase in abortions with no decrease in births requires an increase in pregnancies, which is predicted to occur in this situation.

The intuition for these findings can be summarized by thinking about abortion availability as a form of insurance against an unwanted birth. When an abortion is very costly, a woman will choose to have an unwanted birth rather than have an abortion if she becomes pregnant. If its cost falls, the greater access will enable women to abort that pregnancy, protecting them from the downside risk of having a child that they do not want. But if its cost continues to fall further so that abortion is available at relatively little cost (in all dimensions—not just monetarily), then the primary impact will be on the likelihood of pregnancy. Couples will take fewer steps to avoid a pregnancy since these activities are costly as well, and may become more costly than an abortion.

Much of the remainder of the book was devoted to describing the methods that have been used to test these hypotheses and to summarize the results of empirical tests of them. I described the quasi-experimental methods that have been applied to examine these issues extensively over the past decade or so. These methods use policy changes to create pseudo-treatment and control groups that can be compared over time to arrive at causal estimates of the impact of the change. Although there are limitations to this approach, it represents a significant methodological improvement over past work. Used appropriately, these methods can provide a suitable assessment of the impact of policy changes on individual behavior.

These quasi-experimental methods were employed extensively to investigate the impact of abortion legalization and of subsequent changes in abortion access in the United States along with the impact of changes in abortion policy in Eastern Europe. The results of these analyses generally support the hypotheses generated from the economic models. In the United States, abortion legalization was found to lead to a reasonably large reduction in (presumably) unwanted births. Ignoring the potential role of mobility between states in which abortion was legal and states in which it was not in the early 1970s, the results suggest that the birth rate fell by about 5 percent when a state legalized abortion. Incorporating that mobility—by comparing legal states with far away states in which abortion was illegal—suggested that births fell by perhaps 10 percent in response.

Once abortion was legalized in the United States, subsequent changes focused on imposing moderate restrictions on abortion access through policies like Medicaid funding restrictions, parental involvement laws, and mandatory delay laws. In addition, abortion access has also been reduced through a slow decline in the availability of abortion providers over time. The evidence supports the proposition that pregnancies are the outcome most directly affected by these changes. Each type of restriction on access appears to reduce abortion demand without increasing the number of births. This means that contraceptive use must respond positively or sexual activity negatively to the imposition of a moderate restriction; limited evidence directly supports this proposition regarding the use of contraception.

Eastern Europe also provided a valuable laboratory in which to examine the impact of changes in abortion policies since many of the countries have done so over the past two decades. These policy changes were wide-ranging, encompassing the full spectrum from outlawed abortion to abortion available upon request with little restriction. I reported an empirical investigation of three different broad categories of abortion policies and the changes among them that some countries experienced. These categories included abortion available upon request, abortion available for broad medical and / or social reasons with prior approval, and abortion available only in very limited circumstances like a serious health issue. As in the United States, the results of those analyses indicated that abortion legalization significantly reduced the birth rate. Moving from a regime with moderate abortion restrictions to one in which abortion was available upon request did not have any discernible effect on births, however.

Yet abortions did increase, suggesting that pregnancies had to have risen as well in response to relaxing the abortion laws. Overall, the available evidence from both the United States and Eastern Europe is generally consistent with the predictions of the economic models.

Although our knowledge regarding the impact of abortion policy has grown considerably over the past decade or so, there still remain a number of unresolved questions like those described in chapter 8. In that chapter, I detailed a number of issues that have received some attention in past analyses, but not enough to draw firm conclusions. Those issues largely involved the impact of changes in the legal status of abortion on outcomes for children and mothers that may result from the observed impact on fertility. The fact that legalized abortion was shown to reduce the number of births combined with the proposition that it is doubtful that those births represent a random draw of the population suggests that this policy change may have altered the characteristics of the cohort of children that were born. To date, empirical evidence has shown that infant mortality and children's living circumstances were improved by the legalization of abortion. But controversy exists about the impact on crime, and no work has been conducted so far that examines other outcomes for young adults.

The women who were better able to control their fertility may also have been able to alter other outcomes in their life as a result. Marriage, fertility over the rest of their childbearing years, and educational and career options may have changed for them. Although some work has begun to investigate issues like these, more work needs to be done here.

Implications

What can we learn from these results regarding the design of governmental policy toward abortion? This fundamental question crosses the line between a positive and normative analysis. As I described in chapter 1, economists make a distinction between positive questions that inquire about "what is" and normative questions that ask "what should be." As a field, we are much better equipped to address positive questions rather than normative ones. This entire book up until this point has almost exclusively restricted its attention to positive analysis. In this section I will discuss some of the issues that economic analysis can bring to bear on a normative discussion of abortion policy.

The Private Cost of Abortion

The starting point for this analysis is to make a distinction between the impacts of a particular type of abortion policy on women compared to that for others in society. Abortion policy obviously has implications for women, and changes in those policies may influence their private decision making and alter the private costs that they face. Before extending the discussion to the broader societal impact, it makes sense first to clarify what these private costs are.

Throughout this book, women are assumed to make decisions to maximize their own well-being subject to the constraints facing them. They are always doing what is best for them given the available options to choose from. Within this framework, in virtually all of the analyses provided, less restrictive abortion policy improves their well-being. If abortion policy is very restrictive, say illegal, then a woman is subject to a considerable cost if an unintentional pregnancy occurs and she is forced to choose between an unwanted birth or a costly illegal abortion. Lessening that restriction, through legalization, significantly lowers that cost, and more women may choose to abort rather than give birth. Despite the costs that are incurred from the abortion, they are less than that of the unwanted birth. If not, there would be no abortion.

Further reductions in the cost of abortion continue to improve women's well-being. Economic models suggest that reducing its cost to very low levels may lead some women to substitute abortion for contraception. This is beneficial to them in these models because contraception is costly as well, and they would switch only if abortion were less costly. Moreover, in the extended economic model of abortion presented in chapter 3, greater abortion access provides an additional benefit. If its cost becomes sufficiently low, women can take advantage of the option of becoming pregnant in order to obtain additional information regarding the value of giving birth. This leads some women to receive positive information and have a wanted birth when she would not even had become pregnant otherwise. Even if the information received would lead her to abort the pregnancy, the uncertainty in the process would be reduced for her, which provides some value. In both ways, the information is valuable, and it is the availability of low cost abortion that enables her to receive it.

Not all economic models, however, would support the notion that women are better off when abortion policy becomes less restrictive. In particular, the work of Akerlof et al. (1996) that was described in chapter 8 provides exactly the opposite conclusion. In one of their models, women compete in a marketplace to enter into relationships; a less restrictive abortion policy places those women who are less willing to enter into premarital sexual relationships at a competitive disadvantage. In another model, less restrictive abortion policies reduce women's bargaining power in these relationships, reducing the likelihood that a father will support a child, either financially or through marriage, if a pregnancy results. In both cases, women's well-being diminishes when abortion access improves through a process that these authors label "female immiseration." Although these ideas are intriguing, they have not withstood substantive empirical testing that could validate them. Therefore, the remainder of this discussion will continue to treat abortion availability as if it provides private benefits to women themselves.

Externalities

Based on this discussion, if the only relevant party in an abortion was the woman herself, then economic analysis is clear that it should be provided as readily as possible. The economic reasoning is similar to any other transaction that takes place in a market. Transactions take place only if they benefit all the parties involved, so any restriction imposed upon them can only be harmful. A fully efficient market outcome would be attained if abortion providers were able to operate freely and charge women a market price to obtain their services. No government intervention would be desirable, which also means no subsidies should be available.

In general, economists believe it is appropriate for government to intervene in the marketplace only if there is some form of "market failure." The relevant form of possible market failure here is that of an "externality." With an externality the costs and benefits born by a private individual from undertaking an activity are not the only ones imposed upon society. There may be social costs and benefits that are associated with the activity as well that go beyond those faced by the individual.

The classic example of an externality is pollution. Firms that pollute are imposing a cost on society of which they themselves face only a small part. Although the owners of a polluting firm have to breathe in bad air, which they find costly, they do so because they get to profit from selling goods using less expensive methods of production. Everyone else around the plant, however, has to breathe in the pollution as well, and they do not get to share in the profits. The owners of the firm do not directly face this cost to others and are unlikely to incorporate fully its value in making production decisions, and so "too much" pollution is likely to result. The socially optimal amount would result if the firm incorporated all of the social cost in its decision making, not just its own private cost. In such circumstances, government intervention can improve the outcome over what results in private markets that are allowed to operate freely.

Pollution is an example of what is called a negative externality since its production imposes a cost on society. Positive externalities also may exist, however; education is one example. Education clearly provides private benefits to individuals who attend school. Students value the knowledge they acquire, the friends they make, and the higher earnings they are likely to receive later in life. In a private marketplace, schools would exist that would offer educational services and students would purchase those services. But an individual's decision to obtain more education would ignore the societal impact of his / her decision. A more educated population can foster innovation, advance the electoral process, improve public health, and the like, all of which help society as a whole beyond just the private returns. Without government intervention, individual decision makers weighing just their own returns from obtaining more education ignore these societal impacts and choose less education than society would like. Therefore, government intervention to subsidize education is both desirable and common.

The Externalities Associated with Abortion

Suppose that abortion is strictly a private decision and, regardless of what a woman decides, it would have no impact on others in any way. The greater use of abortion services does impose some external social cost in the form of medical services that are diverted to this use rather than others, but these costs are relatively small and can easily be ignored for our purposes. If there is no externality, abortion should be unrestricted. Women get the advantage of reducing the cost of avoiding an unwanted birth, reducing the cost of contraception, and of obtaining the additional information that presents itself between conception and the abortion decision; no one would be hurt by this.

On the other hand, one can easily imagine that abortion generates externalities that may be either positive or negative. In fact, one can even imbed the traditional debate regarding abortion policy within the framework of externalities. For those who believe life begins at conception and, therefore, philosophically object to abortion, those procedures that take place impose a negative externality on them and, perhaps more importantly, on the unborn children. Similarly for those who believe that a woman has the right to control her own fertility, offering women unrestricted abortion access provides these supporters with a positive externality. In the remainder of this section, however, I will omit further discussion of these arguments since the analysis would quickly devolve back into a face-off between traditional views in a different package. Instead, I will focus on the externalities generated by the behavioral effects that result from changes in abortion policy.

First consider the externalities associated with legalizing abortion. The main behavioral impact of abortion legalization is likely to be the reduction in unwanted births, which the empirical evidence suggests is substantial. One would suspect that this generates a positive externality if society faces costs associated with an unwanted birth beyond those experienced by mothers. These costs may include things like medical expenses, expenditures on social services, the well-being of subsequent generations, and others. Some evidence to this effect was presented in chapter 8. Presumably this is at least part of the reason that there is so much of an emphasis on teen pregnancy prevention in public policy. Legalizing abortion could generate some negative externalities as well, since it may lower the adoption rate. Those families who are unable to conceive and would have been able to benefit from adoption will face more difficulty doing so. Although this effect is certainly important, it is hard to imagine that it would outweigh the positive externalities associated with legal abortion along with the benefits that parents themselves would reap from avoiding unwanted births.

The externalities associated with relaxing moderate restrictions on abortion access are less concrete. The main reason for this is that the evidence does not support the view that such restrictions reduce unwanted births; the externalities associated with that are irrelevant here. The main behavioral impact brought about by relaxing such restrictions is that more pregnancies will occur that will result in abortions. To what extent do these additional pregnancies result in an externality? It is not clear that they do. If there is no externality, then such restrictions should not be imposed because women benefit from the lower cost of contraception and from the additional information they may be able to obtain before making fertility decisions.

This issue provides another example where the relationship between abortion and insurance break down. As I described in chapter 3, standard forms of insurance result in excessive losses because its availability alters individuals' willingness to take risks and this greater risk-taking has negative externalities. In those applications, standard solutions like copayments and deductibles can counteract this. Regarding abortion, one could think of relatively minor restrictions on abortion access as a form of copayment that could reduce the abortion rate. But it is not clear that a copayment in this instance would be in society's best interest because of the difficulty in evaluating the externality associated with additional abortions.

Although the precise form of an externality is difficult to identify, it could be related to public discontent associated with the use of abortion as a form of contraception. Results from opinion polls indicating that the majority of Americans support legal abortion, but only in limited circumstances, may reflect this sentiment. In the presence of a negative externality, the cost to society brought about by relaxing moderate abortion restrictions would have to be incorporated along with the benefits women receive in determining whether such restrictions are desirable.

Final Thoughts

This book began by claiming that the abortion debate has hit a roadblock. The same arguments are made repeatedly by entrenched combatants in an unproductive process that has largely taken an important issue of public policy off the table of public discussion. Regardless of the merits of the philosophical points made in this debate, an alternative framework for thinking about the problem is required if we are ever going to make any progress toward moving past the present impasse.

Although I am not presumptuous enough to assume that the contribution of this book will help lead to that breakthrough, it does offer another approach to thinking about abortion policy. That approach is based on economic reasoning and empirical analysis that is designed to understand better the behavioral implications that abortion policies generate. Those who strongly hold pro-life or pro-choice positions would be unlikely to change their thinking based on this alternative perspective. But for others, they may find it helpful to understand the impact of different types of abortion policies on individual behavior.

The analysis presented here has direct implications for public discussion of abortion policy. Economic models tell us that we should not necessarily expect abortion legalization and relaxing moderate abortion restrictions to have the same type of impact on fertility outcomes. Empirical evidence supports this view. Abortion legalization reduces unwanted births, but subsequent increases in abortion access largely result in more abortions through more pregnancies, with no identifiable decline in unwanted births. Therefore, those who favor liberal abortion policies on the grounds that they prevent unwanted births find mixed support for their position. Broadly legal abortion accomplishes this goal, but relaxing moderate abortion restrictions does not appear to do so.

This does not necessarily imply that such restrictions should be endorsed. Women themselves are still best served by as much freedom as possible in their decision making, and so imposing restrictions would require their actions to have some detrimental effect on society more broadly. Even if such an impact could be supported, one could still oppose restrictions that target one group over another (poor women or minors, for instance) on the grounds that these policies are inequitable. However, the results of this analysis significantly weaken one of the primary arguments against such restrictions.

NOTES

CHAPTER TWO
ABORTION LAW AND PRACTICE

1. The level of detail provided was chosen to portray sufficiently those changes in the legal environment that are necessary for the subsequent analysis. But it is important to recognize that the brevity of this discussion glosses over relevant subtleties of the historical development. For those interested in more detail, Garrow (1994) provides a thorough discussion of these issues; much of this discussion is based on his work.

2. The decision states, "The Constitution does not explicitly mention any right of privacy." It continues, "This right of privacy . . . is broad enough to encompass a woman's decision whether or not to terminate her pregnancy" (Garrow 1994, pp. 590–91).

3. A few states have legal provisions that require minors to be provided counseling before obtaining an abortion, and in this book I will consider these restrictions on minors' access to abortion in conjunction with these parental notification or consent provisions.

4. This statement is not quite correct for two reasons. First, the rate of spontaneous abortion, or miscarriage, may change as well. If a pregnant woman aborts a pregnancy that would have otherwise led to a miscarriage, then these pregnancy outcomes would be substitutes, not abortions and births. Since miscarriages are more likely to occur earlier in a pregnancy than an abortion, I will assume that this problem is relatively small and ignore it here. In addition, a woman who aborts has the ability to get pregnant again within a few months and could give birth anyway, so that the abortion and birth would not be substitutes. Again, I will assume that the likelihood of these events is relatively small and ignore it here as well.

5. These dollar figures are all reported as of 1992. If charges for an abortion rose at the same level as all other consumer prices between 1992 and the present (July 2003), every dollar figure reported should be inflated by a factor of about 1.31.

6. The variation in prices charged among the different forms of nonhospital settings is not large, and so the hospital/nonhospital distinction is the relevant one to make.

7. The distance calculation uses the latitude and longitude of the population center of each county and the latitude and longitude of the population center of the closest county with an abortion provider. These coordinates are used to calculate the distance between the two locations "as the crow flies." The underlying data on counties in which abortion providers are located were graciously provided to me by Lawrence Finer and Stanley Henshaw at the Alan Guttmacher Institute.

8. The problem is similar to that which labor economists have addressed regarding unemployment statistics. At a point in time, most unemployment spells are relatively long in nature. But most individuals who become unemployed spend considerably less time looking for work. The reason is that those individuals who

have long unemployment spells accumulate in the pool of unemployed at a point in time. In a cross-sectional survey they are over-represented.

9. See Saad (2002) for an overview of some of this evidence.

CHAPTER THREE
ECONOMIC MODELS OF FERTILITY AND ABORTION

1. For early examples, see Becker (1960, 1965, 1981), Becker and Lewis (1973), Willis (1973), and Schultz (1973). Montgomery and Trussel (1986) provide a survey of early work in this area.

2. For recent examples, see Hotz and Miller (1988), Heckman and Walker (1990), Rindfuss, Morgan and Offutt (1996), and Staiger and Wilwerding (1999).

3. For recent examples, see Leibowitz (1990), Whittington, Alm, and Peters (1990), Chou and Staiger (1997), and Dickert-Conlin and Chandra (1999).

4. See the discussion in Becker (1981), chapter 5.

5. See, for example, Becker (1981), Hotz and Miller (1988), and Joyce (1987).

6. See Santelli et al. (2003) for a detailed discussion of this terminology and the strengths and weaknesses of our ability to measure them.

7. Students of economics should recognize that this is exactly the same logic used in any form of "marginal analysis" like that which leads a firm to choose a level of output where price equals marginal cost.

8. Research that has incorporated models like this include Kane and Staiger (1996), Akerlof et al. (1996), and Levine and Staiger (forthcoming).

CHAPTER FOUR
METHODS FOR EVALUATING THE IMPACT OF POLICY CHANGES

1. A more detailed description of the "panel-data methods" that are described here is available in Ashenfelter et al. (2003).

CHAPTER FIVE
THE IMPACT OF ABORTION LEGALIZATION

1. Interestingly, no papers of which I am aware followed this approach in response to the *Roe v. Wade* decision; all focused on earlier legalization laws.

2. In the terminology used in table 2.2, this includes both "court" states and "control states." Court states are included as the comparison group because it is unclear whether there was any practical significance of the lower court decisions in those states and because preliminary analyses suggest that they had no impact on fertility behavior.

3. Angrist and Evans (1999) similarly find that teens' exposure to a legal abortion environment significantly reduced their fertility.

4. Specifically, they were obtained from regression models that included the share of women aged 15 to 19, 20 to 24, and 25 to 34 among women of childbearing age, the share of the state population that is nonwhite, per capita income, the crime rate, and the insured unemployment rate in each state and year, state and year fixed effects, and state-specific linear trends.

5. All findings reported here are statistically significant at least at the 10 percent level (for nonmarital births) and generally at a level much smaller than that.

6. These distances are determined by comparing the population center of each of the Roe states with that of the states legalizing abortion early. They are computed using the latitude and longitude of each of these locations and represent the distance "as the crow flies."

7. This discussion follows the analysis reported in Levine et al. (1999).

8. To see this, consider again the graphical exercise reported in figure 5.1. The initial treatment effect in that picture represents the drop in the difference in abortion rates when abortion is legalized in one set of states but remains illegal in other states. The second treatment effect, which is assumed to be of the same magnitude, represents the impact of legalization in the rest of the country. The estimates from this analysis suggest that the size of both of these effects is 4.1 percent. But now suppose that we are in a world where abortion is legal everywhere (i.e., at the right hand side of this picture). Suppose further that abortion was made illegal in some set of states. This is equivalent to moving into the middle region of this figure. The treatment effect associated with this change would still be 4.1 percent, except in the opposite direction. In other words, births in Roe states (which are still defined here to be the those states that did not legalize abortion until the *Roe v. Wade* decision) would rise, reducing the magnitude of the gap between states by 4.1 percent.

9. Some research has also been conducted evaluating the impact of abortion legalization on maternal mortality as well. Having a risky, illegal abortion that may result in the death of the mother certainly reflects the behavior of women whose pregnancies would have resulted in an unwanted birth. Dow and Ronan (1998) utilized a quasi-experimental framework to evaluate the impact of abortion policy on maternal mortality and came up with mixed results. When they compared death rates of women of childbearing age between repeal and nonrepeal states, they did not find evidence supporting a causal reduction in maternal mortality brought about by abortion legalization. But they continued their analysis using changes in the ratio of female-to-male mortality, where male mortality is designed to control for other factors related to the health care system in each state. In those specifications, they find that abortion legalization did reduce female mortality (relative to that of men).

10. New data collection efforts began in the mid-1990s, and so more recent adoption data is available. See Stolley (1993) for a detailed accounting of the availability of adoption statistics.

11. Marianne Bitler graciously provided the adoption data so that I could undertake this task.

12. Moreover, the definitions of repeal states are somewhat different; I impose the definition used throughout the analysis reported here in that New York, California, Washington, Alaska, and Hawaii are defined to be the states that legalized abortion prior to the *Roe* decision, all doing so in 1970. Bitler and Zavodny also define Vermont and New Jersey to be repeal states in 1972 in response to court decisions in those states. Statistics from the Center for Disease Control do not indicate that many abortions were conducted in these states in 1972 (U.S. Department of Health, Education, and Welfare, Centers for Disease Control, 1974), so

I do not classify them that way here. I also include in both regression models the same set of control variables used to generate the results in table 5.2 (see the notes to that table).

13. The impact reported here for white births is considerably greater than that reported in table 5.2 and the discrepancy is largely attributable to the different sample of states/years included in the data.

14. The samples are nonrepresentative in that they over-sample women in certain demographic groups (race and age) as well as certain geographic regions, but sampling weights are provided to correct for this.

15. The respondents' state of residence, which is required to categorize women by their states' repeal status, is not available for public-use versions of these data. Therefore, I am not able to share the data used for this analysis with others. Researchers can access this information, however, by visiting the National Center for Health Statistics and conducting the analysis in their Research Data Center.

16. For instance, the impact on the differential in births in the 1970–72 period is only statistically significant when I impose the restriction that the differential in the 1975–80 period is equal to that in the 1965–69 period. Similarly, the increase in the differential in pregnancies in the 1975–80 period is only significant when I impose the restriction that the differential is constant between 1965–75. The increase in the differential in abortions in the 1970–72 period, as well as in subsequent periods, is statistically significant when no restrictions are imposed. See table A.1 for more details.

CHAPTER SIX
THE IMPACT OF RESTRICTIONS ON ABORTION ACCESS

1. Singh (1986) also examines birthrates and pregnancy rates for adolescent women using cross-sectional data from 1980, but reports complete results only for black teen women.

2. Medoff (1988) recognizes the potential endogeneity between abortion demand and price, estimating his model using two-stage least squares. The first stage equation that predicts the price of abortion includes the number of abortion providers, however.

3. Interestingly, Trussell et al. dismiss this possibility out-of-hand, stating: "Other choices theoretically available to women denied access to Medicaid-funded abortions were avoiding intercourse or improving their contraceptive practice. We believe that neither of these options was of practical significance during the course of the study" (121).

4. In Levine (2003) I also include indicators of Medicaid funding restrictions in my analysis, but little variation in that policy is observed over the sample period examined there.

5. Gruber (1996) reports that the fraction of women of childbearing age that are eligible for Medicaid increased from about 20 percent in 1985 to 45 percent in 1992. The increase is attributed to changes in eligibility standards over this period.

6. Data is also available from AGI by state of residence, but these data are available for fewer years and some assumptions are required for its use, as described in Levine (2003).

7. Levine (2001) also estimated the impact of parental notification laws on sexual activity and contraceptive use drawing upon data from the Youth Risk Behavior Surveillance (YRBS) over the 1991–97 period, but found little impact. A potential explanation for this discrepancy is that the YRBS samples only a subset of the states, and over that sample period only five states (Iowa, Maryland, Mississippi, North Carolina, and Pennsylvania) instituted a parental involvement law and had data both before and after the law change.

8. See Levine et al. (1996) for more details regarding the data used to construct these figures.

9. I am grateful to Ted Joyce for providing me with the data necessary to recreate their figures.

10. I am grateful to Doug Staiger for providing me with the data necessary to re-create their figures.

CHAPTER SEVEN
ABORTION POLICY IN AN INTERNATIONAL PERSPECTIVE

1. The countries that used to comprise the former Yugoslavia are not included in this analysis because of limited data availability and because of the conditions of war that persisted over much of this region in the 1990s. The data sources used to generate the descriptions of international abortion laws include: Childbirth by Choice Trust (1995), David (1999), Henshaw (1990), International Planned Parenthood Federation (1997), Muldoon (1991), Norgren (2001), Rahman et al. (1998), Sachdev (1988), Tietze and Henshaw (1986), and United Nations (1992, 1994, 1995, 1999).

2. These categories, along with the current placement of countries into them, are taken from Alan Guttmacher Institute (1999). Some countries with restrictive abortion policies provide exceptions for cases like rape/incest or fetal defects; such exceptions are noted in the brief description of the policy in the table.

3. Coelen and McIntyre (1978) also investigate the impact of abortion legalization in Hungary over this period and find that fertility responds strongly to such changes.

4. Yugoslavia and the German Democratic Republic did not allow abortion to be available upon request until 1969 and 1972, respectively.

5. In 1987, the abortion rate in Canada and the United States stood at about 11 and 27 abortions per 1,000 women of childbearing age, respectively. In 1995, the comparable values were 16 and 22.

CHAPTER EIGHT
UNFINISHED BUSINESS

1. Lundberg and Plotnick (1990 and 1995) estimate models of all outcomes leading to premarital childbearing, including the decision to marry, as a function of welfare generosity, abortion policy, and other factors. In their empirical models,

however, they explicitly leave out the abortion policy measures from the estimating equation for marriage.

2. Apparently, however, in more recent data, the differences between children of unwanted pregnancies and their controls at age 30 are somewhat smaller than that at younger ages (Kubicka et al. 1995).

3. Grossman and Joyce (1990) is similar to these papers in that it is part of the literature on "health production functions," which tries to relate inputs like prenatal care to outputs like birth weight. In this paper, abortion access is used as a means to control for the selectivity of who gives birth, but its relationship to birth outcomes is never directly estimated.

4. Goldin and Katz (2002) assess similar issues regarding the introduction of the birth control pill.

5. These statistics are generated from two separate statistics reported in Jones and Henshaw (2002). These authors indicate the percentage of "early abortions" (i.e., those eligible for Mifepristone) that are performed medically as well as the percentage of all abortions that are early abortions. The product of these two statistics is the percentage of all abortions that are performed medically, and this is what I have reported here.

6. In contrast, note that within five years of the introduction of the birth control pill, Goldin and Katz (2002) report that 40 percent of all married women under age 30 who were using contraception were using that method.

7. Apparently there is some dispute regarding Henshaw's estimate, however, as a simple search of the internet would uncover. Alternatively, the Alan Guttmacher Institute (1997) also reports that in 1992 only about 15,000 abortions were performed between 20 and 24 weeks of gestation out of the 1.5 million abortions performed that year. This may serve as an extreme upper bound on the frequency of this procedure and still indicates that it is uncommon. In general, late-term abortions are uncommon (Alan Guttmacher Institute 1997). The number of abortions performed at 20 weeks or more of gestation was 16,450 and the number performed at 16 or more weeks of gestation was 76,490 in 1992.

8. One should also note that the level of contraceptive technology does not affect the implications drawn earlier regarding the model's predicted impact on behavior brought about by restrictions on abortion access. Although the specific values of p^* would be different, all of the qualitative predictions made in chapter 3 regarding the impact of a reduction in the cost of an abortion continue to hold.

REFERENCES

Abma, Joyce C., William D. Mosher, and Linda J. Piccinino. 1997. "Fertility, Family Planning, and Women's Health: New Data From the 1995 National Survey of Family Growth." *Vital and Health Statistics* 23 (19).

Akerlof, George A., Janet L. Yellen, and Michael L. Katz. 1996. "An Analysis of Out-of-Wedlock Childbearing in the United States." *Quarterly Journal of Economics* 111 (2): 277–317.

Alan Guttmacher Institute. 1989. *An Analysis of Pre-1973 State Laws on Abortion.* Mimeo.

———. 1997. *Issues in Brief: The Limitations of U.S. Statistics on Abortion.* New York: Alan Guttmacher Institute.

———. 1999. *Sharing Responsibility: Women, Society, and Abortion Worldwide.* New York: Alan Guttmacher Institute.

Althaus, Frances A., and Stanley K. Henshaw. 1994. "The Effects of Mandatory Delay Laws on Abortion Patients and Providers." *Family Planning Perspectives* 26 (5): 228–33.

Angrist, Joshua D., and William N. Evans. 1999. "Teen Fertility, Schooling, and Labor Market Consequences of the 1970 State Abortion Reforms." *Research in Labor Economics* 18: 75–114.

Ashenfelter, Orley, Phillip B. Levine, and David J. Zimmerman. 2003. *Statistics and Econometrics: Methods and Applications.* New York: Wiley.

Baban, Adriana. 1999. "Romania." In *From Abortion to Contraception: A Resource to Public Policies and Reproductive Behavior in Central and Eastern Europe from 1917 to the Present*, edited by Henry P. David. Westport, Conn.: Greenwood.

Bachu, Amara. 1999. "Trends in Premarital Childbearing, 1930 to 1994." *Current Population Reports*, P23–197.

Bankole, Akinrinola, Susheela Sing, and Taylor Haas. 1998. "Reasons Why Women Have Induced Abortions: Evidence from 27 Countries." *International Family Planning Perspectives* 24 (3): 117–27, 152.

Bauman, Karl E., Ann E. Anderson, Jean L. Freeman, and Gary G. Koch. 1977. "Legal Abortions, Subsidized Family Planning Services, and the U.S. Birth Dearth." *Social Biology* 24: 183–91.

Becker, Gary S. 1960. "An Economic Analysis of Fertility." In *Demographic and Economic Change in Developed Countries: A Conference of the Universities-National Bureau Committee for Economic Research.* Princeton: Princeton University Press.

———. 1965. "A Theory of the Allocation of Time." *Economic Journal* 75 (299): 493–517.

———. 1981. *A Treatise on the Family.* Cambridge, MA: Harvard University Press.

Becker, Gary S., and H. Gregg Lewis. 1973. "On the Interaction between Quantity and Quality of Children." *Journal of Political Economy* 81 (2): S279-S288.

Besley, Timothy, and Anne Case. 2000. "Unnatural Experiments? Estimating the Incidence of Endogenous Policies." *Economic Journal* 110 (467): F672–94.

Bitler, Marianne, and Madeline Zavodny. 2001. "The Effect of Abortion Restrictions on the Timing of Abortions." *Journal of Health Economics* 20 (6): 1011–32.

———. 2002. "Did Abortion Legalization Reduce the Number of Unwanted Children? Evidence from Adoptions." *Perspectives on Sexual and Reproductive Health* 34 (1): 25–33.

Blank, Rebecca, Christine George, and Rebecca London. 1996. "State Abortion Rates: The Impact of Policies, Providers, Politics, Demographics, and Economic Environment." *Journal of Health Economics* 15 (5): 513–53.

Bronars, Stephen, and Jeffrey Grogger. 1993. "The Socioeconomic Consequences of Teenage Childbearing: Results from a Natural Experiment." *Family Planning Perspectives* 25 (4): 156–61, 174.

Burtless, Gary. 1995. "The Case for Randomized Field Trials in Economic and Policy Research." *The Journal of Economic Perspectives* 9 (2): 63–84.

Calderone, Mary Steichen, ed. 1958. *Abortion in the United States*. New York: Hoeber-Harper.

Camasso, Michael, Carol Harvey, Radha Jagannathan, and Mark Killingsworth. 1999. "New Jersey's Family Cap and Family Size Decisions: Some Findings from a 5-Year Evaluation." Rutgers University. Mimeo.

Cartoof, V. G., and L. V. Klerman. 1986. "Parental Consent for Abortion: Impact of the Massachusetts Law." *American Journal of Public Health* 76 (4): 397–400.

Chen, Renbao, and S. Philip Morgan. 1991. "Recent Trends in the Timing of First Births in the United States." *Demography* 28 (4): 513–33.

Childbirth by Choice Trust. 1995. *Abortion in Law, History, and Religion*. Toronto, Canada: Childbirth by Choice Trust.

Chou, Y. J., and D. Staiger. 1997. "Fertility and the Cost of Having a Child: Can the Government Influence Fertility through Incentives?" Dartmouth College. Mimeo.

Coelen, Stephen P., and Robert J. McIntyre. 1978. "An Econometric Model of Pronatalist and Abortion Policies." *Journal of Political Economy* 86 (6): 1077–101.

Commission on Presidential Debates. *Debate Transcripts: 2000 Debates*. Retrieved September 5, 2002, from http://www.debates.org/pages/trans2000a.html.

Cook, Philip J., Allan M. Parnell, Michael J. Moore, and Deanna Pagnini. 1999. "The Effects of Short-Term Variation in Abortion Funding on Pregnancy Outcomes." *Journal of Health Economics* 18 (2): 241–58.

Corman, Hope, and Michael Grossman. 1985. "Determinants of Neonatal Mortality Rates in the U.S.: A Reduced Form Model." *Journal of Health Economics* 4 (3): 213–36.

Currie, Janet, Lucia Nixon, and Nancy Cole. 1996. "Restrictions on Medicaid Funding of Abortion: Effects of Birth Weight and Pregnancy Resolutions." *Journal of Human Resources* 31 (1): 159–88.

David, Henry P. 1999. *From Abortion to Contraception: A Resource to Public Policies and Reproductive Behavior in Central and Eastern Europe from 1917 to the Present*. Westport, Conn.: Greenwood.

David, Henry P., Zdeněk Dytrych, Zdeněk Matějček, and Vratislave Schüller. 1988. "The Prague Cohort: Adolescence and Early Adulthood." In *Born Unwanted: Developmental Effects of Denied Abortion*, edited by Henry P. David. New York: Springer.

Deyak, Timothy A., and V. Kerry Smith. 1976. "The Economic Value of Statute Reform: The Case of Liberalized Abortion." *Journal of Political Economy* 94 (1): 83–99.

Dickert-Conlin, Stacy, and Amitabh Chandra. 1999. "Taxes and the Timing of Births." *Journal of Political Economy* 107 (1): 161–77.

Donahue, John J., III, and Steven D. Levitt. 2001. "The Impact of Legalized Abortion on Crime." *Quarterly Journal of Economics* 141 (2): 379–420.

Donahue, John J., III, and Steven D. Levitt. 2003. "Further Evidence that Legalized Abortion Lowered Crime: A Reply to Joyce." National Bureau of Economic Research, Working Paper No. 9532. Cambridge, Mass.: NBER.

Dorbritz, Jürgen and Jochen Fleischhacker. 1999. "The Former German Democratic Republic." In *From Abortion to Contraception: A Resource to Public Policies and Reproductive Behavior in Central and Eastern Europe from 1917 to the Present*, edited by Henry P. David. Westport, Conn.: Greenwood.

Dow, William H., and Nick Ronan. 1998. "Maternal Mortality Effects of Abortion Legalization." University of North Carolina, Chapel Hill. Mimeo.

Ellertson, Charlotte. 1997. "Mandatory Parental Involvement in Minors' Abortions: Effects of the Laws in Minnesota, Missouri, and Indiana." *American Journal of Public Health* 87 (8): 1367–74.

Finer, Lawrence B. and Stanley K. Henshaw. 2003. "Abortion Incidence and Services in the United States." *Perspectives on Sexual and Reproductive Health* 35 (1): 6–15.

Forssman, Hans and Inga Thuwe. 1971. "One Hundred and Twenty Children Born after Application for Therapeutic Abortion Refused." In *Abortion and the Unwanted Child*, edited by Carl Reiterman. New York: Springer.

Frejka, Tomas. 1983. "Induced Abortion and Fertility: A Quarter Century of Experience in Eastern Europe." *Population and Development Review* 9 (3): 494–520.

Gallup Organization. *Poll Topics and Trends: Abortion*. Retrieved March 3, 2003, from www.gallup.com/poll/topics/abortion.asp

Garbacz, Christopher. 1990. "Abortion Demand." *Population Research and Policy Review* 9: 151–60.

Garrow, David J. 1994. *Liberty and Sexuality: The Right to Privacy and the Making of Roe v. Wade*. New York: Macmillan.

Geronimus, Arline T., and Sanders Korenman. 1992. "The Socioeconomic Consequences of Teen Childbearing Reconsidered." *Quarterly Journal of Economics* 107 (4): 1187–214.

Gohmann, Stephen F., and Robert L. Ohsfeldt. 1994. "The Dependent Tax Exemption, Abortion Availability, and U.S. Fertility Rates." *Population Research and Policy Review* 13 (4): 367–81.

Goldin, Claudia, and Lawrence F. Katz. 2002. "The Power of the Pill: Oral Contraceptives and Women's Career and Marriage Decisions." *Journal of Political Economy* 110 (4): 730–70.

Grossman, Michael, and Steven Jacobowitz. 1981. "Variations in Infant Mortality Rates among Counties of the United States: The Roles of Public Policies and Programs," *Demography* 18 (4): 695–713.

Grossman, Michael, and Theodore Joyce. 1990. "Unobservables, Pregnancy Resolutions, and Birth Weight Production Functions in New York City." *Journal of Political Economy* 98 (5): 983–1007.

Gruber, Jonathan. 1996. "Health Insurance for Poor Women and Children in the U.S.: Lessons from the Past Decade." National Bureau of Economic Research Working Paper No. 5831, Cambridge, Mass.: NBER.

Gruber, Jonathan, Phillip B. Levine, and Douglas Staiger. 1999. "Abortion Legalization and Child Living Circumstances: Who is the 'Marginal Child?' " *Quarterly Journal of Economics* 114 (1): 263–92.

Haas-Wilson, Deborah. 1996. "The Impact of State Abortion Restrictions on Minors' Demand for Abortions." *Journal of Human Resources* 31 (1): 140–58.

———. 1997. "Women's Reproductive Choices: The Impact of Medicaid Funding Restrictions." *Family Planning Perspectives* 29 (5): 228–33.

Heckman, James J., and Jeffrey A. Smith. 1995. "Assessing the Case for Social Experiments." *The Journal of Economic Perspectives* 9 (2): 85–110.

Heckman, James J. and James R. Walker. 1990. "The Relationship between Wages and Income and the Timing and Spacing of Births: Evidence from Swedish Longitudinal Data." *Econometrica* 58 (6): 1411–41.

Henshaw, Stanley K. 1990. "Induced Abortion: A World Review, 1990." *Family Planning Perspectives* 22 (2): 76–89.

———. 1995a. "Factors Hindering Access to Abortion Services." *Family Planning Perspectives* 27 (2): 54–59, 87.

———. 1995b. "The Impact of Requirements for Parental Consent on Minors' Abortions in Mississippi." *Family Planning Perspectives* 27 (3): 120–22.

———. 1998. "Abortion Incidence and Services in the United States." *Family Planning Perspectives* 30 (6): 263–270, 287.

———. 2001. "*U.S. Teenage Pregnancy Statistics: With Comparative Statistics for Women Aged 20–24.*" New York: Alan Guttmacher Institute.

Henshaw, Stanley K., and Dina J. Feivelson. 2000. "Teenage Abortion and Pregnancy Statistics by State." *Family Planning Perspectives* 32 (6): 272–280.

Henshaw, Stanley K., and Jennifer Van Vort. 1990. "Abortion Services in the United States, 1987 and 1988." *Family Planning Perspectives* 22 (3): 102–108, 142.

Hotz, V. Joseph, Susan Williams McElroy, and Seth G. Sanders. 1997. "The Impacts of Teenage Childbearing on the Mothers and the Consequences of Those Impacts for Government." In *Kids Having Kids: Economic Costs and Social Consequences of Teen Pregnancy*, edited by Rebecca A. Maynard. Washington, D.C.: Urban Institute Press, 55–94.

Hotz, V. Joseph, and Robert A. Miller. 1988. "An Empirical Analysis of Life Cycle Fertility and Female Labor Supply." *Econometrica* 56 (1): 91–119.

International Planned Parenthood Federation. 1997. *Abortion Legislation in Europe*. London: International Planned Parenthood Federation European Network (February).

Jones, Rachel K., Jacqueline E. Darroch, and Stanley Henshaw. 2002a. "Patterns in the Socioeconomic Characteristics of Women Obtaining Abortions in 2000–2001." *Perspectives on Sexual and Reproductive Health* 34 (5): 226–235.

———. 2002b. "Contraceptive Use among U.S. Women Having Abortions." *Perspectives on Sexual and Reproductive Health* 34 (6): 294–303.

Jones, Rachel K., and Stanley K. Henshaw. 2002. "Mifepristone for Early Medical Abortion: Experiences in France, Great Britain, and Sweden." *Perspectives on Sexual and Reproductive Health* 34 (3): 154–61.

Joyce, Theodore. 1987. "The Impact of Induced Abortion on Black and White Birth Outcomes in the United States." *Demography* 24 (2): 229–44.

———. 1988. "The Social and Economic Correlates of Pregnancy Resolution among Adolescents in New York City, by Race and Ethnicity: A Multivariate Analysis." *American Journal of Public Health* 78 (6): 626–31.

———. Forthcoming. "Did Legalized Abortion Lower Crime?" *Journal of Human Resources*.

Joyce, Theodore, Stanley K. Henshaw, and J. D. Skatrud. 1997. "The Impact of Mississippi's Mandatory Delay Law on Abortions and Births." *Journal of the American Medical Association* 278 (8): 653–58.

Joyce, Theodore, and Robert Kaestner. 1996. "State Reproductive Policies and Adolescent Pregnancy Resolution: The Case of Parental Involvement Laws." *Journal of Health Economics* 15 (5): 579–607.

Joyce, Theodore J., and Naci H. Mocan. 1990. "The Impact of Legalized Abortion on Adolescent Childbearing in New York City." *American Journal of Public Health* 80 (3): 273–78.

Kane, Thomas, and Douglas Staiger. 1996. "Teen Motherhood and Abortion Access." *Quarterly Journal of Economics* 111 (2): 467–506.

Kearney, Melissa Schettini. Forthcoming. "Is There an Effect of Incremental Welfare Benefits on Fertility Behavior? A Look at the Family Cap." *Journal of Human Resources*.

Klerman, Jacob Alex. 1998. "Welfare Reform and Abortion." In *Welfare, the Family, and Reproductive Behavior: Research Perspectives*, edited by Robert A. Moffitt. Washington, D.C.: National Academy Press.

Kubicka, L., Z. Matejcek, H. P. David, Z. Dytrych, W. B. Miller, and Z. Roth. 1995. "Children from Unwanted Pregnancies in Prague, Czech Republic, Revisited at Age 30." *Acta Psychiatrica Scandinavica* 91: 361–69.

Leibowitz, Arlene. 1990. "The Response of Births to Changes in Health Care Costs." *Journal of Human Resources* 25 (4): 697–711.

Levine, Phillip B. 2001. "The Sexual Activity and Birth Control Use of American Teenagers." In *An Economic Analysis of Risky Behavior among Youths*, edited by Jonathan Gruber. Chicago: University of Chicago Press.

———. 2003. "Parental Involvement Laws and Fertility Behavior." *Journal of Health Economics* 22(5): 861–78.

Levine, Phillip B., and Douglas Staiger. Forthcoming. "Abortion Policy and Fertility Outcomes: The Eastern European Experience." *Journal of Law and Economics.*

Levine, Phillip B., Douglas Staiger, Thomas J. Kane, and David J. Zimmerman. 1999. "*Roe v. Wade* and American Fertility." *American Journal of Public Health* 89 (2): 199–203.

Levine, Phillip B., Amy B. Trainor, and David J. Zimmerman. 1996. "The Effects of Medicaid Abortion Funding Restrictions on Abortions, Pregnancies, and Births." *Journal of Health Economics* 15 (5): 555–78.

Lichter, Daniel T., Diane K. McLaughlin, and David C. Ribar. 1998. "State Abortion Policy, Geographic Access to Abortion Providers and Changing Family Formation." *Family Planning Perspectives* 30 (6): 281–87.

Loury, Glenn C. 2000. "Preventing Subsequent Births to Welfare Recipients." In *Preventing Subsequent Births to Welfare Recipients*, edited by Douglas J. Besharov and Peter Germanis. College Park: School of Public Affairs, University of Maryland.

Luker, Kristin. 1997. *Dubious Conceptions: The Politics of Teenage Pregnancy.* Cambridge: Harvard University Press.

Lundberg, Shelly, and Robert D. Plotnick. 1990. "Effects of State Welfare, Abortion, and Family Planning Policies on Premarital Childbearing among White Adolescents." *Family Planning Perspectives* 22 (6): 246–51.

———. 1995. "Adolescent Premarital Childbearing: Do Economic Incentives Matter?" *Journal of Labor Economics* 13 (2): 177–200.

Martin, Steven P. 2000. "Diverging Fertility among U.S. Women Who Delay Childbearing Past Age 30." *Demography* 37 (4): 523–33.

Martin, Joyce A., Brady E. Hamilton, Stephanie J. Ventura, Fay Menacker, and Melissa M. Park. 2002a. "Births: Final Data for 2000." *National Vital Statistics Reports* 50 (5).

Martin, Joyce A., Brady E. Hamilton, Stephanie J. Ventura, Fay Menacker, Melissa M. Park, and Paul D. Sutton. 2002b. "Births: Final Data for 2001." *National Vital Statistics Reports* 51 (2).

Matthews, Stephen, David Ribar, and Mark Wilhelm. 1997. "The Effects of Economic Conditions and Access to Reproductive Health Services on State Abortion and Birthrates." *Family Planning Perspectives.* 29 (2): 52–50.

Maynard, Rebecca A., ed. 1997. *Kids Having Kids: Economic Costs and Social Consequences of Teen Pregnancy.* Washington, D.C.: Urban Institute Press.

McCoy, James. 1996. "Welfare Reform in the Light of Catholic Social Teaching." *Catholic World News* (August 19).

Medoff, Marshall H. 1988. "An Economic Analysis of the Demand for Abortion." *Economic Inquiry* 36 (3): 353–59.

Merz, Jon F., Catherine A. Jackson, and Jacob A. Klerman. 1995. "A Review of Abortion Policy: Legality, Medicaid Funding, and Parental Involvement, 1967–1994." Rand Labor and Population Program, Working Paper No. 95–14.

Meyer, Bruce D. 1995. "Natural and Quasi-Experiments in Economics." *Journal of Business and Economic Statistics* 13 (2): 151–62.

Moffitt, Robert A. 1998. "The Effect of Welfare on Marriage and the Family." In *Welfare, the Family, and Reproductive Behavior: Research Perspectives*, edited by Robert A. Moffitt. Washington, D.C.: National Academy Press.

Montgomery, Mark, and James Trussell. 1986. "Models of Marital Status and Childbearing." In *Handbook of Labor Economics*, edited by Orley Ashenfelter and Richard Layard. Amsterdam: North-Holland.

Moore, Kristin A., and Steven B. Caldwell. 1977. "The Effect of Government Policies on Out-of-Wedlock Sex and Pregnancy." *Family Planning Perspectives* 9 (4): 164–69.

Morgan, S. Philip, Nikolai Botev, and Renbao Chen. 1999. "White and Nonwhite Trends in First Birth Timing: Comparisons Using Vital Registration and Current Population Surveys." *Population Research and Policy Review* 18 (4): 339–56.

Muldoon, Maureen. 1991. *The Abortion Debate in the United States and Canada: A Source Book*. New York: Garland.

Norgren, Tiana. 2001. *Abortion before Birth Control: The Politics of Reproduction in Postwar Japan*. Princeton: Princeton University Press.

Ohsfeldt, Robert L., and Stephan F. Gohmann. 1994. "Do Parental Involvement Laws Reduce Adolescent Abortion Rates?" *Contemporary Economic Policy* 12 (1): 65–76.

Posner, Richard A. 1992. *Sex and Reason*. Cambridge: Harvard University Press.

Potts, M., P. Diggory, and J. Peel. 1977. *Abortion*. New York: Cambridge University Press.

Quick, J. D. 1978. "Liberalized Abortion in Oregon: Effects on Fertility, Prematurity, Fetal Death, and Infant Death." *American Journal of Public Health* 68 (10): 1003–8.

Rahman, Anika, Laura Katzive, and Stanley K. Henshaw. 1998. "A Global Review of Laws on Induced Abortion, 1985–1997." *International Family Planning Perspectives* 24 (2): 56–64.

Rindfuss, Ronald R., S. Philip Morgan, and Kate Offutt. 1996. "Education and the Changing Age Pattern of American Fertility: 1963–1989." *Demography* 33 (3): 277–90.

Rogers, James L., Robert F. Boruch, George B. Stoms, and Dorothy DeMoya. 1991. "Impact of the Minnesota Parental Notification Law on Abortion and Birth." *American Journal of Public Health* 81 (3): 294–98.

Rothstein, Donna. 1992. "An Economic Approach to Abortion Demand." *The American Economist* 36 (1): 53–64.

Saad, Lydia. 2002. *Gallup Poll Special Reports: Public Opinion about Abortion—An In-Depth Review*. Washington, D.C.: The Gallup Organization.

Sachdev, Paul, ed. 1988. *International Handbook on Abortion*. Westport, Conn.: Greenwood.

Santelli, John, Roger Rochat, Kendra Hatfield-Timajchy, Brenda Colley Gilbert, Kathryn Curtis, Rebecca Cabral, Jennifer S. Hirsch, Laura Schieve, and other members of the Unintended Pregnancy Working Group. 2003. "The Measurement and Meaning of Unintended Pregnancies." *Perspectives on Sexual and Reproductive Health* 35 (2): 94–101.

Schultz, T. P. 1973. "A Preliminary Survey of The Economic Analysis of Fertility." *American Economic Review* 63 (2): 71–78.

Shelton, James D., Edward Brann, and Kenneth Schultz. 1976. "Abortion Utilization: Does Travel Distance Matter?" *Family Planning Perspective* 8 (6): 260–62.

Singh, Susheela. 1986. "Adolescent Pregnancy in the United States: An Interstate Analysis." *Family Planning Perspectives* 18 (5): 210–20.

Sklar, June, and Beth Berkov. 1974. "Abortion, Illegitimacy, and the American Birthrate." *Science* 185: 909–15.

Staiger, Douglas and Jonathan Wilwerding. 1999. "Is Teen Childbearing a Rational Choice?" Dartmouth College. Mimeo.

Stolley, Kathy S. 1993. "Statistics on Adoption in the United States." *The Future of Children* 3 (1): 26–42.

Tietze, Christopher. 1973. "Two Years Experience with a Liberal Abortion Law: Its Impact on Fertility Trends in New York City." *Family Planning Perspectives* 5 (1): 36–41.

———. 1975. "The Effect of Legalization of Abortion on Population Growth and Public Health." *Family Planning Perspectives* 7 (3): 123–27.

———. 1984. "The Public Health Effects of Legal Abortion in the United States." Family Planning Perspectives 16 (1): 26–28.

Tietze, Christopher, and Stanley Henshaw. 1986. *Induced Abortion: A World Review 1986*. New York: Alan Guttmacher Institute.

Titkow, Anna. 1999. "Poland." In *From Abortion to Contraception: A Resource to Public Policies and Reproductive Behavior in Central and Eastern Europe from 1917 to the Present,* edited by Henry P. David. Westport, Conn.: Greenwood.

Trussell, James T., Jane Menken, Barbara L. Lindheim, and Barbara Vaugh. 1980. "The Impact of Restricting Medicaid Funding for Abortion." *Family Planning Perspectives* 12 (3): 120–30.

Turturro, Carolyn, Brent Benda, and Howard Turney. 1997. *Arkansas Welfare Waiver Demonstration Project. Final Report*. Little Rock: University of Arkansas, School of Social Work.

United Nations, Population Division, Department of Economic and Social Affairs. 1992. *Abortion Policies: A Global Review. Volume 1: Afghanistan to France.* New York: United Nations.

———. 1994. *Abortion Policies: A Global Review. Volume 2: Gabon to Norway.* New York: United Nations.

———. 1995. *Abortion Policies: A Global Review. Volume 3: Oman to Zimbabwe*. New York: United Nations.

———. 1999. *World Abortion Policies 1999*. New York: United Nations.

U.S. Bureau of the Census. Various years. *Vital Statistics of the United States.* Washington, D.C.: U.S. Government Printing Office.

U.S. Centers for Disease Control and Prevention. 2002 "Abortion Surveillance—United States, 1998." *Morbidity and Mortality Weekly Report* 51 (SS-3).

U.S. Department of Education. 2001. *Digest of Education Statistics*. Washington, D.C.: U.S. Government Printing Office.

U.S. Department of Health, Education, and Welfare, Public Health Service, Center for Disease Control. 1971. *Family Planning Evaluation: Abortion Surveillance*

Report—Legal Abortions, United States, Annual Summary 1970. Washington, D.C.: U.S. Government Printing Office.

———. 1972. *Family Planning Evaluation: Abortion Surveillance Report—Legal Abortions, United States, Annual Summary 1971*. Washington, D.C.: U.S. Government Printing Office.

———. 1974. *Abortion Surveillance: Annual Summary 1972*. Washington, D.C.: U.S. Government Printing Office.

U.S. Department of Labor, Bureau of Labor Statistics. 2003. Tables from "*Employment and Earnings": Annual Average Data*. Retrieved April 25, 2003, from http://www.bls.gov/cps/cpsa2001.pdf.

U.S. Federal Bureau of Investigations. Annual editions. *Crime in the United States: Uniform Crime Reports*. Washington, D.C.: U.S. Federal Bureau of Investigations.

U.S. Food and Drug Administration, Center for Drug Evaluation and Research. 2001. *Mifepristone Medication Guide*. Washington, D.C.: U.S. Government Printing Office.

U.S. House of Representatives, Committee on Ways and Means. 2000. *The 2000 Green Book: Background Material and Data on Programs within the Jurisdiction of the Committee on Ways and Means*. Washington, D.C.: U.S. Government Printing Office.

Vassilev, Dimiter. 1999. "Bulgaria." In *From Abortion to Contraception: A Resource to Public Policies and Reproductive Behavior in Central and Eastern Europe from 1917 to the Present*, edited by Henry P. David. Westport, Conn.: Greenwood.

Ventura, Stephanie J., and Christine Bachrach. 2000. "Nonmarital Childbearing in the United States, 1940–1999." *National Vital Statistics Reports* 48 (16).

Whittington, L. A., J. Alm, and H. E. Peters. 1990. "Fertility and the Personal Exemption: Implicit Pronatalist Policy in the United States." *American Economic Review* 80 (3): 545–56.

Willis, Robert J. 1973. "A New Economic Approach to the Economic Theory of Fertility Behavior." *Journal of Political Economy* 81 (2): S14-S64.

Wu, Lawrence L., and Barbara Wolfe, eds. 2001. *Out of Wedlock: Causes and Consequences of Nonmarital Fertility*. New York: Russell Sage Foundation.

INDEX

Page numbers in italics refer to tables or figures in the text.